"To Read and To Know"

TYNDALE THEOLOGICAL SEMINARY THESES SERIES

SERIES EDITORS

T. J. Marinello

H. H. Drake Williams III

CONTRIBUTING EDITOR

Octavian Baban

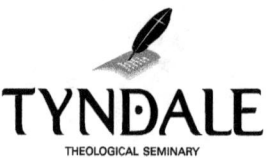

The TYNDALE THEOLOGICAL SEMINARY THESES SERIES contains volumes on topics to include pastoral ministries and intercultural studies, systematic and historical theology, and the biblical languages.

Titles in the series include:

"Blessed are the Peacemakers," but How Does a Christian Make and Preserve Peace? Peacemaking in Nigeria and Rwanda
Adeshina Jayeola and Jean Pierre Methode Rukundo
[Copies of this volume may be ordered from Tyndale Theological Seminary, the Netherlands, by emailing your request to info@tyndale-europe.edu]

"To Read and To Know"

Proper Biblical Translation as a Key to Commentaries and Theology

Bogdan Costea and Alexandru Costea

WIPF & STOCK · Eugene, Oregon

"To Read and To Know"
Proper Biblical Translation as a Key to Commentaries and Theology

Copyright © 2024 T. J. Marinello, H. H. Drake Williams III, the contributors, and Tyndale Theological Seminary in the Netherlands. All rights reserved. Except for brief quotations in critical publications or reviews, no part of this book may be reproduced in any manner without prior written permission from the publisher. Write Permissions, Wipf and Stock Publishers, 199 W. 8th Ave, Suite 3, Eugene, OR 97401

Wipf & Stock
An Imprint of Wipf and Stock Publishers
199 W. 8th Ave, Suite 3
Eugene, OR 97401

PAPERBACK ISBN: 979-8-3852-0839-5
HARDCOVER ISBN: 979-8-3852-0840-1
EBOOK ISBN: 979-8-3852-0841-8

Unless otherwise indicated, all Bible quotations are from *The Holy Bible, English Standard Version®* (ESV®), copyright © 2001 by Crossway, a publishing ministry of Good News Publishers. Used by permission. All rights reserved.

Tyndale Theological Seminary
PO Box 242
Wheaton, IL 60187
USA

Egelantierstraat 1
1171 JM Badhoevedorp
The Netherlands

info@tyndale-europe.edu

"Christ desires His mysteries to be published abroad as widely as possible. I would that [the Gospels and the epistles of Paul] were translated into all languages, of all Christian people, and **that they might be read and known**."

William Tyndale quoting Desiderius Erasmus

"Mark the plain and manifest places of the Scriptures, and in doubtful places see thou add no interpretation contrary to them; but (as Paul saith) let all be conformable and agreeing to the faith."

William Tyndale, *Preface to the New Testament*, 1526.

Contents

Series Foreword ix
Contributors xi
Preface xiii

BOOK 1
The Genre of New Testament Commentary and the Romanian Context: A Parallel Study on the Book of Revelation with a Proposed Commentary Sample
Bogdan Costea

Abstact 3

Dedication 5

Abreviations 9

Introduction 11

Chapter 1 15
   The Genre of Biblical Commentary

Chapter 2 29
   The Exegesis of Commentaries

Chapter 3 43
   Bible Translation in Commentaries

Chapter 4 55
   The Exposition of Commentaries

Chapter 5 67
   An Evaluation of Biblical Commentaries

Chapter 6 79
   A Proposed Commentary on Revelation 2:18–29

Final Conclusions 99

Bibliography of Works Cited 101

BOOK 2
Translation of σῴζω in the Romanian Orthodox Bible and Its Implications for Soteriology

Alexandru Costea

Abstract 111

Dedication 113

Contents 115

Acronyms and Abbreviations... 117

Introduction.. 119

Chapter 1 123
    History of the Translation of the Romanian Bible and Bible Translation Principles

Chapter 2 135
    An Analysis of the Greek Voice

Chapter 3 153
    Σῴζω in the Canonical Gospels

Chapter 4 165
    Soteriology in the Eastern Church Fathers

Conclusion and Recommendations... 177

Bibliography of Works Cited 183

Series Foreword

William Tyndale was an English Reformer in the sixteenth century. He was an outstanding scholar of the original languages. For him as well as other Reformers, the entire Bible was the first and only authority for faith and practice. For this reason William Tyndale labored to put the Scripture in the language of the people so that every man, woman, and child could have access to it in the English language. He was determined to make the Scripture accessible.

On one occasion in the early sixteenth century, Tyndale found himself responding to a learned clergyman. This man claimed that people were better with the Pope than with the Scripture. To this Tyndale famously replied, "I defy the Pope and all his laws. If God spare my life ere many years, I will cause a boy that driveth the plough shall know more of the scripture than thou dost."

This determination for making the Scripture accessible continues at a school that bears this Reformer's name, Tyndale Theological Seminary in Badhoevedorp, The Netherlands. Founded in 1985 by Dr. Arthur P. Johnston with the encouragement of Billy Graham, Tyndale Theological Seminary equips international Christian leaders so that the Scripture can be understood better worldwide. As part of that vision, Johnston assembled a cadre of missionary academics to staff the classroom; this staffing by missionary academics continues to this day. Since 1985, Tyndale has graduated more than 380 students who serve the Lord in over eighty different countries.

The seminary is recognized by the Dutch government as a university of applied science. Her Master of Evangelical Theology (MET) program is accredited by the *Nederlands-Vlaamse Accreditatieorganisatie* (NVAO) as well as the European Council for Theological Education (ECTE) [formerly European Evangelical Accrediting Association (EEAA)]. The seminary's Master of Divinity (MDiv) program is accredited by the ECTE.

This volume is the second of a planned series of books which display the seminary's focus on the study of the Bible with its practical application. As does this one, each of these volumes will contain two selected master's theses with similar or complimentary topics authored by Tyndale graduates. While these are edited theses, these contributions largely are the thoughts and argumentation of the students who wrote them. Accordingly, the Tyndale Theological Seminary Thesis Series presents the passion of the authors of the theses to affect issues confronting Christianity in their home lands. The series is oriented to practical concerns, paying attention to a particular need in the Church or a particular country. Each thesis proceeds by examining the need in relation to the classic theological disciplines within one or more of Tyndale's three divisions: Biblical and Exegetical Studies; Theological and Historical Studies; Intercultural Studies and Practical Ministries. The conclusion applies the findings to the need in the particular country.

Contributors

Bogdan Costea lives with his wife Ela in Romania. He is a PhD candidate at VID Specialized University, Oslo, pursuing his doctorate in theology. His dissertation is entitled "The Frame of the Righteous Sufferer as the Substructure of 1 Peter: An Intra- and Inter-Textual Linguistic Study."

Alexandru Costea lives with his wife Ruth in California where he is doing his doctoral studies at Gateway Seminary.

Preface

We are living in a time in which biblical resources are plentiful. While many Bible translations and commentaries exist in printed or digital form, frequently they are in English, French, German, and Spanish. Many language groups do not have biblical resources in their own tongue. Some of these language groups are seeing the church expand rapidly, but they do not have adequate resources for biblical study if any resources at all are available.

In some language groups, Bible commentaries and translations are of lesser quality, often due to the lack of training in Greek, Hebrew, and Aramaic for their authors and translators. Skills to translate, systematize and apply the text also are less available. Additionally, many commentaries are authored by those who are unfamiliar with the language, church, and culture of the target audience. Further, commentaries which are translated from other languages very often import the culture of that language as well as address issues not germane to the culture into which the commentary is translated.

Some language groups also struggle with the quality of translations of the biblical text itself. At times, a translation may not come from the biblical languages but from a Bible translation in another modern language.. This can result in the theological perspective of the previous translators being unwillingly written into the subsequent translation. How can these deficiencies be addressed?

In this installment of the Tyndale Theological Seminary Theses Series, two brothers, Bogdan and Alexandru Costea, address biblical studies issues in Romania. Bogdan writes about the importance of having a Romanian commentary series that compares the biblical languages with Romanian Bible versions that are used by Evangelicals and interacts with the Church fathers, and then applies the results to Romanian needs. Alexandru evaluates the meaning of σῴζω in the Romanian Orthodox Bible, a word commonly translated as "save" in many English contexts. He then comments on the implications his study has for understanding of salvation. While these topics may appear somewhat technical to the casual reader, this type of work is part of the goal of education at Tyndale Theological Seminary. The training received at the seminary has allowed these two men to grapple with the core issues related to commentary production suitable for the Romanian context as well as provided a model for other language contexts.

Bogdan's thesis was supervised by Assistant Professor Dr. Octavian Baban, the Director of the Department of Pastoral Theology at Baptist Theological Institute of Bucharest (BTIB), Romania. His doctorate was completed at London School of Theology, Brunel University, UK (1999). He has taught New Testament studies at BTIB since 1998, and also from the same year at the Baptist Theology Faculty of the Bucharest University. From 1998 he served as a Bible studies and counselling pastor at the Biserica Creştină Baptistă „Sfânta Treime" din Bucureşti. The second reader was Professor Doctor Marius Cruceru, the Director of the Department of Theology, Music and Socio-Human Sciences at Universitatea Emanuel in Oradea, Romania. His doctorate was completed at Universităţii din Bucureşti (2006). He has taught on the faculty at Universitatea Emanuel since 1994. He also served as a pastor for twenty years at Biserica Creștină Baptistă „Sfînta Treime" din Aleșd and is a chaplain at Fundației Hospice Emanuel Oradea.

Alexandru's thesis was supervised by Dr. H. H. Drake Williams III, one of the editors of this series and its founder. He completed his doctorate at Aberdeen University, Scotland (1999). Dr. Williams served for many years as Professor of New Testament Language and Literature at Tyndale as well as its Vice President of Academic Affairs and Academic Dean. He presently is Associate Professor of New Testament at Evangelische Theologische Faculteit in Heverlee/Leuven, Belgium, and Minister of Mission and Theology at Central Schwenkfelder Church in Lansdale, Pennsylvania. He also is a multi-published author at both the scholarly and popular level. Alex's second reader was Dr. Baban.

Dr. Williams has a special interest in these two theses as does Dr. Baban and Dr. Cruceru since all three are writers in Seria Comentarii Exegetice Românești, an evangelical Romanian commentary series. During the preparation of this volume, the importance of Tyndale training those who may choose to become part of the next generation of Romanian biblical scholars was brought into sharp focus with the passing of Corneliu Constantinaneau, one of Romania's foremost evangelical biblical scholars. And so, with an eye on the ongoing task of evangelical scholarship dedicated to the support of the Church midst the uncertainties of life, and with heartfelt thanks to the Lord of glory, this volume comes to print.

T. J. Marinello, PhD, FRHistS
H. H. Drake Williams III, PhD

BOOK 1

The Genre of New Testament Commentary and the Romanian Context:
A Parallel Study on the Book of Revelation with a Proposed Commentary Sample

Bogdan Costea

Abstact

This book is advocating for the contribution of exegetical commentaries based on biblical languages in the Romanian evangelical context of today. It starts from the analysis and presentation of the genre of biblical commentary. Then, main resources that are available for church leaders such as Bible translations and Bible commentaries are analyzed and evaluated to this end. This process reveals, in this book, the need for better tools in the hands of church leaders in order to do their ministry, like autochthonous exegetical Bible commentaries based on the biblical languages that compare and engage with the various Romanian translations of the Bible and existing Romanian commentaries. Throughout this book it will be clear that such kind of exegetical commentaries are needed in the Romanian evangelical context, especially in the fifth chapter which compares and reveals the differences between Romanian and English commentaries. Finally, an example of an exegetical Bible commentary from a passage in the Book of Revelation is presented in order to better illustrate the type of commentary proposed.

Dedication

To my wife Ela. Thank you for those long evening walks that kept us close to each other and close to God.

Contents

Abreviations 9

Introduction 11
    Purpose   11
    Necessity and relevance   11
    Objectives   12
    Terminology   12
    Delimitations   13
    Methodology   13

Chapter 1 15
    The Genre of Biblical Commentary
    A Historical Analysis of the Genre   15
        Short Introduction to the Definition and Genre of Commentary   15
        A Short History of Biblical Interpretation   16
        The Development of the Art of Commentary Writing   20
    A Classification of the Variety of the Genre   21
        Types of Commentaries   21
        The Methodology of Commentaries   21
        The Purpose of Commentaries as Shaped by Audience   23
        The Publishing Format and Content of Commentaries   25
    Final Remarks   25
        The Spectrum of Commentaries   25
        Implications in the Romanian Context and a Working Definition   26

Chapter 2 29
    The Exegesis of Commentaries
    Exegesis: Definition and Methodologies   29
    Historical or Text Oriented Approaches to Exegesis   35
    Reception History   38
    Conclusion   41

Chapter 3 43
    Bible Translation in Commentaries
    Description, Definition and Categories   44
    Advocates for the Positions   46
    Theological Foundations   47
    Addressing the Main Issues   48
    Implications for Biblical Commentaries   50
    The Romanian Specific Context   51
    Conclusion   53

Chapter 4 55
    The Exposition of Commentaries

The Text of the Commentary	55
Commentary as a Form of Communication	56
The Major Parts of Commentaries as a Form of Communication	57
The Writer	58
The Reader	58
The Text	59
The "What" and "How" of Commentary's Task	60
Issues of Content	61
Priorities in Commentary Writing	61
Main Mistakes in Commentaries	62
Important Elements in Commentary Genre	63
Conclusion	65

Chapter 5 67
An Evaluation of Biblical Commentaries

Preliminary Concerns	67
English Commentaries on Revelation	69
Romanian Commentaries on Revelation	72
Conclusion	75
An Evaluation of the Romanian Commentaries on Revelation	75
The Type of Commentary Proposed	76

Chapter 6 79
A Proposed Commentary on Revelation 2:18–29

Translation	79
Short Overview of the Reception History of Revelation 2:18–29 in the Church Fathers	80
Exposition	81
Revelation 2:18	83
Revelation 2:19	85
Revelation 2:20	86
Revelation 2:21	89
Revelation 2:22	89
Revelation 2:23	91
Revelation 2:24	92
Revelation 2:25	94
Revelation 2:26	94
Revelation 2:27	95
Revelation 2:28	96
Revelation 2:29	97
Summary	97
Conclusion	98

Final Conclusions 99

Bibliography of Works Cited 101

Abreviations

ASB	American Standard Bible
BDAG	W. Bauer, F. W. Danker, W. F. Arndt, F. W. Gingrich, *A Greek English Lexicon of the New Testament*, 3rd ed.
CBTEL	*Cyclopedia of Biblical, Theological and Ecclesiological Literature*
CE	*The Catholic Encyclopedia*
EB	*The New Encyclopedia Britannica*
ICC	International Critical Commentary
ISBE	*International Standard Bible Encyclopedia*. Edited by G. W. Bromiley
KJV	King James Version
NA27	*Novum Testamentum Graece,* Nestle-Aland 27th ed.
NSHERK	*New Schaff-Herzong Encyclopedia of Religious Knowledge*. Edited by S. M. Jackson
NIGTC	New International Greek Testament Commentary
NICNT	The New International Commentary of the New Testament
NLV	New Life Version
NTR	Biblia, Noua Traducere
NTC	Noul Testament Catolic
TLN	Traducerea Literară Nouă
NTPBA	Noul Testament și Psalmii traducerea Bartolomeu Anania
NTSBIR	Noul Testament SBIR
NIV	New International Version
RSV	Revised Standard Version
UBS[4]	*The Greek New Testament,* United Bible Societies, 4th ed.
WBC	Word Biblical Commentaries

Introduction

This present book sets out to explore the genre of biblical commentary in order to relate it to the Romanian context with the purpose of proposing a certain type of biblical commentary that is needed in today's Romanian context. Besides a personal interest and desire, the motivation for this research is to adventure in helping the advancement of this particular field of research. This can be done by synthesizing the various information about the genre of biblical commentaries. Some dictionaries and encyclopedias indeed engage in talking about biblical commentaries, but the articles are very few and short. More than that, these articles present a historical account of different commentary writers as opposed to a presentation of the genre of biblical commentary.

There is also little or no writing about the genre of biblical commentary in the Romanian academic context. In order to know the direction and the next step, we need to know and comprehend the larger picture. For us to know what kind of biblical commentaries we need in a particular context, we need to understand what the Bible commentaries are about and what has been done so far in their development.

This enterprise is valuable for the sake of the advancement of God's kingdom in Romania, and for the sake of academic advancement and dialogue. This is accomplished by providing a good biblical commentary as a tool to all church leaders who want to understand the text of the Bible and explain the differences in the Romanian Bible versions and commentaries.

Purpose

In recent times, Romania has developed in terms of biblical scholarship. More and more ministers complete postgraduate studies in the field of theology or biblical studies. This is reflected in the Christian bookshops, where more biblical commentaries, translations of the Bible, and other scholarly books are sold. The goal of this book is to analyze the genre of biblical commentary in the light of this Romanian context. Since the Romanian book market is seeing a greater number of biblical commentaries, now is the right time to ask what kind of biblical commentaries we have so far, and what do we need for the future. By analyzing the genre of biblical commentary and by then comparing the existing commentaries with a more developed English market, we will be able to propose a further step in this field and the type of commentary needed in the Romanian context.

Necessity and relevance

When one thinks of the tools a preacher or a teacher uses for a sermon, lecture, exposition, Bible study or simply ministry preparation, one of the most important ones is a Bible commentary. Many would feel that it is indispensable. It is clear that the great majority of Christian leaders use Bible commentaries on a regular basis, and thus, it is also clear that it is a necessary tool. In a sense we can say that there is a constant need for up-to-date commentaries in any language. Even though the Evangelical community in Romania is under 4% of the population, there are only a few Bible commentaries and fewer are addressed to Romanians in particular.

The reality is that Romanian preachers, pastors and leaders can benefit from a critical Bible commentary only if they know English or another more widespread language. There is a need for Romanian critical Bible commentaries. The challenge is to make the Romanian community aware of this situation, first of all, and then to address it by encouraging the writing of good Bible commentaries.

Because the number of Romanian Christians acquainted with the biblical and classical languages was so few, the approach of Romanian Bible commentators was to write more of a Bible study, reflection-on-the-text type of commentary or to bring to discussion the opinion of foreign Bible commentators. The commentaries of Beniamin Fărăgău were very helpful for a developing and growing Romanian church under communism. They served many local churches by providing good material for Bible studies during regular worship services. In today's context of different Bible translations and commentaries, however, a different type of commentary is necessary which reflects the recent changes in Romania. In other words, we need more critical or exegetical Bible commentaries in addition to what we have. Bad translations can lead to minute errors or misinterpretation; as the Italian saying brought to attention by Benedetto Croce goes, "Traduttore, traditore," (translator, traitor).

That is why we need exegetical Bible commentaries based on the original languages not on the Romanian or English texts. But the problem is that most of the existing Romanian commentaries do not deal with the original languages. We need good, Evangelical exegetical commentaries that bring to discussion the difference in translations.

Objectives

Objectives:
- To analyze and define the genre of biblical commentary.
- To show what is involved in the process of writing a Bible commentary.
- To evaluate the existing Romanian biblical commentaries on Revelation and to compare them with the English Bible commentaries.
- To make the Romanian community conscious of the need for Romanian exegetical commentaries that will interact with the Romanian context, scholars, and translations.
- To present an example of a part of a Romanian exegetical Bible commentary based on the original languages that treat a chosen passage of Scripture.

Terminology

Bible commentary, exegesis [exegetical Bible commentary], Dumitru Cornilescu, Romanian Evangelical community, [Romanian] Bible translation, Greek New Testament, the Book of Revelation, Revelation 2:18–29, historical criticism, literary criticism, reception history, formal equivalence, functional equivalence.

Delimitations

First, the treatment of the genre of biblical commentary is not meant to be exhaustive, but merely to serve as a springboard for our later evaluation and model proposal. Second, this book will not show or explain all the reasons why the Romanian community needs exegetical Bible commentaries based on the original languages, but rather it will address some of the existent problems pointing to the need. Third, the analysis of English biblical commentaries is limited to the ones on Revelation and to the ones that are viewed as important for the comparison with Romanian commentaries. Finally, the presentation of the example of Romanian exegetical Bible commentary will be limited to one short passage in the book of Revelation.

Methodology

This book will use examine written sources such as Bible commentaries, Bible translations, Romanian Bible translations, and other Romanian sources along with English sources. Analysis, comparison, and exegesis will be the main method used towards the latter part of the book.

Even though many biblical commentaries were written and continue to be written, one can find very few writings *about* commentaries. Very few biblical dictionaries and encyclopedias have an article dedicated to commentaries. More than that, there are only a small number of journal articles that treat this topic, and they are usually meant as a reflection on the experience of writing a commentary. Also, few scholarly reviews of commentaries refer to the overall genre of commentary. From all these, it is easy to see the need to first analyze and define the genre of biblical commentary. This will be done in the first chapter of this book.

The second chapter will be dedicated to the first part of the process involved in writing a biblical commentary, namely, the research or exegesis of the commentary. Because a biblical commentary sets out to interpret and explain the text of Scripture, a thorough research needs to be applied to every passage. But this exegetical process is complex, and we need to understand it in order to recognize different methodologies, approaches, and goals of commentaries.

Oftentimes, translation serves as a bridge between the interpretation and the explanation of the biblical text. This is the reason why many commentators prefer to offer their own translation of the book being commented on. By doing so, the interpretation proposed is reflected in translation, and it provides a good starting point for the exposition of the biblical passage. Since translation plays such an important role, and since there are many different views on its process, it is only proper to dedicate an entire chapter to it. So, the third chapter will embody it in our discussion of biblical commentaries.

The fourth chapter deals with the last part involved in the general purpose of the biblical commentary. When the research or exegesis is done, and when the Scripture passage has been translated, a certain interpretation of it needs to be expanded. But this needs to be done in a compelling, attractive and simple way. Some elements are in order at this point, and some mistakes need to be avoided to achieve this goal.

After describing the genre of biblical commentary and after understanding the processes it entails, it is time to focus our attention on the context of the country where the contribution is intended. If we have the big picture of what a biblical commentary is about, we can better observe the need in a particular context. So, an evaluation of the Romanian market of Bible commentaries will be the heart of the fifth chapter. This evaluation will be narrowed down only to commentaries dealing with the book of Revelation, or a section of it. Towards the end of the chapter, a certain type of biblical commentary will be proposed, based on all the data gathered to this point.

The sixth chapter will simply be an example of the kind of commentary that is proposed for the Romanian context. Because of space limitations, this book will only present a commentary on Revelation 2:18–29. This passage was chosen because of the various questions related to translation and text critical issues. This will be followed by a chapter of final conclusions for the entire book.

Chapter 1

The Genre of Biblical Commentary

This chapter will provide a better understanding of the phenomenon of biblical commentaries by looking at some of its common characteristics. It is true that, a genre "is identified by the recognizable similarity among a number of texts."[1] For this reason, this chapter will reveal common elements in the genre of biblical commentaries. This will be done by looking at the history of commentary writing, its development as an art, its types, methodologies, purposes, and publishing formats. A look at the spectrum of commentaries will offer further information. A working definition will be proposed at the end, together with an analysis of the implications in the Romanian context of the genre of biblical commentaries. This will provide a basis for analyzing the present state of commentaries in Romania. It will also give us important guiding elements and characteristics we should include in the proposed model of the type of commentary needed for the present Romanian context.

A Historical Analysis of the Genre

Short Introduction to the Definition and Genre of Commentary
Many teachers, pastors, preachers, scholars, church members, students of the Bible and others turn on a regular basis to commentaries in order to find help in understanding, applying or teaching the word of God. Very few, however, stop and wonder about the literary and theological nature of a commentary in itself. Frequently, a good commentary does such a good job in linking the reader with the text of the Bible that such features go almost unnoticed. An important tool as a Bible commentary should be assessed in terms of its method and general purpose, in terms of the style and philosophy it uses in order to facilitate the connection between the reader and the biblical text. Thus, the question regarding the quality and the method of any given commentary becomes an important one. It needs to be further pursued and analyzed for definitions, guidelines and relevant assessment criteria.

Very few dictionaries and encyclopedias have an entry on commentaries. Frederic W. Danker mentioned *CE*, *ISBE*, and *CBTEL* to which we add *EB* and *NSHERK*. For example, the *CBTEL* affirms that "*commentary*, in its theological application, is usually meant an exhibition of the meaning which the sacred writers intended to convey; or a

---

1 John Joseph Collins, "Introduction: Towards the Morphology of a Genre," *Semeia* 14 (1979), 1, accessed 11 January 2021, *ATLA Religion Database with ATLASerials*, EBSCO*host*.

development of the thrust which the Holy Spirit willed to communicate to men for their saving enlightenment."² *ISBE* offers the following explanation:

> Etymologically, a commentary (from Lat. *commentor*) denotes jottings, annotations, memoranda, on a given subject or perhaps on a series of events; hence its use in the plural as a designation for a narrative or history, as the *Commentaries* of Caesar. In its application to Scripture the word designates a work devoted to the explanation, elucidation, illustration, sometimes the homiletic expansion and edifying utilization, of the text of some book or portion of Scripture.³

The short entry of *CE* gives the following short definition, "commentaries are explanatory writings on the books of the *Bible*," to which it adds that "[s]trictly speaking these are not works of biblical criticism but are for the study and understanding of the texts of Scripture."⁴ The rest of the mentioned encyclopedias talk in general terms about exegesis and hermeneutics.

At this point, we can attempt to give a provisory definition to the genre of biblical commentary. From what we have seen so far, a commentary developed from the desire to elucidate or explain the meaning of the biblical text. Therefore, we can say a biblical commentary is a literary work which offers explanation to the biblical text after a process of interpretation, for the benefit of a specialized or general reader. Therefore, one can find a homiletic commentary oriented towards preachers; an exegetical commentary aimed at students and well trained specialists; or a devotional commentary used for meditation, prayer, application. This definition will be used again, later, and will be developed.

A Short History of Biblical Interpretation

It is important to give a history of interpretation here because it will better describe the development of the genre throughout centuries. It will also offer explanation about the form, content and methodology used in today's commentaries.

Commentaries followed the trends of biblical interpretation shaped by the various circumstances of the time they were written, the culture, the major philosophical schools of that time, and the stage and development of religious life and thinking. The origins of biblical interpretation and commentary go back to the Bible itself, as has been demonstrated by Michael Fishbane, among others.⁵ It has been suggested that, in the process of the canonical formation of the Old Testament, we can observe different practices, such as scribal interpretation or large exegetical comments (*e.g.*, the

---

2 John McClintock and James Strong, "Commentary", in *Cyclopedia of Biblical, Theological, and Ecclesiastical Literature* (Grand Rapids, MI.: Baker Book House, 1981), 2:427.

3 James Orr and Frederic W. Danker, "Commentaries," in *International Standard Bible Encyclopedia*, ed. Geoffrey W. Bromley (Grand Rapids, MI: William B. Eerdmans Publishing Company, 1979), 1:737.

4 Robert C. Broderick, "Biblical Commentaries," in *The Catholic Encyclopedia, Revised and Updates Edition*, ed. Robert Broderick (Nashville, TN: Thomas Nelson Publishers, 1987), 125.

5 See Michael A. Fishbane, *Biblical Interpretation in Ancient Israel* (Oxford: Clarendon Press, 1988).

Chronicles) on the already established authoritative texts.[6] It is also well known that the New Testament writers often exegeted Old Testament texts or sayings of Jesus. Thus, biblical interpretation is recorded in the text of the Scriptures themselves.

In the process of translating the Jewish canonical writings, whether in their Greek or Aramaic form, one can see the tendency to explain or interpret different idioms, expressions or sentences.[7] The Aramaic translations are also viewed by many scholars as commentaries.[8] This can be seen in Targum Onqelos to some extent but more clearly in Targum Jonathan and Targum Pseudo-Jonathan.

Gradually, commentaries were made on the sacred texts in the Jewish and Christian tradition. Philo of Alexandria, the Qumran community, the rabbinic tradition, and the patristic tradition are all examples of different prominent efforts to make plain the text of the Scripture by interpreting and commenting upon it.[9]

The tradition around the Hebrew Bible was very strong especially after the exile. This is evident from Ezra onwards. From the time of Ezra we have the beginning of the oral commentaries on the Torah which, in their written form received the name of Midrash.[10] The Sopherim and then the Tanaim (teachers of the Law) were followed by Jewish teachers called Rabbis who formed schools of interpretation with moral influence.

Philo of Alexandria (c. 20 BC–c. 50 AD) was a Jew belonging to a prosperous priestly family in Alexandria.[11] His writings on philosophy and interpretation of the Jewish sources are particularly of interest even today. He wrote exegetical works as *Questions and Answers on Genesis and Exodus*, *Allegorical Interpretations of Genesis*, *Legum Allegoriae*, and others that give mostly two levels of interpretations: a literal and an allegorical one.[12] His method of interpretation stands in contrast with Palestinian Judaism, as a representative of the Hellenistic Diaspora Judaism, though he would often contradict Hellenistic Jews also. Similarly, he would sometimes argue against the literal interpretation of the Old Testament that sought to undermine Jewish tradition, and other times against the allegorical interpretation of it that had the same goal. In his view, "the allegorical [interpretation], though higher and more important, practically never invalidates the literal."[13]

The Qumran community and their library was a great discovery for many reasons like textual criticism, cultural and social understanding of their time period, comparative

---

6 Fishbane, *Biblical Interpretation*, 23, 152.

7 Frederick F. Bruce, "Exegesis and Hermeneutics, Biblical," *The New Encyclopaedia Britannica*, 15th ed. (Chicago: Encyclopedia Britannica, 1978), 17:65.

8 Roy A. Stewart, "Commentaries, Hebrew," in *International Standard Bible Encyclopedia*, ed. Geoffrey W. Bromley, (Grand Rapids, MI: William B. Eerdmans Publishing Company, 1979), 1:743.

9 Bruce, "Biblical Exegesis," 65–67.

10 Stewart, "Commentaries, Hebrew," 744.

11 Peder Borgen, "Philo of Alexandria," in *Anchor Bible Dictionary*, vol. 5, ed. David Noel Freedman (New York: Doubleday, 1992), 333–42.

12 Borgen, "Philo," 333–42.

13 Borgen, "Philo," 60–68.

literature study, etc. Another contribution of the findings of the Dead Sea Scrolls is in the field of the history of interpretation. This community produced a good number of exegetical works on the Old Testament, because of their dedication to *midrashic* study.[14] They are especially known for their principle of interpretation called *pesher*. Because the community thought the teachings of the Scriptures refer "essentially to the end of time," they believed "it was the task of the commentator to discover, or rather to divine, all these mysterious teachings by means of superior intuition."[15] This process of interpretation was called *pesher*, which was "an explanation of the hidden significance, a revelation of the secrets concealed in the divine books, which only inspired commentators, prophets, or initiates were able to discover."[16] They claimed the prophetic texts of the Jewish Scripture were fulfilled in their community, thus their hermeneutic is best explained as a fulfillment hermeneutic.[17] It is well known also the fact that to the Palestinian Talmud (A.D. 400) and the Babylonian Talmud (A.D. 600) both functioned as commentaries to the oral interpretation of the Torah, called Mishnah.[18]

The patristic commentary literature was mostly divided in two schools of interpretation: the Alexandrian and the Antiochian School. The Alexandrian School was influenced by Philo's interpretations, and it has been argued that what Philo's interpretation and that of the representatives of the patristic Alexandrian School have in common is the apologetic purpose of interpretation.[19] Because both the Greek philosophers and the Gnostics claimed to have a special mystical knowledge revealed only to them, it seems only natural that allegory would be used for apologetic purposes by Philo and church fathers alike.

Of the Alexandrian School, Origen is the prominent representative. He believed that "[j]ust as in man there is body, soul and spirit, so in scripture there is a threefold meaning—the literal, the moral and the spiritual."[20] The Antiochian School is best represented by Theodore of Mopsuestia and Chrysostom. It is believed that it was founded by Lucian (martyred A.D. 312), its real head being Diodorus of Tarsus (d. ca. 347) and Theodore of Mopsuestia (d. ca. 428). The Antiochian school promoted the literary interpretation of the Bible. Its representative figure is Chrysostom (b. ca. 347). "Schaff speaks of Chrysostom as 'the prince of commentators among the Fathers.' In the

---

14 André Dupont-Sommer, *The Essene Writings from Qumram*, trans. G. Vermes (Cleveland, OH: World Publishing Company, 1961), 306.

15 Dupont-Sommer, *The Essene Writings*, 255.

16 Dupont-Sommer, *The Essene Writings*, 255.

17 For a better understanding of the Qumranic interpretation and the *pesher* method Charlesworth's book is of great value. James H. Charlesworth, *The Pesharim and Qumran History: Chaos or Consesus?* (Grand Rapids, MI: William B. Eerdmans, 2002).

18 Jacob Neusner, "Talmud," in *International Standard Bible Encyclopedia*, ed. Geoffrey W. Bromley (Grand Rapids, MI: William B. Eerdmans Publishing Company, 1979), 4:717.

19 Robert M. Grant and David Tracy, *A Short History of the Interpretation of the Bible*, 2nd ed. (Philadelphia: Fortress Press, 1984), 54.

20 M. F. Wiles, "Origen as Biblical Scholar," in *The Cambridge History of the Bible*, vol. 1, *From the Beginnings to Jerome* (Cambridge: Cambridge University Press, 1975), 454–89.

West, Ambrose of Milan (ca. 339-397) and Jerome (ca. 346-420) wrote commentaries."[21] Theodore's nickname was "Interpreter" because he was an expounder of the biblical text.[22]

Biblical interpretation in the Middle Ages is a very vast and diverse topic that is hard to cover in a paragraph. It essentially consisted of an equivalence between interpretation and theology. Talking about the development of patristic commentaries and theology, Robert Grant observes the development from catena to glosses. "The catena had generally been marginal, sometimes even surrounding the text entirely, the gloss, on the other hand, was sometimes marginal, sometimes interlinear, and sometimes separate and continuous. Later theological questions were introduced, and finally these questions came to circulate separately."[23] The main interpretation of the Bible was predominantly allegorical. The system of allegorization with its four meanings is well known through the following verse:

> *Littera gesta docet, quid credas allegoria,*
> *Moralis quid agas, quo tendas anagogia.*[24]

During the time of the Reformation, the genre of commentary was developed and commentaries had basically the form that is now familiar to us. See for example, Martin Luther's *A Commentary on St. Paul's Epistle to the Galatians*, or Calvin's commentaries. There has been a transition in form and content from the patristic literature to German scholarship. Understanding this development helps us grasp more easily what biblical commentaries are.

It is evident that much more can be said about the history of interpretation, especially from the time of Reformation to the present. Yet, the information above serves to prove that the genre of biblical commentary had an early beginning and was characterized by various shapes and developments, depending on the historical and social context. One thing can be noticed here—that the characteristics of commentaries were dependent also on the development of society in general and technology in particular. Such factors as the cost of parchments, the invention of the printing machine and the invention of the computer (with its search engines), to mention but a few, influenced the length of commentaries or their research quality. One thing is certain—that the originality and inventions of Scripture commentators took on a great variety. This will be our next focus, as we try to compare the format of contemporary commentaries with different expressions of biblical commentaries.

---

21 Orr and Danker, "Commentaries," 738.

22 M. F. Wiles, "Theodore of Mopsuestia as Representative of the Antiochene School," in *The Cambridge History of the Bible*, vol. 1: *From the Beginnings to Jerome*, ed. P. R. Ackroyd and C. F. Evans (Cambridge: Cambridge University Press, 1975), 490.

23 Grant and Tracy, *A Short History of the Interpretation of the Bible*, 83.

24 Grant and Tracy, *A Short History of the Interpretation of the Bible*, 84.

The Development of the Art of Commentary Writing

Together with the development of manuscript transmission, scribes came up with creative ideas to help readers. Thus, the τίτλοι (titles) were invented to accompany each κεφάλα (chapter) in order to help the readers find their way in the text. The titles consisted in a short "summary heading placed in the margin and describing the content of the chapter."[25] It was to be understood that the summary offered by the scribes was characterized by subjectivity. Different prologues called hypothesis (ὑπόθεσις) were meant for "supplying the reader with certain amount of information concerning the author, content, and circumstances of composition of the particular book."[26] Also,

> [f]or Acts and the Epistles, a considerable apparatus of auxiliary materials circulated under the name of Euthalius or Evagrius," which "[b]esides chapter divisions and hypotheses . . . included a lengthy sketch of the life, writings, and chronology of the apostle Paul; a brief statement of the martyrdom of Paul; a table of Old Testament quotations in the Epistles; a list of places at which the Epistles were thought to be written; and a list of the names associated with Paul's in the headings of the Epistles.[27]

The superscriptions and subscriptions of the manuscripts were short and simple and indicated simple titles of books or the close of books. However, as time passed, they "became more elaborate and often included traditional information regarding the place at which the book was thought to be written and sometimes the name of the amanuensis."[28]

In the same line of transmitting manuscripts, Metzger helps us understand what glosses, scholia and catenae were. The *glosses* were short definitions or "brief explanations of difficult words or phrases;"[29] while the *scholia* were "interpretive remarks of a teacher placed beside the text in order to instruct the reader."[30] From the *Schaff-Herzog Encyclopedia of Religious Knowledge*, glosses were "the simplest form of elucidation" meant to explain an obscure or uncommon expression, "and that scholia were marginal notes on the text for use in schools."[31]

The next step was the *commentary* which was a systematic development of scholia in order to continuously elucidate "the entire text, rather than being merely random notes on certain passages."[32] The *catenae* (chains) were links of "comments extracted from older ecclesiastical writers."[33]

---

25 Bruce M. Metzger and Bart D. Ehrman, *The Text of the New Testament: Its Transmission, Corruption, and Restoration*, 4th ed. (New York: Oxford University Press, 2005), 36.
26 Metzger and Ehrman, *The Text of the New Testament*, 39.
27 Metzger and Ehrman, *The Text of the New Testament*, 40.
28 Metzger and Ehrman, *The Text of the New Testament*, 41.
29 Metzger and Ehrman, *The Text of the New Testament*, 41.
30 Metzger and Ehrman, *The Text of the New Testament*, 41.
31 Henry S. Nash, "Exegesis or Hermeneutics", in *The New Schaff-Herzong Encyclopedia of Religious Knowledge*, ed. Samuel Macauley Jackson (Grand Rapids, MI: Baker Book House, 1949–50), 4:243.
32 Metzger and Ehrman, *The Text of the New Testament*, 41.
33 Metzger and Ehrman, *The Text of the New Testament*, 43.

Translations are now also viewed as a type of commentaries, especially the Old Testament targumim. It is a known fact that the Targum or the Aramaic translation of the Hebrew Bible might be considered as a commentary because it was not "a mere translation, but a combination of translation and commentary, resulting in paraphrase, or an interpretative translation, with its origin in exegesis."[34]

We cannot talk about a clear chronological development of the form of commentaries from translation and scribal insertions to scholia, catenae, annotations, and commentaries as independent works separated from the manuscripts. However, comparing these forms of commentary to what we now consider commentaries to be helps us understand the genre of commentaries. In the next subchapter we will deal with the variety of commentary types in order to be able to offer a working definition and to help us identify important constituents of the genre.

In conclusion, we can see how there was always a need to explain the sacred text and to systematize the beliefs of the church. As a result, different forms of commentaries were developed.

A Classification of the Variety of the Genre

Types of Commentaries

Teachers are frequently asked by students and others to tell which commentary is the best on a certain book of the Bible. Later in this study, we will see that this is too complex to answer. Carson agrees in terms of commentaries, that "it is clear that what is 'best' can vary from reader to reader and depends on what kind of information a particular reader is looking for—quite apart from the theological orientation of particular commentaries."[35] There are different types of commentaries as there are different ways of approaching the biblical text, and commentators have their own contributions in the study of a certain book of the Bible. For example, as we will see below, commentaries can fit in different categories such as: exegetical, homiletic, historic, etc., depending on the methodologies applied to the biblical text and the readers addressed by them. Like any other literary work, commentaries have different purposes and different goals that they achieve through their different approaches. Exegetical or scholarly commentaries can be easily identified by the complexity of language. The more technical the language of a commentary, the more scholarly it is. The simpler the exposition and style of a commentary, the more accessible it is to laity.

The Methodology of Commentaries

There are a variety of commentaries depending on the type of exegesis applied to the biblical texts. For example, the primary focus of commentaries before the Enlightenment was to offer a literal, moral, allegorical and anagogical interpretation of the Latin translation of the Bible. With the Enlightenment and the Reformation, there was a return

---

34 Stewart. "Commentaries, Hebrew," 743.

35 Donald Arthur Carson, *New Testament Commentary Survey*, 6th ed. (Grand Rapids, MI: Baker Academic, 2007), 153.

to the sources, *ad fontes*. Then, the historical-critical method ruled the methodology of commentaries. The goal was to reveal the historical context that gave rise to the biblical text. A response to this method was the literary-critical method which focused on the text, rather than the historical context. Besides these different methodologies that produced different types of commentaries, we also witness a difference in the actual style of the commentary, shaped on different audiences. For example, we have on one end, the critical commentary written for scholars, and on the other end the popular commentary addressed to the laity.

In "Commenting on Commentary," Frank Gorman, Jr. has a rather interesting assessment of the genres of biblical commentary.[36] Even though he exemplified his research by using the book of Leviticus, in addressing general issues, his comments are relevant also for New Testament commentaries. Gorman divides the practice of commentary writing into two distinct periods: premodern and modern, and, accordingly, he identifies two types of biblical commentary.

First, he argues that in the premodern type of interpreters focused on two areas, mainly, on the text and on the community. The community shaped, copied, interpreted, and reinterpreted the text, and the text would shape the community.

The author talks about how the biblical text bears witness to how communities like those of Israel and the church used hermeneutical processes like "commentary, adaptation, explication, interpretation and reinterpretation." This was done in order to attempt "to define both themselves and their practices in the context of newly emerging social, cultural and historical contexts through textual interpretation and commentary."[37]

The interpreters of the premodern era shared several concerns, such as understanding the biblical text in relation to the community, understanding the nature of the religious community, its constitution, its faith, and its practices; to define "the other" by contesting textual meanings and to understand the present in relation to the past.

The modern period of commentary writing has a primary historical goal and focused on "understanding the biblical book as a document of the past, associated with a past community and addressing issues concerned with the past life of the book."[38] Gorman goes on to say that in "Germany, a new genre of commentary writing developed, the "Introduction." This so called "'[i]ntroduction' was designed to deal with historical questions of textual origins and development."[39] The biblical commentary "has become a standard genre of scholarly writing and practice." Thus, "Commentaries generally present three basic types of material: the development of a new historical/interpretive argument, the development of a new reading based on already existing argument, a statement concerning the current state of the discipline."[40] This has forced the writers

---

36 Frank H. Gorman, Jr., "Commenting on Commentary: Reflections on a Genre," in *Relating to the Text: Interdisciplinary and Form-Critical Insights on the Bible*, ed. Timothy J. Sandoval and Carleen R. Mandolfo (London: T&T Clark International, 2003), 100–19.

37 Gorman, "Commenting on Commentary," 100–101.

38 Gorman, "Commenting on Commentary," 104.

39 Gorman, "Commenting on Commentary," 104.

40 Gorman, "Commenting on Commentary," 104.

of commentaries to raise the standard, but at the same time, often failing to meet the needs of lay people in the church communities.

In the next chapter we will better understand how the methodology of exegesis relates to the type of commentary produced. We will briefly look at the critical approaches in biblical studies.

The Purpose of Commentaries as Shaped by Audience

The purpose of a commentary is intimately related to the concept of intended audience. It is easy to see how the purpose and audience of a literary work that is in essence an act of communication can determine the type of that work.

Although they are brief, biblical dictionaries and encyclopedias offer information about commentaries which in turn speak about their situation and purpose. For example, in the *Cyclopedia of Biblical, Theological and Ecclesiological Literature* we find that

> [t]here are two kinds of commentary which we shall notice, viz. the critical and the popular. The former contains grammatical and philological remarks, unfolds the general and special significations of words, points out idioms and peculiarities of the original languages, and always brings into view the Hebrew or Greek phraseology employed by the sacred writers.[41]

From this, we can see not only the two types mentioned but the two categories of readers addressed: *scholars* and *laymen*.

An article in *The Zondervan Pictorial Encyclopedia of the Bible* admits that "[t]he actual nature of a commentary depends on a number of factors, such as the attitude of the writer toward the Scripture, his knowledge of the original languages, the purpose of his writing the commentary, and the subjects of his major interests."[42] The article also says, "[c]ommentaries vary radically in purpose and in kind."

J.B. Green provides an important emphasis, stressing the difficulty and the complexity of the commentary as a literary and theological genre. He makes the following statement in his article about commentary:

> [T]he genre of biblical commentary today is difficult to describe. This is because the late twentieth century witnessed the genesis of numerous commentary series, each justifying itself by purporting to represent a different approach to the task of commenting on biblical texts. Each attempt to serve an increasingly well-defined audience, and each subtly redraws the boundaries of the genre to meet its own ends.
>
> Generalizations about commentary are also made problematic by the increasingly pervasive recognition that the enterprise of commentary writing has entered a critical era.[43]

---

[41] McClintock and Strong, "Commentary," 428.

[42] Wilbur M. Smith, "Commentaries," in *The Zondervan Pictorial Encyclopedia of the Bible*, ed. Merrill C. Tenney (Grand Rapids, MI: Zondervan Publishing House, 1976), 1:920.

[43] Joel B. Green, "Commentary," in *Dictionary for Theological Interpretation of the Bible*, ed. Kevin J. Vanhoozer (Grand Rapids, MI: Baker Academic, 2005), 123.

Further, in the following sections, we will look at a number of different series (and types) of commentaries.

The text of the commentary itself provides many clues about its situation, purpose and recipients. For example, the title of the *Life Application Bible Commentary* has much to say about its purpose. As the name suggests, *The NIV Application Commentary* is focused on the practicality or relevance of the biblical text. Yet the series introduction insists that the commentaries published are "commentaries, not popular expositions" and that they are "works of reference, not devotional literature."[44] Much of the exposition in this series is concerned with the contemporary significance of the text. It is more on the popular end of the scholarly-popular commentary spectrum.

The Ancient Christian Commentary on Scripture series of biblical commentaries is a compilation of the comments of the church fathers "from the end of the New Testament era to A.D. 750."[45] According to the editors, this commentary targets primarily "lay persons," but also the "pastor, exegete, student and lay reader."[46] The variety of the readings mirrors the diverse communities and traditions represented, such as "Protestant, Catholic and Orthodox."[47] It is not easy to determine where this commentary is situated on the popular-scholar axis since it contains different readings from different authors in different times. However, it also contains texts belonging to the pre-critical era of biblical studies.

The *New International Greek Testament Commentary* series identifies its target as being represented by the "students of the Greek text" and its content label as providing "something less technical than a full-scale critical commentary." The editors also identify the audience as being "international in character" representing a "spread between different countries."[48]

The framework of evangelicalism is openly admitted by the *World Biblical Commentary* series. The editorial preface lets the reader know of the contributors' "broad stance," that is evangelicalism.[49] As for its audience, the dustcover of the series announces its audience of scholars, students and preachers. The language is technical, but it offers translation to words and quotes in other languages.

---

44 Craig S. Keener, *Revelation*; *The NIV Application Commentary* (Grand Rapids, MI: Zondervan, 2000), 9.

45 William C. Weinrich, ed., *Ancient Christian Commentary on Scripture, New Testament*, vol. 12, *Revelation* (Downers Grove, IL: InterVarsity Press, 2005), xi.

46 Weinrich, ed., *Revelation*, xi.

47 Weinrich, ed., *Revelation*, xii.

48 Gregory K. Beale, *The Book of Revelation: A Commentary on the Greek Text*, New International Greek Testament Commentary (Grand Rapids, MI: Wm. B. Eerdmans Publishing Co., 1999), xvii.

49 James D. G. Dunn, *Word Biblical Commentary*, vol. 38A, *Romans 1–8*, ed. Ralph P. Martin (Dallas, TX: Word Books, 1988), xii.

The technicality and specialized language such as the one of the WBC is raised in the *International Critical Commentary*. The Greek and Latin citations are not translated, thus making it inaccessible to many students and pastors.[50]

Shortly in this book we will have a closer look at many different commentaries in order to see what they communicate in relation to their purpose, audience, methodology, language, etc. This analysis will be conducted for the purpose of comparing the variety of commentaries on the English market with the Romanian market.

We will see later from Hartman's model of communication that the audience and its environment represent an important element in the communication process, especially in its written form, since it is more susceptible to misinterpretation. It is understood that the majority of leading commentaries today are written in and for the English and German speaking cultures. This fact makes evident the limits of their use in Majority World Countries.

The Publishing Format and Content of Commentaries

In terms of publishing distinctiveness which reflect the need of the market, commentaries can be independent ones proposed by authors writing outside commentary series, one volume biblical commentaries, or commentaries in series proposed by different publications.[51]

From the assessments of many bibliographic books on the biblical studies, one-volume commentaries are good for introducing the reader to the books and issues encountered. Interdependent contributions outside commentary series rarely exhibit a high level reading, though exceptions exist. None of the writers of these bibliographic books venture to say what one particular series of commentary is the best. This is because taken individually on particular books of the Bible, some are better and some are worse. That is why suggestions are given on each book of the Bible separately and only infrequently will one see a particular series being in the top recommendations for every book.

In terms of content, the market of biblical commentaries is full of variety. One can find commentators who choose to interpret a book of the Bible in its entirety and commentators who focus on interpreting only a passage in a Bible book. As we saw above, there are others who choose to spread their interpretation to all of the New or Old Testament. Today it is even rare to see an author dedicating his interpretative work to the whole of the Bible.

Final Remarks

The Spectrum of Commentaries

Speaking on a larger, global level, we can look at commentaries as being defined by a spectrum with two ends. In ISBE the biblical commentaries are differentiated in two opposite sides, according to their purpose. Some are more scholarly, and others are more

---

50 Carson, *New Testament Commentary Survey*, 24.
51 Carson, *New Testament Commentary Survey*, 15.

popular.⁵² Likewise, the *Cyclopedia* advises that "there are two kinds of commentary ... the *critical* and the *popular*" (original emphasis).⁵³ This same article on commentary goes on to define what a critical commentary is by saying that it

> contains grammatical and philological remarks, unfolds the general and special signification of words, points out idioms and peculiarities of the original languages, and always brings into view the Hebrew or Greek phraseology employed by the sacred writers ... [I]t takes a wide range, while it states the processes which lead to results, and shrinks not from employing the technical language common to scholars.⁵⁴

On the other hand, the popular commentary "states in perspicuous and untechnical phraseology the sentiments of the holy writers, usually without detailing the steps by which that meaning has been discovered."⁵⁵

This kind of distinction is made also by bibliographic books on biblical studies. For example, talking about commentaries on the book of Revelation, Carson gives a first list of commentaries recommended for "the preacher's or student's first requirements" and then he gives a second list of commentaries which he calls "more substantial works" for "those with adequate training." After these, a list of standard commentaries follows on the Greek text together with a list of commentaries at "the very popular level."⁵⁶ Therefore, no matter in what terms we may speak of biblical commentaries, we can always see them within the framework of this popular-scholarly/critical spectrum.

Implications in the Romanian Context and a Working Definition

With this background, the question remains as to what from the Romanian context will better inform the purpose, audience, type and approach of Romanian biblical commentaries?

In the preliminary results in 2011 of the 2012 census in Romania the percentage of population divided by religion was: the Orthodox Church with 85.9% followed by the Roman and Greco-Catholic Church with 4.6%, Reformed Church with 3.2%, Pentecostal Church with 1.9%, Baptist Church with 0.6%, Seventh Day Adventist Church with 0.5%, no religion or atheism 0.2% and others 1.8%.⁵⁷ The Baptist, Pentecostal, Brethren, Seventh Day Adventist and Evangelical Church formed the Romanian Evangelical Alliance in 1990.⁵⁸ When referring to the evangelicals in Romania, these Neo-Protestant churches are mainly in view. From this data it is evident that a Romanian biblical

---

52 Orr and Danker, "Commentaries," 738.
53 McClintock and Strong, "Commentary," 428.
54 McClintock and Strong, "Commentary," 428.
55 McClintock and Strong, "Commentary," 428.
56 Carson, *New Testament Commentary Survey*, 145, 146, 150.
57 Comunicat de presa, accessed 10 August 2020, http://www.recensamantromania.ro/wp-content/uploads/2012/08/Comunicat-presa_Rezultate-preliminare.pdf.
58 Cultele Neoprotestante (Evanghelice): Baptist, Adventist de Ziua a Şaptea, Penticostal, Creştin după Evanghelie, Biserica Evanghelică Română), accessed 16 January 2021, http://web.archive.org/web/20120130012119/http://www.culte.ro/DocumenteHtml.aspx?id=1738.

commentary will have to be aware and address (maybe even incorporate) elements from the Orthodox tradition. However, since the archpriest and theologian John Beck sincerely admits in his introduction of *Sfânta Scriptură în Tradiția Bisericii* that "the Orthodox biblical scholars write commentaries very rarely,"[59] the most logical thing to do is to frequently interact with the church fathers, especially the Greek ones.

Considering the audience of possible Romanian biblical commentaries, the need is for more scholarly/critical commentaries addressed to scholars, students and workers in the churches with evangelical background in an Orthodox immersed culture. In his master thesis, Dragoș Manea has shown that "the present and the future of biblical language study in the Romanian evangelical context can go deeper and further than it is now."[60] The need is for scholarly fit tools such as biblical commentaries but presented in a manner accessible to those who have limited or no biblical languages skills.

Following the rules of definition, it is possible to give a working, intensive definition of the commentary genre. However, given the fact of the abundant variety of methodologies of research and exposition, it is almost impossible to give an extensive definition of it.[61]

A working definition of a biblical commentary would be the following: a biblical commentary is a literary work designed to research and interpret in order to explain the content and meaning of one of the books of the Christian Scriptures, or parts, collections, even the whole of it, for the benefit of general or specialized readers. A side purpose of many biblical commentaries is also to offer a translation of the Greek text as a point of reference and initialization of the exposition. At the heart of this definition we find the verbs *research* and *explain*. In explaining the commentary genre, it is vital to refer to these two parts involved in the process of producing a biblical commentary. The following chapters will deal with these parts.

---

59 John Beck, *Sfânta Scriptură în Tradiția Bisericii* trans. Ioana Tămăian (Cluj-Napoca, Romania: Patmos, 2008), 13.

60 Dragoș Ștefăniță Manea, "A Short Exploration on the Importance of Greek Language Study for the Romanian Evangelical Church" (MET thesis, Tyndale Theological Seminary Badhoevedorp, The Netherlands, 2010), 89.

61 For a better understanding of the issues involved in the act of defining, see Raziel Abelson, "Definition," in *The Encyclopedia of Philosophy*, 2nd ed., ed. Donald M. Borchert (Farmington Hills, MI: Macmillan Reference USA, 2006), 2:664–77.

CHAPTER 2

The Exegesis of Commentaries

The main goal of this chapter is to discuss one of the two major tasks of commentary writing, namely the task of exegesis. After we have identified some of the common elements present in the genre of biblical commentary, we have considered a working definition of the biblical commentary. From this definition we have seen that at its core, a commentary is an exposition of the interpretation given to the biblical book(s) or portions of books. This entails research to start with, which, applied to the biblical text, is frequently being called biblical exegesis. By describing the process of exegesis in this chapter, we not only enrich our understanding of biblical commentaries in general, but we also present a basis for recognizing different methodologies and approaches to writing a commentary. This will be helpful when we will evaluate the Romanian market of commentaries. This chapter is also important for offering background information and viable ingredients for the proposed mode of biblical commentary needed today in the Romanian context.

Most dictionaries and Bible encyclopedias agree that commentaries come in a great variety. They also agree on their description and purpose. Thus, Joel B. Green can say they "[e]ach reflects (1) the hermeneutical imperative, which proceeds from the twofold observation that these texts must be interpreted if they are to function as Scripture, and that biblical texts are not self-interpreting; and (2) the imperative needs and aims of the world within which the commentary was produced."[1] Commentaries have, therefore, a twofold task: exegesis and expounding, which flows from exegesis and is a natural step of simply explaining the biblical text in written or oral form after understanding it through exegesis.

Exegesis: Definition and Methodologies

Exegesis is a term that usually refers to the explanation of a literary work.[2] The word comes from the Greek verb *exegeomai* which in the noun form refers to 'interpretation' or explanation."[3] Related to biblical studies, exegesis refers to an extended and critical interpretation of the Bible[4] or to the "exposition, critical analysis, or interpretation of

---

[1] Green, "Commentary," 125.

[2] Francis Andrew March and Francis Andrew March, Jr., *A Thesaurus Dictionary of the English Language* (Philadelphia: Historical Publishing Company, 1913), 377.

[3] John H. Hayes and Carl R. Holladay, *Biblical Exegesis: A Beginner's Handbook* (Atlanta: John Knox Press, 1982), 5.

[4] Webster's Online Dictionary with Multilingual Thesaurus Translation, accessed 24 July 2012, http://www.websters-online-dictionary.org/definitions/exegesis.

a word, literary passage, etc., especially of the Bible.[5] It is often considered similar to interpretation or explanation of a text or portion of Scripture. However, there are three distinct terms in biblical studies that were often seen similar and thus confused: exegesis, Bible interpretation and hermeneutics. The tendency has been to correctly define and separate these three terms though many writers have had different opinions on this matter. *The International Standard Bible Encyclopedia* offers the following clarification

> Hermeneutics traditionally has been understood as part of a triangular relationship with exegesis and interpretation, although the distinctions once made are no longer always so clearly drawn. Exegesis was that part of the process of the study of biblical texts that had to do with determining the meaning of the text for its author and addressees. Interpretation had to do with determining the text's meaning for the present age, and hermeneutics then referred to the rules and methodology applied in the movement from exegesis to interpretation. There is a degree of overlap and synonymity that can be detected already in the ancient use of the Gk. terms *hermeneia* and *exegesis*. This also carried over into their Latin counterparts, *interpretatio* and *expositio*, and it persists in English.[6]

The *New Encyclopedia Britannica* also separates exegesis from hermeneutics, but it does so implying that "[b]iblical exegesis is the actual interpretation of the sacred book, the bringing out of its meaning; hermeneutics is the study and establishment of the principles by which it is to be interpreted."[7]

From this clarification, one can clearly see the need to start the process of writing a commentary with exegesis. From exegesis he or she then moves to interpretation and application under the government of hermeneutics. So, "hermeneutics aims to establish methodological principles necessary to interpret the biblical text, while exegesis aims to apply these principles in the actual process of unfolding the meaning of the text. In general, hermeneutics is related to exegesis as theory to practice."[8]

But what precisely is exegesis? I. Howard Marshall, in the introduction of the book which he edited called *New Testament Interpretation: Essays on Principles and Methods,* offers (though not in a direct manner) some steps involved in exegesis. These are: textual criticism, translation, historical background, source criticism, form criticism, context information, levels of understanding (historical, the writer's and the interpreter's level) and what the text meant in the mind of its original author for his intended audience.[9] Part

---

[5] Jean L. McKechnie, ed., *Webster's New Twentieth Century Dictionary of the English Language, Unabridged: Based Upon the Broad Foundations Laid Down by Noah Webster*, 2nd ed. (Grand Rapids, MI: Collins World, 1979), 640.

[6] David G. Burke, "Interpret; Interpretations," in *International Standard Bible Encyclopedia: E-J*, rev. ed., ed. Geoffrey W. Bromiley (Grand Rapids, MI: Eerdmans Pub. Co., 1979), 863.

[7] Bruce, "Biblical Exegesis," 60.

[8] John D. Grassmick, *Principles and Practice of Greek Exegesis: a Classroom Manual* (Dallas, Texas: Dallas Theological Seminary, 1976), 8.

[9] I. Howard Marshall, *New Testament Interpretation: Essays on Principles and Methods* (Grand Rapids: William B. Eerdmans Pub. Co., 1979), 11–15.

two of this book deals with the critical methods in interpretation. The following terms are introduced as part of the methods in interpretation: semantics, questions of introduction (authorship, date, purpose etc. of the document), religious background, historical criticism, source criticism, form criticism, tradition history, and redaction criticism.

Gordon Fee sees exegesis as a part of hermeneutics. He affirms that "[h]istorically, the broader term for the science of interpretation, which includes exegesis, was *hermeneutics*."[10]

Conzelmann and Lindemann mention five preconditions required by the exegetical task: "the wording of the text must be established; the meaning of the words then needs to be ascertained; the literary characteristics of the text must be recognized and defined; the historical locus of the text must be determined as narrowly as possible. The questions regarding the theology of the text can be addressed only after these issues are settled."[11] Two paragraphs later they also add translation as a part of the exegetical task. The authors try to explain the relationship between exegesis and hermeneutics. They say that the goal of exegesis is understanding. But the conditions to which understanding is subjected are dealt with by hermeneutics.[12] The same authors also propose two methods of exegesis under the umbrella of the term scholarly doubts. The two doubts are centered on the authorship of the New Testament books and the historical reality in the presentation of the words and deeds of Jesus in particular.[13]

The exegesis manual from the year 1976 used at Dallas Theological Seminary defines exegesis as both a science and an art of the "skillful application of sound hermeneutical principles to the biblical test in the original language with a view to understanding and declaring the author's intended meaning."[14] The same manual defines hermeneutics as "the setting forth of methodological principles and techniques necessary to interpret the biblical text."[15] Exegesis is defined as "the application of the hermeneutical principles to the biblical text in order to understand and explain it."[16]

At this point, it needs to be said that some see differently the dynamics between exegesis and hermeneutics. For example, it may be argued that the difference between exegesis and hermeneutics could be seen as the difference between studying the ancient text in its historical meaning (exegesis), and studying the ancient text in its contemporary significance (hermeneutics). Even from this explanation, we see that hermeneutics entails a further step than exegesis related to the interpretation of the Bible to bridge the "then and there" to "here and now."

---

10 Gordon D. Fee, *New Testament Exegesis: a Handbook for Students and Pastors*, 3rd ed. (Louisville, KY: Westminster John Knox Press, 2002), 1.

11 Hans Conzelmann and Andreas Lindemann, *Interpreting the New Testament: an Introduction to the Principles and Methods of N.T. Exegesis* (Peabody, MA: Hendrickson Publishers, 1999), 4.

12 Conzelmann and Lindemann, *Interpreting the New Testament*, 1.

13 Conzelmann and Lindemann, *Interpreting the New Testament*, 32.

14 Grassmick, *Principles and Practice*, 7.

15 Grassmick, *Principles and Practice*, 7.

16 Grassmick, *Principles and Practice*, 8.

The editor of the book *Introducing New Testament Interpretation (Guides to New Testament Exegesis)*, Scot McKnight and its authors focus on the next disciplines as part of the exegesis methodology: background information, textual criticism, Greek grammatical analysis, word analysis, sociology, theological analysis and the function of the Old Testament in the New.[17]

Hayes and Holladay introduce two degrees of difficulty when it comes to exegesis of any type and seven factors of complexity when it comes to the process of exegesis. The degrees of difficulty depend on the degree in which the sender and the recipient share a common ground and on the degree in which the message or content of the text or document is specialized or technical. These seven factors are: the so called "'third-party perspective'" which basically means that the interpreter is not one of the original parties in the communication event; "when the text or document is composed in a language different from that of the interpreter;"[18] the cultural gap; the historical gap; the fact that documents are sometimes the product of collective and historical growth; the existence of multiple and differing texts of the same documents; and "some texts are considered sacred and thus different in some fashion from all other works."[19] Then, the book explains how these seven factors apply to biblical exegesis. The suggestion of the book is that in order to succeed in the process of biblical exegesis one must lower as much as possible the degrees of difficulty and factors of complexity. This is done through the consideration of seven types of criticism: textual, historical, literary, form, grammatical, tradition and redaction criticism.[20]

Michael J. Gorman proposes seven elements of exegesis in his book *Elements of Biblical Exegesis: a Basic Guide for Students and Ministers*. These elements are: survey (preparation and overview), contextual analysis (consideration of the historical and literary contexts of the text), formal analysis (of the form, structure, and movement of the text), detailed analysis (of the various parts of the text), synthesis (of the text as a whole), reflection, (on the text today), and expansion and refinement (of the initial exegesis).[21]

Gorman's presentation provides an excellent introduction and is a comprehensive and encompassing treatment of the subject of exegesis. The author displays both a clear panorama and a sharp care for the details concerning this discipline. He sums up the methods involved in the exegetical process in three methods: synchronic, diachronic and existential.

He rightly observers that two terms are frequently used to describe these methods: analysis and criticism. He explains:

---

17 Scot McKnight, ed., *Introducing New Testament Interpretation*, Guides to New Testament Exegesis (Louisville, KY: Baker Academic, 1990).
18 Hayes and Holladay, *Biblical Exegesis*, 9.
19 Hayes and *Holladay, Biblical Exegesis*, 13.
20 Hayes and Holladay, *Biblical Exegesis*, 8–13.
21 Michael J. Gorman *Elements of Biblical Exegesis: a Basic Guide for Students and Ministers* (Peabody, MA: Hendrickson Publishers, 2001), 26.

The Exegesis of Commentaries 33

Interpreters of the Bible employ a variety of general approaches and specific methods to understand and engage the text. Some of these methods are called *criticisms*. The use of the term *criticism*, as in *redaction criticism*, does not necessarily imply negative judgment; the primary meaning of the term is analysis, though it may also mean judgment—whether negative, positive, or both—about the historical, literary, or theological value of a text.[22]

Under the category of the synchronic approach, Gorman lists: literary criticism and genre and form analysis

(the quest to understand the text as literature by employing either traditional or more recent models of literary criticism that are employed in the study of literature generally). [There he lists] narrative criticism (a subset of literary criticism, the quest to understand the formal and material features of narrative texts or other texts that have an implicit or underlying narrative within or behind them). Rhetorical criticism [is next presented] (the quest to understand the devices, strategies, and structures employed in the text to persuade and/or otherwise affect the reader, as well as the overall goals or effect of those rhetorical elements). Lexical, grammatical, and syntactical analysis follows (the quest to understand words, idioms, grammatical forms, and the relationship among these items according to the norms of usage at the time the text was produced). [The next is] semantic or discourse analysis (the quest to understand the ways in which a text conveys meaning according to modern principles and theories of linguistics). The last is social-scientific criticism (the quest for the social identity, perceptions of the world, and cultural characteristics of the writes, readers/hearers, and communities suggested by the text . . . usually divided into two distinct subdisciplines, social description and social-scientific analysis).[23]

Under the diachronic approach, or the historical-critical method, Gorman lists textual criticism; historical linguistics; form criticism; tradition criticism; source criticism; redaction criticism; and historical criticism.

Text criticism is the quest for the original wording of the text. Historical linguistics is the quest to understand words, idioms, grammatical forms, and the relationship among these items, often with attention to their historical development within a language. Form criticism is the quest for the original type of oral or written tradition reflected in the text, and for determining out of what sort of situation such a tradition might have developed. Tradition criticism is the quest for understanding the growth of a tradition over time from its original form to its incorporation in the final text. Source criticism is the quest for the written source used in the text. Redaction criticism is the quest for perceiving the ways in which the final author of the text purposefully adopted and adapted sources.

---

22 Gorman, *Elements of Biblical Exegesis*, 12.
23 Gorman, *Element of Biblical Exegesis*, 13.

Historical criticism is the quest for the events that surrounded the production of the text, including the purported events narrated by the text itself.[24]

The existential approach is the author's proposed term (with no connection to existentialism philosophy intended) and is viewed as a part of the exegetical method or process even though some scholars oppose this view. The existential approach contains

> canonical criticism (exegesis is done in the context of the Bible as a whole); theological exegesis and spiritual reading (exegesis is done in the context of a specific religious tradition and for religious purposes); embodiment or actualization (exegesis is done in the context of attempting to appropriate and embody the text in the world); advocacy criticism, liberationist exegesis, and ideological criticism (exegesis is done in the context of struggle for justice or liberation).[25]

Werner Stenger in *Introduction to New Testament Exegesis* brings further clarification to the methods of biblical and especially New Testament exegesis. He simplifies the methodology to two goals: philological and historical. He writes, "The subdisciplines of exegesis fall into three basic groups: Some seek to describe a text's *linguistic form* and underlying structures, others look into the circumstances surrounding a text's *origin* and seeks to identify its initial addresses. Finally, other methods investigate the *reception* a text has had in the course of its history and has in the present."[26] This aspect of reception will be dealt with in the second part of this chapter. The same author continues with the following remarks, "But this third group of methods—when the text in question is the New Testament—is the task of every theological discipline, including ethics. Therefore, we must understand the specific discipline of *New Testament* exegesis as obligated in particular to describe the text's linguistic form and investigate the circumstances of its origin. New Testament exegesis is thus "directed primarily toward *philological* goals, and within this dual focus is called *historical-critical* exegesis."[27] The author admits that even this historical-critical method "possesses a more colorful palette of possibilities because of . . . methodological developments."[28] He mentions here form criticism with discourse analysis and rhetorical analysis and sociological and psychological approaches. With all these developments, he advises the reader to "keep in mind the basic ordering of exegetical methods described above. Some methods describe a text's linguistic form ("philological" methods), and some investigate the circumstances in which the text came into being ("historical" methods)."[29] He warns that even with this exegetical task completed, another task remains: "to make that qualitative transition from the historical

---

24 Gorman, *Element of Biblical Exegesis*, 15–16.
25 Gorman, *Element of Biblical Exegesis*, 19.
26 Werner Stenger, *Introduction to New Testament Exegesis*, trans. Douglas W. Stott (Grand Rapids, MI: William B. Eerdmans Publishing Company, 1993), 3.
27 Stenger, *Introduction to New Testament Exegesis*, 3.
28 Stenger, *Introduction to New Testament Exegesis*, 4.
29 Stenger, *Introduction to New Testament Exegesis*, 5.

elements of biblical texts to theological statements that are relevant for today."[30] This is what he calls "the theological problem of the historical-critical method"[31] implied in the hermeneutical process. He concludes with the warning that "[e]xegesis, like all the theological disciplines, continually breaks its teeth on this hard nut."[32]

As we have seen from these approaches, the process of exegesis is complex and cannot be reduced to some fixed steps. There is no standard approach to exegesis. Nevertheless, we have seen some common features that point to important elements of exegesis. When exegeting a passage, the text needs to be established and attention should be paid to morphology, semiotics, syntax, literary analysis, and other grammatical and philological issues, together with the historical context. All these should be done considering the theological and/or canonical context.

It is safe to conclude from these definitions that exegesis is seen as a multi-oriented task that considers at least the philological and the historical dimensions of a text. The criteria used for explaining these different exegetical approaches can be best explained in a bipolar way, as we will see in the next section as John Sailhamer did. This explanation offers two extremes of exegesis: one is focusing on the historical context behind the text, and the other is focusing on the text itself. Another way of explaining these differences in exegesis is by looking at the theological or philosophical presuppositions behind them. Thus, a more liberal theology is usually characterized by a more critical analysis, while a more conservative theology will use a more textual, canonical approach, starting from the presumption of verbal inspiration.

Historical or Text Oriented Approaches to Exegesis

This section will survey the tendencies and scholarly disciplines related to the field of interpretation. With this in mind, the next paragraphs will present an overview of biblical criticism in the light of John Sailhamer's contribution to this topic.

One revealing and insightful book concerning the discernment of different approaches in biblical scholarship was written in relation to Old Testament theology but serves as a guide for biblical studies and theology in general. John Sailhamer's book, *Introduction to Old Testament Theology: A Canonical Approach* is written from a scholarly evangelical perspective.[33] The author applies an analytical linguistic procedure that puts in contrast essential hermeneutical approaches like: a text versus event-oriented approach; a canonical versus a critical approach; a confessional versus a descriptive approach; and a diachronic versus a synchronic approach. He argues that the exegete's opinion on the locus of divine revelation will dictate his methodology. If the exegete or theologian views historical events as the locus of revelation, the text of Scripture serves only for reconstructing those events (or texts). If, however, the exegete sees Scripture as the revelation of God, his or her approach will be oriented to the text and the author's (or

---

30 Stenger, *Introduction to New Testament Exegesis*, 7.
31 Stenger, *Introduction to New Testament Exegesis*, 5.
32 Stenger, *Introduction to New Testament Exegesis*, 7.
33 John H. Sailhamer, *Introduction to Old Testament Theology: A Canonical Approach* (Grand Rapids, MI: Zondervan Publishing House, 1995).

Author's) intent. In the former approach, historical criticism as a methodology will be adapted; in the latter approach, canonical and literary criticism will prevail.

In the *New Schaff-Herzong Encyclopedia of Religious Knowledge* under the title "Exegesis or Hermeneutics," Henry S. Nash identifies three kinds of exegesis: "philological, revealing the structure and vocabulary of the language; historical, setting forth the text as the result of certain actual conditions of origin, contents and purpose; and stylistic, building on the other two and leading to the valuation of the text."[34] It follows that the process of biblical exegesis and biblical criticism falls in these categories. Most of the scholars would agree to divide biblical criticism in three: text criticism, historical criticism and literary criticism.

Textual or lower criticism is dealing with, and informing, all the three departments of exegesis. It is a historical enterprise in recovering data from a biblical manuscript that influences the wording of the text. According to ISBE "the function of textual criticism is the restoration of the original wording of a document when alterations have been introduced (deliberately or inadvertently) in the course of copying and recopying" the original manuscripts.[35] Textual criticism is a careful comparative study of the extant copies of the original manuscripts.[36] The text we read as a final product of textual criticism must be as close to the original as possible. Bruce Metzger describes textual criticism as follows: "The science of textual criticism deals with *(a)* the making and transmission of ancient manuscripts, *(b)* the description of the most important witnesses to the New Testament text, and *(c)* the history of the textual criticism of the New Testament as reflected in the succession of printed editions of the Greek Testament."[37] He goes on to say that "[t]he art of textual criticism refers to the application of reasoned considerations in choosing among variant readings."[38] Through these two descriptions he defines textual criticism as being both a science and an art. The criteria used for doing text criticism can be summarized in the simple maxim "choose the reading which best explains the origin of the others."[39]

The other Bible criticism methods (or higher criticism) will be shortly introduced here. Part of the arrangement of these methods is indebted to *The Anchor Bile Dictionary* and John H. Hayes and Carl R. Holladay. Higher criticism is generally divided into historical criticism and literary criticism.

---

34 Nash, "Exegesis or Hermeneutics," 239.
35 Frederick Fyvie Bruce, "Criticism," in *International Standard Bible Encyclopedia*, ed. Geoffrey W. Bromiley (Grand Rapids, MI: William B. Eerdmans Publishing Company, 1979), 1:818.
36 See Kurt Aland and Barbara Aland. *The Text of the New Testament: An Introduction to the Critical Editions and to the Theory and Practice of Modern Textual Criticism* (Grand Rapids, MI: W.B. Eerdmans, 1989).
37 Metzger and Ehrman, *The Text of the New Testament*, i.
38 Metzger and Ehrman, *The Text of the New Testament*, i.
39 Metzger and Ehrman, *The Text of the New Testament*, 207.

Historical criticism has the purpose to achieve a historical understanding, and for this, the text has to be viewed in its historical and cultural context.[40] A good exegete will have to pay attention to the historical situations described in the text and the historical situations behind the text which gave rise to the text (or the history in the text and the history of the text).[41] History of religions or *religionsgeschichte* is basically a study of comparative religion (Greco-Roman religions or cults) under historical criticism. Form criticism refers to the study of oral tradition behind the text and the *Sitz im Leben* (situations in life) that led to its development.[42] Form criticism can also be used in literary criticism where it deals with genre analysis and the relation of the text to the larger literary unit in which it is situated.[43] Tradition criticism analyses the origin and development of units of tradition which are cited within the biblical text and the way biblical authors adapted those materials. Closely tied to tradition criticism is oral tradition criticism. Sociological interpretation is another form of criticism that has to do with the *Sitz im Leben* and makes use of social sciences (sociology and cultural anthropology).[44]

Literary criticism may have concerns with historical aspects, but its focus is on the text itself. We agree with Joel B. Green's worry for not decisively separating the historical from the literal in our methodologies. This is because "the history to which the biblical text gives witness was isolated from the biblical text that provides this such a witness."[45] It is to be noticed that "early works in literary criticism dealt with vocabulary, grammar, style and rhetorical figures."[46] Source criticism had to do with the source of the Synoptic Gospels. Redaction criticism is concerned with the final composition (employing form, tradition and source criticism) and focuses on the final written form.[47] This is important for the study of the Synoptic Gospels (and not only) where one event or saying is reported sometimes in three, four different ways.[48] Another critical method has to do with the "identification and analysis of the literary type or classification to which a particular text belongs."[49] Its name is genre criticism.

The new literary criticism was a reaction against the traditional historical criticism. It sees the text "exclusively as literature" and that is the only "objective of investigation"[50] (historical investigations and the author's concern not being of importance). Rhetorical criticism tries to uncover "the personal aspects of the author's thought" and the context.[51]

---

40 William Baird, "Biblical Criticism," in *The Anchor Bible Dictionary* (New York: Doubleday, 1992), 1:732.
41 Hayes and Holladay, *Biblical Exegesis*, 42.
42 Baird, "Biblical Criticism," 732.
43 Hayes and Holladay, *Biblical Exegesis*, 77.
44 Baird, "Biblical Criticism," 733.
45 Green, "Commentary," 123.
46 Baird, "Biblical Criticism," 733.
47 Baird, "Biblical Criticism," 733–34.
48 Hayes and Holladay, *Biblical Exegesis*, 95.
49 Baird, "Biblical Criticism," 734.
50 Baird, "Biblical Criticism," 734.
51 Baird, "Biblical Criticism," 735.

Narrative criticism intends to restore the narrative features of the Bible which can refer some scholars to human experience in general.[52] Reader response criticism focuses on the role of the reader who is to be differentiated from the critic. This methodology uses notions like the ideal (the reader the author images) and real reader; the ideal (the author the reader images) and real author; and temporal and linear reading. The task of structuralism is to decode the text that is encoded with deep structures (unconscious mythic patterns with ontological significance) that are binary or dichotomous.[53]

Brevard Childs was one of the first to use canonical criticism, even though he rejected the title coined by J. A. Sanders.[54] Canonical criticism implies canonical hermeneutic which is "the investigation of how canonical texts are interpreted in the ongoing development of the tradition."[55]

For a historical-critical approach, one can refer to German scholars and the Tübingen School and to works of Martin Dibelius and F. Schleiermacher, F. C. Baur, D. F. Strauss, R. Bultmann, etc. For more text oriented commentaries, one can turn to such writers as Richard I. Pervo, Brevard Childs, even Silviu Tatu, Beniamin Fărăgău, etc.

It is now time to consider how a commentary should approach these methods. John Hayes and Carl Holladay insist there should be no hierarchical or mechanical process in exegesis, but rather, an exegete should let the questions and issues arise from the text itself.[56] They suggest six principles summarized here: (1) "Allow the text to set the agenda"; (2) "Let the questions point to the appropriate methodology, exegetical technique or type of criticism"; (3) Use the appropriate tools for each methodology; (4) Correlate the questions and answers addressed to this point; (5) Conclude the analysis; and (6) "Synthesize the findings into a coherent interpretation of the passage."[57]

Reception History

Earlier in the book we mentioned that Werner Stenger viewed the method of analyzing the *reception* that a text has had in the course of its history and has in the present, as part of the exegetical task. This will prove to be a valuable point especially when it comes to the Romanian context. The reality is that the majority of pastors, teachers, and leaders in the Evangelical communities are not in touch with Orthodox theology and practice. Analyzing the way a biblical passage was and is received in the Orthodox tradition will throw light not only on the exegetical part of a commentary, but also on its application part. D. H. Williams is right when he says

> the Christian Church has a long tradition of commentary on the Bible, far older (and richer) than the scholarship of the late nineteenth and twentieth centuries on which nearly all present methods and studies are based. This is a matter that Bible schools,

---

52 Baird, "Biblical Criticism," 735.
53 Baird, "Biblical Criticism", 735.
54 Baird, "Biblical Criticism", 736.
55 Baird, "Biblical Criticism", 736.
56 Hayes and Holladay, *Biblical Exegesis*, 105.
57 Hayes and Holladay, *Biblical Exegesis*, 110–12.

lay institutes, seminaries, and faculties of theology should pay heed in their training of students in biblical interpretation.[58]

He goes on to say "[p]atristic and medieval forms of 'pre-critical' exegesis—scriptural and theological—need to be retrieved as having an important value for biblical interpretation and application."[59]

What is meant by reception history? In a review essay by Jonathan Roberts and Christopher Rowland in the *Encyclopedia of the Bible and Its Reception*, the authors open with these statements:

> The reception history of the Bible has been, and continues to be, developed in a number of different ways. Much of the intellectual groundwork of reception history was done in the philosophical tradition that culminates in the philosophical hermeneutics of Hans Georg Gadamer. Gadamer's work began to be developed in the context of literary studies by, amongst others, Hans Robert Jauss, and in a theological context in the work of Ulrich Luz on Matthew's gospel.[60]

These three authors (Gadamer, Jauss, and Luz) will guide our understanding of reception history and its role in biblical exegesis and commentaries.

Hans Georg Gadamer (1900–2002), in his *magnum opus*, the book titled *Truth and Method* sets the basis for reception history. He says: "The horizon is the range of vision that includes everything that can be seen from a particular vantage point. Applying this to the thinking mind, we speak of narrowness of horizon, of possible expansion of horizon, of opening up of new horizons, and so forth."[61] He then goes on to say,

> in the sphere of historical understanding, too, we speak of horizons, especially when referring to the claim of historical consciousness to see the past in its own terms, not in terms of our contemporary criteria and prejudices but within its own historical horizon. The task of historical understanding also involves acquiring an appropriate historical horizon, so that what we are trying to understand can be seen in its true dimensions. If we fail to transpose ourselves into the historical horizon from which the traditionary text speaks, we will misunderstand the significance of what it has to say to us. To that extent this seems a legitimate hermeneutical requirement: we must place ourselves in the other situation in order to understand it.[62]

---

58 D. H. Williams, *Evangelicals and Tradition: The Formative Influence of the Early Church* (Grand Rapids, MI: Baker Academic, 2005), 162.

59 Williams, *Evangelicals and Tradition*, 162.

60 Jonathan Roberts and Christopher Rowland, review of *Encyclopedia of the Bible and Its Reception*, in *Relegere: Studies in Religion and Reception* 1, no. 2 (2011), 351, accessed 12 September 2012, http://www.relegere.org/index.php/relegere/article/viewFile/473/556.

61 Hans-Georg Gadamer, *Truth and Method*, 2nd rev. ed., trans. Joel Weinsheimer and Donald G. Marshall (New York: Continuum, 2004), 301.

62 Gadamer, *Truth and Method*, 302.

He then gives the example of conversation saying that we normally try to discover the other person's horizon. He comments:

> In a conversation, when we have discovered the other person's standpoint and horizon, his ideas become intelligible without our necessarily having to agree with him; so also when someone thinks historically, he comes to understand the meaning of what has been handed down without necessarily agreeing with it or seeing himself in it. . . .
>
> In fact the horizon of the present is continually in the process of being formed because we are continually having to test all our prejudices. An important part of this testing occurs in encountering the past and in understanding the tradition from which we come.[63]

Gadamer is known for the metaphoric description of the hermeneutical horizons, admitting: "however if there is no such thing as these distinct horizons, why do we speak of the fusion of horizons and not simply of the formation of the one horizon, whose bounds are set in the depths of tradition?" He continues on the same metaphorical line: "In the process of understanding, a real fusion of horizons occurs—which means that as the historical horizon is projected, it is simultaneously superseded. To bring about this fusion in a regulated way is the task of what we called historically effected consciousness."[64] In hermeneutics, Gadamer emphasized the "critical reflections both on the activity of interpreting texts and from assessments of the 'effective history' (*Wirkungsgeschichte*), or the results and consequences of interpretation over time."[65]

Hans Robert Jauss was the one who decisively shaped reception history. For him, "[r]eception history demonstrates both continuities and discontinuities or 'provocations' . . . in the history of interpretation. The former stresses the role of tradition; the latter is more in tune with so-called postmodern approaches."[66]

As we have seen, Gadamer's concept of *Wirkungsgeschichte* was the basis for Jauss's reception theory, and both were the foundation for Luz's methodology in his commentaries. Ulrich Luz is best known for his commentary on Matthew's Gospel. "Luz works from within a particular faith tradition, and his work remains principally concerned with the theological, ecclesiastical, and (in quite a conservative sense) artistic reception history of Matthew's gospel."[67] Luz "has built significantly on Gadamer's stress on the 'effective history' of texts and has reopened important questions about the role of the history of interpretation and its methodological implications for biblical scholars. Luz illustrates what he terms *Wirkungsgeschichte* (Gadamer's term) in his four-volume commentary on Matthew."[68] For Luz, *Wirkungsgeschichte* "includes both the influence of the text on its successive reception and the influence of successive

---

63 Gadamer, *Truth and Method*, 302, 305.
64 Gadamer, *Truth and Method*, 306.
65 Gerald T. Sheppard and Anthony C. Thiselton, "Biblical Interpretation in Europe in the Twentieth Century," in *Dictionary of Major Biblical Interpreters*, ed. Donald K. McKim (Nottingham, England: Inter-Varsity Press, 2007), 81.
66 Sheppard and Thiselton, "Biblical Interpretation", 81.
67 Roberts and Rowland, review of *Encyclopedia of the Bible and Its Reception*, 351–52.
68 Sheppard and Thiselton, "Biblical Interpretation," 81.

'receptions' on later understanding of the text. These include 'history, reception and actualizing of a text in media other than commentary, e.g., in sermons, canonical law, hymnody, art, and in the actions and sufferings of the church.'"[69]

Conclusion

So far we have shown that the methodology of most commentaries involves a double task: the exegetical task, and the expounding task. In this first chapter we dealt with the exegetical task and we concluded that the exegetical methodology is concerned with the historical and philological aspects of the text. We went through all sorts of methodologies in order to show that biblical criticism is divided in two major scholarly tendencies (besides lower or textual criticism): historical criticism and literary criticism. Though many other methodologies can be mentioned besides the ones approached in this book, they all fall in one of the two. However, a separation of the two is forced.

In this book we also included a relatively modern approach in biblical studies: reception history. As the editors argue in the preface of the first issue of *Relegere: Studies in Religion and Reception*, "the goal of reception history is not to recover the original meaning of a text or to establish an authoritative reading, or even worse, to redeem a troublesome text."[70] Reception history is a helpful enterprise when it comes to understanding the Romanian Orthodox (or Evangelical) tradition and practice, and serves as a connecting bridge and catalyst of interaction and dialogue between Orthodoxy and Evangelicalism. Nevertheless, due to the limits of this work, reception history is to be applied only from the literary perspective. This is to say that in this book we will limit the analysis of the reception of a chosen passage to written works, and the will be on the Greek Church fathers. In our analysis of biblical commentaries in the next chapters, the methodology applied by their authors will be categorized as such (i.e., historical-critical, literary-critical, etc.).

The methodology of the commentary proposed in the final chapter will incorporate the historical and philological analysis and will be text oriented, canonical, confessional, but not ahistorical. Starting from a belief in the verbal inspiration of the Scriptures, any interpretation applied to the text will be within the borders of the canon of the New Testament, the theology of that canon, the interpreter's confessional beliefs (which are viewed as a help and not a hindrance, as long as they are admitted in the process of engaging in the "hermeneutical spiral"), and the grammatical-philological and historical-social context of the text.

---

69 Sheppard and Thiselton, "Biblical Interpretation," 81.

70 Eric Repphun, Deane Galbraith, Will Sweetman, and James Harding, "Beyond Christianity, the Bible and the Text: Urgent Tasks and New Orientations for Reception History," *Relegere: Studies in Religion and Reception* 1, no.1 (2011): 10, accessed 11 January 2021, http://www.relegere.org/index.php/relegere/article/viewFile/391/494.

CHAPTER 3

Bible Translation in Commentaries

In the previous chapters we started to gain a perception on biblical commentaries by seeing them as a genre with common characteristics and by observing the research process involved in writing them. We also stated that a commentary assumes two major parts: exegesis and exposition. In this chapter we will be considering the process of translation which is the bridge between the two. It is a starting point for the explanations presented in the text of the commentaries. The translation of the biblical text found in the commentary may explain issues that were probably unclear in some translations or may need further explanations.

A discussion of biblical translation as a part of the commentary text is required here because of its importance in the process of explaining the text. In fact, the explanation of the biblical passage may well start with its translation. This discussion around the process of translation will start with its description, definition and categories. It will then point to the advocates of different approaches of biblical translations and their theological presuppositions. Then it will address the main issues involved in translation, together with its implications for biblical commentaries. Finally, the discussion will consider some of the special implications raised in the Romanian context.

The issue of translation is treated separately here because it may be considered as a discipline in and of itself outside the exegetical process. However, there is a major dimension of translation that is of concern here: that of interpretation. Translation as interpretation is often offered in many commentaries. This kind of translation is intentionally more literal or more dynamic, because it has to be in line with the exegesis offered by the author.

The tradition of Bible translation is very rich and diverse extending not only to the past, but also to our present times. The Scriptures have "been translated in more languages than any other piece of literature."[1] Even from the close of the second or the beginning of the third century, Christians undertook the responsibility of translating Scripture from the Greek and Hebrew in languages that were spoken in different important regions. In this manner the Bible has been translated in languages such as Syriac, Latin, Coptic, Gothic, Armenian, Georgian, Ethiopian, Arabic, Sogdian or Nubian. According to United Bible Societies, out of 6,600 languages in the world, portions of the Bible have been translated into 2,527 languages and about other 2,000

---

[1] Bruce M. Metzger, *The Bible in Translation: Ancient and English Versions* (Grand Rapids, MI: Baker Academic, 2001), 8.

are in process of translation. The complete Bible has now been translated into 475 languages and the New Testament into 1,240.[2]

Description, Definition and Categories

In the article on the verb *to translate* in the *International Standard Biblical Encyclopedia*, we find the following specifications:

> [A]ny translation requires that the translator not attempt to retain a word-for-word or structure-for-structure rendering of the old into new. Rather the translator must take every effort to express accurately in the receptor language the precise meaning of the original, a procedure that demands interpretation. The people in biblical times understood this, because all the words noted above that are rendered 'translation' or 'translate' have as their fundamental meaning 'interpretation' or 'interpret.'[3]

This subjective aspect of the translation process is also evidenced by the saying: "One cannot translate in a vacuum."[4] We need to understand better this process of translation. The problem is how to translate a passage in order to communicate it to the target audience/readers, or what translation should one choose from many versions on the market for the same purpose. The answer to these questions can be given only after an analysis of the theory of biblical translation.

What exactly is Bible translation and what are the issues involved in the translation process? There are a good number of Bible translation philosophies, and at first it seems that every new version of the Bible in any given language has a different approach to the translation methodology.[5] The question, *"What does a good Bible translation look like?"* is answered in terms of the purpose of that translation. In the spectrum of Bible translations there are two major types generally admitted. The first type of translation focuses on the source language and tries to be faithful to its form, or words with the result that many times it neglects the message. This is usually called a "literal" or "word-for-word" translation.[6] The second type of translation focuses on the message and function (in terms of the response of the addressees) of both languages with the result that the form is many times sacrificed. This is called a dynamic or a "thought-for-thought"

---

[2] United Bible Societies, accessed 5 August 2012, http://www.unitedbiblesocieties.org/sample-page/bible-translation/.

[3] G. F. Hawthorne, "Translate," in *International Standard Bible Encyclopedia*, ed. Geoffrey W. Bromiley (Grand Rapids, MI: William B. Eerdmans publishing Company, 1979), 4:890.

[4] Richmond Lattimore cited in Eugene Nida, *Towards a Science of Translation: With Special Reference to Principles and Procedures Involved in Bible Translating* (Leiden, Netherlands: E. J. Brill, 1969), 148.

[5] Some writers argue for the fact that translation is not a science. See for example George Steiner, *After Babel: Aspects of Language and Translation*, 3rd ed. (Oxford: Oxford University Press, 1998). He called translation an exact art.

[6] Gordon D. Fee and Mark L. Strauss, *How to Choose a Translation for All It's Worth: A Guide to Understanding and Using Bible Versions* (Grand Rapids, MI: Zondervan, 2007), 25.

translation.⁷ The discussions today use the term *formal equivalence* in reference to the former type of translation and *functional equivalence* in reference to the latter.

The last term comes from translation theorist Eugene A. Nida. He is one of the major authors on the subject of translation, and at least two of his books are still a point of reference when it comes to the contemporary debate: *The Theory and Practice of Translation* coauthored with Charles A. Taber and *Toward a Science of Translating: With Special Reference to Principles and Procedures Involved in Bible Translating*. Nida identifies three types of translations: "intralingual," "interlingual" and "intersemiotic," out of which interlingual translation is "the translation proper."⁸ Bible translating, in particular, surpasses all the other various types of translations in: (1) the range of subject matter (e.g. poetry, law, narration); (2) linguistic variety (directly or indirectly from Greek and Hebrew into more than 1,200 other languages and dialects); (3) historical depth (from the third century B.C. to the present); (4) cultural diversity (there is no cultural area in the world which is not represented by Bible translating); (5) volume of manuscript evidence; (6) number of translators involved; (7) conflicting viewpoints; and (8) accumulation of data on principles and procedures employed.⁹

Nida gives a definition for dynamic equivalence in the glossary provided in his book *The Theory and Practice of Translation*: "[Dynamic equivalence is the] quality of a translation in which the message of the original text has been so transported into the receptor language that the RESPONSE of the RECEPTOR is essentially like that of the original receptors. (his emphasis)"¹⁰ He also gives a definition of formal correspondence in the same glossary. He says formal correspondence is the "quality of a translation in which the features of the form of the source text have been mechanically reproduced in the receptor language. Typically, formal correspondence distorts the grammatical and stylistic patters of the receptor language, and hence distorts the message, so as to cause the receptor to misunderstand or to labor unduly hard; opposed to DYNAMIC EQUIVALENCE."¹¹ (his emphasis).

According to these definitions and clarifications, we can now see the entire spectrum of translations or Bible versions and their classification. At the extremity of the dynamic translation, many have put paraphrase versions of the Bible (or portions of Bible). They view it as a subjective and loose or free translation. However, Eugene Nida helps us once again to understand that the process of paraphrasing is a technical term from linguistics and related disciplines, and is characterized by three specific features: (1) it is intralingual rather than interlingual, *i.e.*, it is 'another way of saying the same thing' in the *same* language; (2) it is rigorous, in that there are no changes in the

---

7 Philip W. Comfort, *Essential Guide to Bible Versions* (Wheaton, IL: Tyndale House Publishers, 2000), 104.

8 Eugene A. Nida, *Toward a Science of Translating: With Special Reference to Principles and Procedures Involved in Bible Translating* (Leiden, Netherlands: E. J. Brill, 1969), 3–4.

9 Nida, *Toward a Science of Translating*, 4.

10 Eugene A. Nida and Charles R. Taber, *The Theory and Practice of Translation*, 2nd ed. (Leiden, Netherlands: E. J. Brill for UBS, 1982), 200.

11 Nida and Taber, *The Theory and Practice of Translation*, 201.

semantic components: no additions, no deletions, no skewing of relationships, only a different marking of the same relations between the same elements; (3) specifically as it relates to back-transformation, it is aimed at restatement at a particular level, that of kernels."[12] The back-transformation process he is referring to is the analysis into kernels of the surface structure of a discourse in the same language.[13] Even though he uses the term in back-transformation, it is helpful to notice paraphrasing is not a translation from a language into another and as a consequence it should not be included in the classifications or spectrum of translations (though it might be viewed as a version of the Bible). In a sense, therefore, paraphrase "occupies a middle place between translation and commentary."[14]

This leaves us with two ends of the translation spectrum. At one end we have form and at the other we have function.[15] Thus, Bible versions are generally grouped into three categories on account of their translation of the Hebrew and Greek: formal equivalence, mediating and functional equivalence.[16] To give examples from the English versions of the Bible, we can talk about *New American Standard Bible*, *New King James Version* and the *New Revised Standard Version* as being in the category of formal equivalence;[17] the *Good News Translation* (*Today's English Version*; *Good News Bible*) and *Contemporary English Version* as being in the category of functional equivalence;[18] and the *Today's New International Version* and *New English Bible* in the mediating category.[19] Even though Gordon Fee and Mark Strauss consider *The Living Bible* to be a functional equivalence translation, if we take into account Nida's definition, this version is a paraphrase because Taylor used the *ASV* as a base text for his translation.[20]

Advocates for the Positions

If the old focus in translation was the form of the message with "particular delight in being able to reproduce stylistic specialties, *e.g.*, rhythms, rhymes, plays on words, chiasmus, parallelism and unusual grammatical structures,"[21] Nida helped to place the focus on message, audience and receptor language. Even before Nida, some Bible translators favored functional equivalence.[22] His contribution awoke translators from the naivety of word-for-word translation.

For Nida "[t]ranslating consists in reproducing in the receptor language the closest natural equivalent of the source-language message, first in terms of meaning and

---

12 Nida and Taber, *The Theory and Practice of Translation*, 47.
13 Nida and Taber, *The Theory and Practice of Translation*, 197.
14 McClintock and Strong, "Commentary," 428.
15 Fee and Strauss, *How to Choose a Translation*, 28.
16 Fee and Strauss, *How to Choose a Translation*, 26.
17 Fee and Strauss, *How to Choose a Translation*, 147–48.
18 Fee and Strauss, *How to Choose a Translation*, 154.
19 Fee and Strauss, *How to Choose a Translation*, 149, 151.
20 Fee and Strauss, *How to Choose a Translation*, 153.
21 Nida and Taber, *The Theory and Practice of Translation*, 1.
22 See for example Jerome's preference for a "sense for sense" translation explained in Philip W. Comfort's *Essential Guide to Bible Versions*, 105.

secondly in terms of style."²³ This is possible if the translator focuses on the near kernel levels because "if one can reduce grammatical structures to the kernel level, they can be transformed more readily and with a minimum of distortion."²⁴ He emphasizes the fact that "[t]ranslating must aim primarily at 'reproducing the message'" and that "[t]he best translation does not sound like a translation."²⁵

The same author suggests a set of four priorities in translation: "(1) contextual consistency has priority over verbal consistency (or word-for-word) concordance, (2) dynamic equivalence has priority over formal correspondence, (3) the aural (heard) form of language has priority over the written form, (4) forms that are used by and acceptable to the audience for which a translation is intended to have priority over forms that may be traditionally more prestigious."²⁶ All this is done in the light of "the fundamental procedures of translating: analysis, transfer, reconstructing and testing."²⁷

On the side of dynamic equivalence, we can say that Eugene Nida was its important supporter, as it has been proven so far. It is also clear that the advocates of form equivalence translations are usually found in the ranks of the KJV supporters (even NASB, or RSV), because of the version's fame for its literal translation. This is implied by Ryken when he states his choice for an essentially literal translation is in the King James tradition.²⁸

Theological Foundations

It is important to understand that form equivalence was preferred because of the view of biblical inspiration and inerrancy. The editors of *The Challenge of Bible Translation* affirm that "the reason of some (not all) conservative evangelicals begins to shift from defensible doctrine to questionable inference. Each individual word of Scripture, the questionable reasoning suggests, was specifically selected by God and delivered to us from above in a manner very similar to dictation. The words were sent down, one at a time, like crystal droplets. Each word is an autonomous integer, separate from the rest, and each is to be treasured like a sacred gem and cherished inviolate for all time." ²⁹ That is why "[t]hose who view Scripture this way ... favor attempts at word-for-word translation." In the same line of thought, "evangelicals are to get beyond their current impasse over translation theory," and realize the need for "a more profound doctrine of biblical inerrancy—one that continues to respect the inspired words of the original

---

23 Nida and Taber, *The Theory and Practice of Translation*, 12.
24 Nida and Taber, *The Theory and Practice of Translation*, 39.
25 Nida and Taber, *The Theory and Practice of Translation*, 12.
26 Nida and Taber, *The Theory and Practice of Translation*, 14.
27 Nida and Taber, *The Theory and Practice of Translation*, vii.
28 Leland Ryken, *The Word of God in English: Criteria for Excellence in Bible Translation* (Wheaton, IL: Crossway Books, 2002), 18.
29 Glen G. Scorgie, Mark L. Strauss and Steven M. Voth, eds., *The Challenge of Bible Translation: Communicating God's Word to the World* (Grand Rapids, MI: Zondervan, 2003), 23.

text but also acknowledges that these words are mere instruments in the service of a higher purpose, namely, the communication of meaning."[30]

Not only those who view the inspiration of the Bible at a dictation level advocate the formal equivalence or the essentially literal translation. Those who do probably emphasize the suggested common denominator is the verbal inspiration belief of the evangelicals.[31]

Concerning the dynamic equivalence position, the theological understanding of translation finds its main source in a neo-orthodox view of inspiration, with focus not so much on the word that is inspired, but on the experience. Robert Thomas lists Moffatt's translation as one among the modern/dynamic equivalence versions moving away from verbal inspiration. He affirmed that his methodology of translation was "freed from the influence of the theory of verbal inspiration."[32]

Dynamic equivalence supporters also can stress that a translation should be comprehensive and natural for the reception language. Robert Thomas, who was mentioned earlier, demonstrated in his article that the majority of advocates of dynamic equivalence come from the missionary field and are concerned with contextualizing the message of the gospel through translations. There remains to be proven, however, that this is the defining role of a Bible translation. As we will see further, they tend to believe a translation should replace the work of a missionary. This approach has its weaknesses and when it comes to commentaries, the translation they use should be more literal in order to be more helpful for the study of the text.

Addressing the Main Issues

Some of the important issues in Bible translation will now be shortly introduced here. It is vital to understand what principles a good translation should take into account. The discussion about Bible translation usually uses the principles of accuracy, clarity, naturalness, and audience-appropriateness. Accuracy means a translation should reflect the meaning of the text as closely as possible. A translation should also be clear in the receptor language, but without transculturation. This means the genitive, some verbal aspects and the word order should not be rendered mechanically. When it is said a translation should be natural, it usually means the idioms of the source language should not be translated *ad literam*. Nevertheless, it must respect and retain the author-intended ambiguity. A good translation is always appropriate for its audience.[33] This is to be understood as a qualifier of the other criteria. From his definition of dynamic equivalence, Eugene Nida stressed the fact that a translation must try to get a similar reaction from its audience as the original text produced for its original audience.

---

30 Glen Scorgie et al., *The Challenge of Bible Translation*, 23.

31 This is implied by professor Robert L. Thomas in "Dynamic Equivalence: A Method of Translation or System of Hermeneutics," *The Master's Seminary Journal* 1, no. 2 (Fall 1990), 164–65, accessed 13 January 2021, http://www.tms.edu/tmsj/tmsj1g.pdf.

32 James Moffatt cited by Thomas, "Dynamic Equivalence: A Method of Translation or System of Hermeneutics," 165.

33 Fee and Strauss, *How to Choose a Translation*, 36–41.

However, this must be understood as referring to linguistic priorities alone.[34] For liturgical purposes, a translation should have a natural flow and sound good when read out loud.[35] Faithfulness or fidelity to the original language can also be a criterion for translations. The problem is that all versions claim to be faithful, but they give priority either to the meaning or to the form of the source language. The last criterion for a good translation summarizes the others: a translator should respect the genius of the source and the receptor language, pay attention to literary genre issues (like rhythm in poetry), and try to produce a literary work.[36] All these are important because "the biblical text represents a spiritual and cultural treasure which must be elegantly, and modernly translated."[37]

From the impact of Nida's theory of translation the domination of functional equivalence did not mean it was accepted unanimously. Ryken makes this very clear, and he adds that now, people that disagreed with the functional equivalence modern versions have an alternative in the English Standard Version to modern translations on the one hand and the Authorized Version (KJV) or Revised Standard Version on the other hand.[38] D. A. Carson, Leland Ryken, Raymond C. Van Leeuwen, and others have shown the limitations and even dangerous tendencies of the functional equivalence translation theory. Among others we mention the tendency to interpret the passage for the reader; to eliminate any ambiguity, even those intentioned by the author; to put more emphasis on the reader than the text; the tendency to reductionism; to destabilize the biblical text; transculturation brought by a contextualization desire and evangelistic zeal and so on.

Therefore, when it comes to Bible translation, we have to remember five important points. First, there will always be a degree of loss in the process of translation. One cannot render in another language exactly what was present in the source language. Therefore, we must understand any translation has a degree of subjectivity and interpretation. Secondly, a translation can and should not replace the work of evangelists and preachers. Thirdly, a translation that is too literal is not natural and many times not understandable in a receptor language. Fourthly, dynamic equivalence versions of the Bible sacrifice their uniqueness or "otherness" by over-contextualizing it. Finally, the entire discussion between the two opposite camps tends not to recognize the fact that meaning cannot be utterly divorced from form.

---

34 Donald Arthur Carson, "The Limits of Functional Equivalence Translation—and other Limits, too," in Glen G. Scorgie, Mark L. Strauss and Steven M. Voth, eds., *The Challenge of Bible Translation: Communicating God's Word to the World* (Grand Rapids, MI: Zondervan, 2003), 93.

35 Ryken, *The Word of God in English*, 288.

36 Nida, *The Theory and Practice of Translation*, 4.

37 Octavian Baban, "Reflecţii asupra locului Bibliei şi a traducerilor ei în mărturia şi viaţa Bisericii Baptiste," *Jurnal Teologic* 5, (2006): 135.

38 Ryken, *The Word of God in English*, 16.

Implications for Biblical Commentaries

One of the concluding thoughts on the translation debate is that the two major camps give the impression that form and meaning are totally separate in a literary text. We have to remember that in many ways "form is meaning,"[39] and the two must not be brutally separated.[40] Many times translation theorists write as though a translation of the Bible can solve all the problems in understanding. If this would be the case, we would not need missionaries, evangelists, preachers, teachers, expositors, or the Holy Spirit.[41] It is true that interpretation and translation intersect in their purpose, but they are not identical. We have to be aware of the limitations both formal and functional equivalence have and remember that we always have the option to footnote a text (limited to neutrally theological matters of linguistics, history and culture).[42]

Which versions or translations are good then? The answer to that question depends on the purpose of the reader. According to Nida and many other translators and translation theorists, a functional equivalence translation is what people need, but he also admits the need for different types of translation.[43] Gordon Fee and Mark Strauss suggest the use of more than one version of the Bible: a mediating version would be overall useful for a primary Bible; a form equivalent version would serve as a tool for study purposes; and a functional equivalence version would provide a fresh eye on the text.[44] The need for a variety of translations is also maintained by the literal translation theorist Leland Ryken.[45] In these authors we see the generally admitted need for more than one translation, because a translation can never be free from subjectivism and can never be perfect.[46]

Stenger believes that, "[a] text translated from its original language into a target language invariably undergoes alterations of many kinds. The simple core meaning might be translatable, but it is impossible to transfer fully the phonological and grammatical elements of the original language."[47] This and the importance of having a group of scholars involved in the process of translation are evidenced also by Philip Comfort. Since "the translator must enter the same thought as the author," he affirmed that a "functionally-equivalent or a thought for thought translation should be done by a group of scholars (to guard against personal subjectivism), who employ the best

---

39 Ryken, *The Word of God in English*, 31.

40 See the argument made by D. A. Carson in *The Limits of Functional Equivalence* mentioned above.

41 Carson, "The Limits of Functional Equivalence," 103–104.

42 Carson, "The Limits of Functional Equivalence," 91–93.

43 Nida and Taber, *The Theory and Practice of Translation*, 31, cited in Y. C. Yang, "To Whom is a Translator Responsible—Reader or Author?," in Stanley E. Porter and Richards S. Hess, eds., *Translating the Bible: Problems and Prospects* (London: T&T Clark International, 2004), 59n28.

44 Fee and Strauss, *How to Choose a Translation*, 29.

45 Ryken, *The Word of God in English*, 10.

46 For an extended discussion of this issue generally and subjectivity specifically, see Thomas, "Dynamic Equivalence," 149–69.

47 Stenger, *Introduction to New Testament Exegesis*, 8.

exegetical tools."[48] This is the case, however, when one has in view the translation of the whole Bible or one Testament. Some books on exegesis include the translation in the exegetical task in two stages: the first stage is to give a provisional translation of the passage selected in order to get acquainted with the passage and the second stage which is optional, is to provide a final translation.[49] Probably Matthew Brook O'Donnell is the first one to suggest the idea of creating an "interpretative translation" as a result of the exegetical task.[50] His idea is built, among other arguments, on the observation that many commentaries "include a new translation of each pericope as part of their format" and that "[t]hese translations often reflect interpretative decisions."[51]

Probably all commentators will want to produce a translation which is closer to the literal end of the spectrum. Just because of the reality of various translations present in English, commentaries in the same language often include a translation of their own and discussions around the options of expressing a certain biblical passage in that language. There are three kinds of commentaries in this regard. We may have commentaries that use a (authorized) translation; commentaries that offer only their translation; and commentaries that offer their translation and then interact with other translations. Usually, the methodology of approaching translations is chosen by the editors.

We have to be aware of the truth expressed by Hays and Holladay. They asserted that when translations are made they are themselves already interpretations, since it is never possible for a translation to be an exact one-to-one transference from one language to another.

> An interpretation of a translation is what might be called a 'second-level interpretation.' A first-level interpretation is the interpretation made of the original, whether by a native speaker or hearer or by one who has acquired knowledge of the original language. What appears in a translation is the translator's understanding of the original. The second level of interpretation enters the picture when an interpreter seeks to understand the content of the translation.[52]

Perhaps, this is the case in Romanian Bible translations. Interpretations of translations or "second-level interpretations" become the only choice of a majority of pastors. This is due to the relative lack of commentaries dealing with the Greek text and its rendering in Romanian.

The Romanian Specific Context

Considering all the data about the theory and practice of translation that we covered so far, what kind of translation is Dumitru Cornilescu's and what are the implications

---

48 Comfort, *Essential Guide to Bible Versions*, 105–106.
49 E.g., Fee, *New Testament Exegesis*, 10–11, 35.
50 Matthew Brook O'Donnell, "Translation and the Exegetical Process, Using Mark 5.1–10, 'The Bidding of the Strongman', as a Test Case," in *Translating the Bible: Problems and Prospects*, ed. Stanley E. Porter and Richard S. Hess (London: T&T Clark International, 2004), 163.
51 O'Donnell, "Translation and the Exegetical Process," 163.
52 Hayes and Holladay, *Biblical Exegesis*, 9.

for the theory of Bible commentary writing in the Romanian context? In 2004, Marius David Cruceru, professor at Emanuel University of Oradea wrote an article in the evangelical periodical *Creștinul Azi* with the title *"Cornilescu" față de alte traduceri ale Sfintelor Scripturi în limba Română. Propunere de sistem de grile analitice pentru ediții ale Bibliei după 1989, în cadrul mișcării evanghelice din România*[53] (*"Cornilescu" compared to other Romanian translations of the Holy Scriptures. A Proposed analytical grading system for Bible editions after 1989 in the frame of the evangelical movement in Romania*). Cruceru set a number of criteria for Bible translations in Romania after 1989. His research included investigating one hundred Christian evangelical families. Most of his criteria in his investigation had to do with things like classification, identification, selection, comparative analysis and internal analysis. For the limited purpose of this book we will focus only on the internal analysis criteria.

The first two terms Cruceru uses are often encountered in Romanian translation theorists or philologists: denotation and connotation. Denotation is the sense of a word from the source language in the receptor language established through the use of dictionaries.[54] Connotation is basically what a word means in different contexts, namely, a meaning that goes beyond the definition taken from dictionaries.[55]

Professor Cruceru affirms that "a good translator will look not only for denotation . . . but he will look for that unique sense which will fit perfectly into the new context created by the text to be translated."[56] He goes on saying that the word order is important only in the case of word play and that the reason many translations sound bad is because the translator keeps the word order of the source text. In his opinion, a good translator also seeks to emphasize the same thing the author wanted to emphasize. A good translator transposes himself in the manner and mood the author expressed the text (phonologically, lexically, grammatically and linguistically) and controls his or her emotions. The last criterion mentioned by Cruceru is style. He cites Virgil Nemoianu saying that the relationship between the translation and the original work and the relationship between the translation and the Romanian culture are important.[57] Other tasks of the translator are: to understand the essence of the text and its meanings, to know thoroughly the two languages, to honor the meaning not the word order, to create a clear version without unnecessary embellishments, to compose in a pleasant style. After having set these criteria and analyzed 13 editions of the translation of the entire Bible or portions of it in Romanian, Cruceru concludes that the most popular and accepted edition is still Cornilescu's translation and editions of it accompanied by helping tools such as study notes. He advises that the wisest thing to do is reprint and reedit Cornilescu's text with

---

53 Marius David Cruceru, '"Cornilescu" față de alte traduceri ale Sfintelor Scripturi în limba Română. Propunere de system de grille analitice pentru ediții ale Bibliei după 1989, în cadrul mișcării evanghelice din România,' in *Creștinul Azi* 4 (January 2004): 2–13.

54 Leon D. Levițchi, *Îndrumar pentru traducătorii din limba engleză in limba româna* (Bucharest, Romania: Editura Științifică și Enciclopedică, 1975), 19.

55 Levițchi, *Îndrumar*, 174.

56 Cruceru, *"Cornilescu" față de alte traduceri*, 5.

57 Cruceru, *"Cornilescu" față de alte traduceri*, 6.

study tools for at least two decades. During this time Romanians are encouraged to "sharpen our instruments," that is to prepare a monumental new contemporary relevant translation as a product of a developed authentic school of translation. Cruceru admits that Cornilescu's translation does not pay careful attention to details presented by the Hebrew and Greek text, but he believes it has great insight combined with the hard work of an exceptional translator.[58] He encourages the use of the original language in writing commentaries.

To this analysis by Cruceru, we can add the criteria of accuracy, clarity, naturalness and audience-appropriateness and apply them to Cornilescu's translation of the Bible. In his master's thesis Dragoș Manea showed examples of passages and expressions from Cornilescu's translation that are less accurate. For example, to mention a few, the translation of: ἁμαρτίαν οὐ ποιεῖ by "does not sin," οὐ δύναται ἁμαρτάνειν by "he cannot sin,"[59] τῷ πάντοτε θριαμβεύοντι ἡμᾶς ἐν τῷ Χριστῷ by "always carries us in His triumphal chariot in Christ,"[60] ῥίζα γὰρ πάντων τῶν κακῶν ἐστιν ἡ φιλαργυρία by "the love of money is the root of all evil,"[61] and εἰ δέ τις ἀγνοεῖ, ἀγνοεῖται by "and if someone does not understand, let him not understand!"[62] These examples illustrate the lack of accuracy in some places in Cornilescu's translation and clarity in his rendering of some verbal aspects. Even though Cornilescu's syntax and flow of text is good and natural, the contemporary audience is also growing ignorant of the meaning of some words that he used in his translation.

Most would agree that Dumitru Cornilescu achieved a monumental accomplishment by translating the Bible. Today, however, more and more, scholars are conscious that there is a need for good, contemporary translations of the Bible in Romanian.

Conclusion

In the Romanian context it is important to provide a personal translation of the passage commented upon simply because the most accepted and popular Romanian translation used today, Cornilescu, is unclear in places. At times, the archaic language raises difficulties in understanding the passage.

Since translations have an element of interpretation, it is better to avoid translating commentaries from other languages into Romanian. It is also better to provide an understanding of the extant translation options by offering one's own translation and initiating a dialogue between them in the corpus of the commentary. Probably the best solution is to provide a more literal translation in the first part of the comment on a biblical passage and then to explain idioms, tense nuances, genitive constructions, textual variants, etc. and compare them with the Cornilescu version in the latter part of the commentary. The Cornilescu version is probably still more satisfactory than many

---

58 Cruceru, *"Cornilescu" față de alte traduceri*, 11.
59 Manea, "A Short Exploration," 47.
60 Manea, "A Short Exploration," 53.
61 Manea, "A Short Exploration," 59.
62 Manea, "A Short Exploration," 65.

other versions. Romanians now hope to have a better translation and there is encouraging movement in this direction.

CHAPTER 4

The Exposition of Commentaries

The exposition found in biblical commentaries is the other side of the process involved in writing a commentary. After thoroughly exegeting the biblical text, some things must be left out because of their redundancy, lesser importance or irrelevance to the reader. However, what should be included in the explanations and what should be excluded? A list of the important elements of which text is required for the evaluation of Romanian commentaries in particular. Thus, it is vital to clarify this in our remaining two chapters.

After a short introduction, we will examine the idea that biblical commentaries are in essence an act of communication. We will then address the parts involved in this communication. Further, some advice will be considered for the text of a biblical commentary. This will be followed by creating an awareness of the major mistakes some biblical commentators make. At the end of the chapter we will list some important elements that must be present in the text or exposition of the biblical commentary.

The Text of the Commentary

So far this book has looked at the type and amount of research involved in the writing of a commentary and at the issues related to the principles of translation. This has involved the perspective of the Bible translation, particularly on the original text. The next step is to finally look at the actual process through which a commentator puts into writing the considerable amount of personal study notes and technical observations on the text. It is also important to look at the commentator's motivation for writing a new commentary.

One of the most common questions every reader meets in various commentary prefaces is one that almost all biblical commentators ask themselves, "Why write yet another commentary on this book of the Bible?" The question is legitimate considering the multitude of commentaries being printed each year.

The answer is always going to be contained in the author's desire to communicate something of her or his interpretation of the biblical text. From this fact we can presume that a biblical commentary is an act of communication. We will look at this aspect in the following pages. However, the question may be asked why this communication necessarily has to be in the form of commentary and not in another form of ministry like preaching, teaching, article writing, etc. Every form of ministry in the Church, involving the proclamation of the Word, is informed in this form of communication called commentary. As we will see later in this chapter, even the "prince of preachers," C. H. Spurgeon, advised his students to consult commentaries before preaching.

The same advice can be applied to all Word-proclaiming ministries in the Church or academia. For example, in a reflective article about the motives of commentary writing, John Nolland writes,

While we are grateful for monographs, journal articles and other specialist studies, there persists an instinct that there is a need for coming to terms with a work in its entirety and not just in this or that respect. And as valuable as may be the contribution of commentators present and past, this coming to terms with is never something that can be done once and for all, but is in need of constant renewal, influenced as it is and should be by context and time. So we keep on producing commentaries; and there continues to be a market for them.[1]

The second question biblical commentators have to ask themselves is how to go about writing the actual commentary. Are there any guiding principles, outside the methodology of exegesis, having to do with the actual content and aspect of a commentary?

At this stage of our research, one should note that we will be next considering the general elements for writing a commentary, and not the particular ones depending on the focus of the writer and the chosen methodology. The kind of commentary we will imply in this quest is one that is most common to all and does not reflect those that are very popular or very critical. For instance, devotional commentaries do not have the same format as scholarly ones and have in common few elements besides the text.

The important elements of a commentary discussed in the conclusions are in no way normative. Rather they are descriptive, revealing what is encountered in the genre of biblical commentaries. By pointing out some important elements for the aspect of the commentary, we are not trying to suggest an ideal commentary, but rather to draw attention to what is already recognized as particular to the commentary genre.

Commentary as a Form of Communication

Since every literary work employs communication and a commentary is a literary work, it is understood that every commentary is a form of communication. One of the most helpful articles about commentaries seen in this perspective is *A Commentary: A Communication about a Communication* by Lars Hartman.[2] Hartman proposes a working definition for the phenomenon of writing a commentary as a communication act. He speaks about the communication that has to consider the author of the biblical text to the original ancient audience and the purpose and situation giving rise to that communication. All these are referred to by applying the superscript "1" to these words. Then he talks about the biblical commentator with his text to his recipients and their purpose and situation. This latter act of communication is referred to by applying the superscript "2." This, he calls "a communication about a communication." Hartman affirms that the communication mentioned can be described this way: "Through a Text^2 a Sender^2/the Interpreter, in a Situation^2 and with a Purpose^2 interprets a Text to a Recipient^2 as containing the Message of the Sender^1 with a certain Purpose^1 to

---

1 John Nolland, "The Purpose and Value of Commentaries," *Journal for the Study of the New Testament* 29, no. 3 (March 2007): 305, accessed 13 January 2021, DOI: 10.1177/0142064X07076314.

2 Lars Hartman, "A Commentary: A Communication about a Communication," *Novum Testamentum* 51, no. 4 (2009): 389–400.

Recipient,¹ who is in a given Situation.'"³ If to this definition we add the variable of interpretation or hermeneutics (which, according to Hartman may have two levels: one of clarifying the text interpreted, and a second, stronger one of not only a clarification, but a deepening of the contents of the text interpreted), we will probably have to distinguish the following cases:

1. The Interpreter/Sender² provides Recepients² with a rephrasing interpretation of Message¹ to Recipients.¹
2. The same as 1 above, but presupposing that Message¹ is also the Message² to Recepients.²
3. The same as 1 above but in addition also interpreting Message¹ in a deeper or more wide embracing way; still, however, the focus is on Message¹ to Recipients.¹
4. The same as 3 above, but adding a Message² which applies Message¹ to Recipients².⁴

Eugene Nida talks about three fundamental parts of communication: "the sender, the message, and the receptor."⁵ So, seeing a commentary as a communication act, one can clearly say something about its sender, message, purpose, and recipients. But a commentary presupposes to communicate something about a communication (i.e., the one initiated by the biblical writer), which interposes the communication of the divine author to the original and extended recipients. Understanding this reality means understanding the multitude of different types of commentaries and the complexity of their making.

By looking at the different parts of this communication act we can better explain what is expected from a biblical commentary. It is implied here that the biblical commentator has an understanding of the original author of the biblical text and his recipients, purpose and situation. This understanding about this side of the communication employed in a commentary was ideally achieved by applying hermeneutical principles to the exegesis that was mentioned in Chapter 2.

The Major Parts of Commentaries as a Form of Communication
Seeing the task of the biblical commentator in this framework provided by Hartman, simplifies our task of observing their rhetoric, intentions, method and so on. Since every book has to be actively read with discernment,⁶ biblical commentaries have to be judged also. One of the ways to do just that is to observe the three important parts involved in the communication: the sender (the commentator), the message (the text), and the receptor (the readers). That is why even interpretive approaches mold, in general, according to

---

3 Hartman, "A Commentary," 391.
4 Hartman, "A Commentary," 399.
5 Eugene Nida, *Signs, Sense, Translation* (Cape Town, South Africa: Bible Society of South Africa, 1984), 2.
6 Mortimer J. Adler and Charles van Doren, *How to Read a Book: The Classic Guide to Intelligent Reading* (New York: Simon and Schuster, Inc., 1972), 5.

the author, text and reader.⁷ This is also argued by Gorman in his article, "Commenting on Commentary: Reflections of a Genre." He states that "a commentary requires three initial elements: a writer, a reader and a text."⁸ Thus, acknowledging their importance, the next sections will focus on assessing the role of each of these three items as major parts of the communication process.

The Writer

It is vital to understand that the writer has a background, a situation, purpose, strengths and weaknesses, and so on. Just as we have seen that a translator cannot translate in a vacuum, so a commentator cannot interpret without certain presuppositions.⁹ Understanding where the writer is coming from and what baggage she or he carries, will be of great help to the reader. This is necessary because the "writer exists within a complex set of institutional and disciplinary structures and practices" (like university, seminary, faith community, grant-giving agencies, the publishing industry and the critical review industry). This is why some biblical commentators think it is important to share their theological and/or training background with the readers.

As we have seen in the first chapter, there are two major tendencies for the exposition of the Bible: one pre-modern and the other modern. Before the rise of German scholarship, the expositors of the Scripture had the Church as their audience. The setting of academia, on the other hand, tends to be a closed, inaccessible circle to the Church, because of its highly specialized language. Of course, this is not to say that all academic settings are beyond the reach of the laity, or that all ministers in academic settings address only their colleagues in a specialized language. The point is that a correct understanding of the two different audiences addressed by commentators, enable us to see why we have two opposite sides (as the popular and the scholarly) in the spectrum of commentary genre. So, in writing a scholarly commentary, an author might be led by the desire "to demonstrate a professional and technical competence." In the end, the "effectiveness and value of the commentary will be decided, primarily, within the context of the scholarly community."¹⁰

The Reader

Ever since the impact of Bultman's theology , together with the French speech theories and the New Criticism, the role of the reader has been greatly emphasized. If it is true that "pure objectivity" cannot be achieved in Bible interpretation, and that the reader will always have a set of presuppositions approaching the text, how much liberty does

---

7 Octavian Baban, *Curs de hermeneutica biblica*, unpublished notes, (București, România, 2009), accessed, 23 December 2012, http://obinfonet.ro/docs/herm/herm_c.pdf.

8 Gorman, "Commenting on Commentary," 106.

9 See for example the conclusions of Walter C. Kaiser, Jr., and Moisés Silva in *Introduction to Biblical Hermeneutics: The Search for Meaning*, rev. and exp. ed. (Grand Rapids, MI: Zondervan, 2007), 292–93. This approach goes back to Schleiermacher and his philosophy of hermeneutics.

10 Gorman, "Commenting on Commentary," 106.

the reader have in interpreting the text "ahistorically?"[11] In any case, the fact that a reader of the Bible is reading a commentary is a good indicator that she or he is willing to hear the text of the Bible speaking for itself through a voice of a "prophet," if you will, or a commentator. This is yet one more reason for the commentator to have not only a sound methodology of interpreting the text, but also a good exposition of it, accompanied by additional information about the writer's orientation provided in the preface or introduction.

In the process of communicating the meaning of the Bible in writing, we should consider also the discourse of the biblical commentator and his rhetoric.

> Because the commentary is a written form of interpretation, and because it is designed to do something, it must be located within the context(s) of the reading public. Not only is it designed to demonstrate exegetical analysis, it is also designed to convince the reader of a particular reading of a text.[12]

Their purpose is to "employ specific rhetorical practices in order to persuade the reader."[13]

Following in the lines of discourse analysis approaches, Gorman identifies three types of biblical commentary readers. These are: "the intended reader (an 'audience' usually constructed by editors and publishers), the real reader (a person who actually reads the book), and the ideal reader (the reader that the writer has in mind in writing)."[14] However, he proposes that the writer of the commentary "views the writing-self as the ideal reader." This can work against the effectiveness of the communication by means of biblical commentaries. Impediments on the reader's side can be added to this problem, because the real reader "also exists within institutional and personal contexts" (university, seminary, faith community, etc.). His way of looking at the text of the commentary can be biased, just as interpreters can be biased in writing a biblical commentary. Thus, the concluding question Gorman asks is, "Do scholars write for the same reasons that readers read?"[15]

The Text

The text is the last important element in the communication of biblical commentators to their readers. Here we also can encounter problems. First of all,

continuing the investigation of his chapter, Gorman addresses specific issues concerning the text. He first posts the question, "which text will serve as the basis for the commentary?" He then says that "the historical methods insist that biblical texts be located in their ancient contexts, for example, original context, usage in the community, collection into texts, construction of 'books.'" Then he asks several questions: "do

---

11 For a better understanding of this discussion, see Moisés Silva, "Contemporary Approaches to Biblical Interpretation," in Kaiser and Silva, *Introduction to Biblical Hermeneutics*, 275–93.
12 Gorman, "Commenting on Commentary," 105–106.
13 Gorman, "Commenting on Commentary," 106.
14 Gorman, "Commenting on Commentary," 106.
15 Gorman, "Commenting on Commentary," 108.

origins, original contexts and compositional history control meaning?" and " . . . how crucial are specific and concrete contexts for determining and delimiting the meaning of texts?" Thirdly, he asserts that the history of interpretation "has significant implications for contemporary interpretations," and this is made clear by the scholarly bibliography which serves two purposes. The first is to demonstrate that "the writer has undertaken and completed appropriate research." The second is to demonstrate that "the writer is aware of alternative readings that need to be discussed and, when necessary, dismissed."[16]

The "What" and "How" of Commentary's Task

It is true that "no book has produced anything like the vast amount of commentaries on the Holy Scripture."[17] Yet, what exactly are these commentaries assumed to do? One answer comes from the *Interpreter's Dictionary of the Bible*:

> A biblical commentary takes a section of scripture and seeks to make its meaning clear, or at least clearer, to the man of the author's own day. Typically it begins with the commentator's conclusions on the questions of introduction—who wrote it, why, etc. But some commentaries proceed inductively, leaving the reader to gather these matters in the original or in translation. The comment must deal to some extent with textual, grammatical, and lexical problems of the original; some do little more.[18]

The same article in this dictionary describes the main task of commentaries:

> The primary function of a good commentary is to furnish an exact interpretation of the meaning of the passage under consideration; it should also show the connection of ideas, the steps of argument, and the scope and design of the whole, in the writing in question.[19]

This definition comes with a competence explicitly affirmed by the author of this article. He believes the process of commentary writing

> can be successfully accomplished only with a knowledge of the original language of the writing and of the historical setting of the particular passage; by careful study of the context and of the author's general usages of thought and speech; and by comparison of parallel or related texts.[20]

Besides articles in biblical dictionaries, valuable advice comes from the prince of preachers, C. H. Spurgeon. In *Commenting and Commentaries*, Spurgeon described to his student the portrait and duty of a biblical commentator. He believed that a biblical commentator should be able to "read the Bible in the original;" to "point out very carefully wherever a word bears a special sense;" to explain the obscure sentences;

---

16 Gorman, "Commenting on Commentary," 109.
17 Smith, "Commentaries," 1976), 920.
18 Kendrick Grobel, "Commentary," in *The Interpreter's Dictionary of the Bible: An Illustrated Encyclopedia*, ed. George Arthur Buttrich (Nashville: Abingdon Press, 1962), 1:663.
19 Grobel, "Commentary," 663.
20 Grobel, "Commentary," 663.

and to "make the word plain." In very metaphorical language, Spurgeon affirmed that a commentator's duty is to "gather out the stones and leave the fruitful field of Scripture for your people to till."[21] He also believed that a biblical commentary should be applicative. In other words, after revealing the meaning of the Scripture passage, the commentator should give guidance in applying that very passage. This is what he considered the most important duty of a commentary should be. He said,

> The chief part of your commenting, however, should consist in applying the truth to the hearts of your hearers, for he who merely comprehends the meaning of the letter without understanding how it bears upon the hearts and consciences of men is like a man who causes the bellows of an organ to be blown, and then fails to place his fingers on the keys; it is of little service to supply men with information unless we urge upon them the practical inferences therefrom.[22]

Issues of Content

Priorities in Commentary Writing

Acknowledging the main role of biblical commentaries to reveal the meaning of the text to its readers, John Nolland said

> There is plenty of room for difference of judgment about the precise balance of priorities, but for me an overriding priority is for a commentator so to write as to aid his or her readers in engaging with the text rather than offering the readers an alternative to engagement with the text. We cannot stop readers using our commentaries as replacement text, but we can make it difficult for them.[23]

Standing back from the detail is as important as becoming immersed in the detail. He continues,

> I have found that a close attention to structure and flow of thought have been invaluable in lifting me beyond detail to reflect on the role of material in relation to the larger shape of the story. Attention to thematic development, literary linkages and structural markers all help to ensure that one has travelled up through the levels of questions from those that relate to detail to those that relate to the big picture. A good commentary is one that can successfully move between levels, attentive to detail, but assisting the reader to gain a grasp of the whole.[24]

Commentaries exist to enable their readers to engage more successfully with biblical texts.

---

21 Charles H. Spurgeon, *Lectures to My Students*, vol. 4, *Commenting and Commentaries* (Peabody, MA: Hendrickson Publishers, 2010), 584–88.
22 Spurgeon, *Commenting and Commentaries*, 588.
23 Nolland, "The Purpose and Value of Commentaries," 310.
24 Nolland, "The Purpose and Value of Commentaries," 310–11.

Main Mistakes in Commentaries

The following subchapter is not an enumeration of exegetical mistakes. Some of the mistakes encountered in different Bible commentaries may be categorized as errors pertaining to exegesis.[25] However, there are mistakes particular to commentaries, especially in their exposition of the exegesis applied to biblical texts. These kinds of errors will be treated in the following section.

Gordon Fee in *Reflecting on Commentary Writings* mentions five faults of commentaries:

> expounding the obvious while skirting the difficult; erring on the side of "exposition" without paying adequate attention to exegetical details (textual issues, lexicography, grammar); its opposite, expounding on the nuance of every preposition or participle without an adequate exposition of the text; engaging in a running debate with scholarship without adequately engaging in conversation with the biblical author; and expounding verses seriatim without adequate discussion of the historical and literary contexts.[26]

A mistake that a beginning exegete might do is to unfold the analysis

> in a verse-by-verse fashion or in a series of word studies. . . . The most important consideration in deciding on the structure of an exegesis is whether it is sufficiently comprehensive to do justice to all the important aspects of the passage, yet at the same time whether it is pliable enough to provide the framework for unfolding an illuminating and coherent interpretation.[27]

It must be mentioned, however, that some commentaries present a verse-by-verse approach to the analysis or exposition of the text, and also have a summary or overview of the interpretation of the entire section or pericope. Though, many times, a verse-by-verse approach may fragment the text, it is preferred for two simple reasons. First, the most basic and elementary unit of text analysis is a sentence, which usually comprises a Bible verse. Secondly, in conversations, sermons, books, articles, etc., arguments or questions come from Bible verses, which are usually made up of one or two sentences. It is in our tendency to express affirmations or questions in this form, and so, a correct understanding of those verses is independent in a way, though understood in its larger context.

The purpose of the popular commentary is to present the thoughts of the writers in an attractive form in order to "vividly impress the mind and interest the heart."[28] A common mistake of some commentaries is prolixity (the length of some commentaries contain the wandering away of compositors, presenting prosaic musings and not confining to

---

25 For an excellent book on exegetical errors, see Donald Arthur Carson, *Exegetical Fallacies*, 2nd ed. (Carlisle, England: Paternoster, 1996).

26 Gordon Fee, "Reflections on Commentary Writing," *Theology Today* 46, no. 4 (1990): 387. *ATLA Religion Database with ATLASerials*, EBSCO*host*.

27 Hayes and Holladay, *Biblical Exegesis*, 110.

28 McClintock and Strong, "Commentary," 428.

exhibiting the text as a result of a sustained mental effort "to apply severe and rigid examination to each sentence and paragraph of the original").[29] Another mistake is the collection of the opinions of others without sifting them (even though an array of names is impressive, the commentator should be preoccupied with the right meaning of the text); the dwelling on the easy and evading the difficult passages; and the tendency to cover too much text at one time resulting in a superficial work (the ambition to write on the whole of the Bible may explain this phenomenon, but it must be countered by a concentration to the study of one book or letter over many years).

From all these enumerations, we understand many commentaries incorrectly when they present a lengthy exposition of the text, with other commentators' opinions and not so much their own. Also, presenting a short and superficial explanation is not helpful either. The biblical commentator has to engage the biblical author more than other scholars, and he or she must also present his or her own definite conclusion.

Important Elements in Commentary Genre

In terms of the structure, Gorman identifies three common elements in commentaries: an introduction which addresses issues like: title, structure and content, authorship, origins, etc.; the commentary proper; and a bibliography.[30] The great majority of biblical commentaries, even those focused more on application, contain an introductory section. Any serious commentator of the Bible has to deal with introductory issues before jumping to interpretation. This is particularly true for the book of Revelation, where dating its composition plays an important role in its interpretation.

The issue of the translation of the passage being commented upon is often brought up by commentaries. The great majority of the scholarly commentaries offer their own translation of the biblical passage. This helps in the process of explaining the text. The translation of the text reflects the interpretation of the passage and facilitates the explanation of the text. A good translation is always done after the exegesis of the passage, and it often reflects the exegetical decisions of the commentator or translator. The concerns involved in the translation of the biblical passage are present also in the popular commentary. Though the authors of such commentaries do not offer their own translations, they oftentimes resort to comparing translations or appeal to a particular version, in order to express a particular meaning or interpretation of the text.

Also, many critical commentaries give a special bibliography used for the study and exegesis of the passage explored. This gives a better flow to the main text containing the exposition, or the commentary proper, the writer not having to footnote every sentence, and thus, interrupting the lecture of many meticulous readers.

Some biblical commentaries have a section with the summary of the paragraph. In this summary, they try to present the main argument of the passage and its connection to the immediate context, the book as a whole, and the larger context of the New Testament and Bible. The usefulness of this section in the commentary is understood and promoted also by Orr and Danker when they say a good commentary "should also show the

---

29 McClintock and Strong, "Commentary," 428.
30 Gorman, "Commenting on Commentary," 110.

connections of ideas, the steps of argument, and the scope and design of the whole, in the writing in question."[31] Gorman adds, "Commentary, then, is always a theoretical and practical engagement with questions concerning the relationship between the parts and the whole. The central concerns of the discipline are linguistic, lexical and syntactic."[32]

In terms of the function of commentaries, Adele Reinhartz's four ideas are relevant. First, commentaries are comprehensive. They treat every verse even though not all receive the same length of treatment. The passages posing particular problems and those that are of particular interest to the commentator receive special attention. Second, commentaries involve several dimensions of the text: philological, conceptual, historical and literal. Third, a commentary provides a guide to the primary source and the history of interpretation. Fourth, the publisher or editor of the series sets a number of constraints about the length, cost and intended audience. Finally, commentaries are works of reference that are many times consulted not in their entirety. Therefore they need to be coherent and comprehensible on every passage, but also to carry themes throughout the entire work.[33]

Also Henry S. Nash mentions reception history as an important element in good commentaries. A good exegete is aware of the various interpretations a particular book or Bible passage has had in history. This empowers him or her to be aware of his or her own preconceived ideas about that passage. That is why a "commentary of the Bible must keep in view not merely the Bible, but also the history of its interpretation if it is to present adequately the present status."[34] However, gathering information about the interpretation of a certain passage in the Bible is not enough. As we have seen earlier, a catena is different than a biblical commentary. This means the author of the commentary must give his own input and interpretation of the passage. This is because, as Gorman warns, "The general reader is a naïve postmodernist: 'all interpretations are equally valid, although I have not really thought about why or why not that is the case'."[35] According to the *Cyclopedia of Biblical, Theological, and Ecclesiastical Literature* the characteristics of commentaries are: "an elucidation of the meaning belonging to the words, phrases, and idioms of the original;" pointing out "the particular meaning belonging to a term in a particular place, together with the reason of its bearing such a sense;" explaining "the construction of sentences, the peculiarities of the diction employed, the difficulties belonging to certain combinations of words, and the mode in which they affect the general meaning."[36] The exhibition of the writer's purpose and his arguments, his train of thought or reasoning pursued throughout the book or

---

31 Orr and Danker, "Commentaries," 737.

32 Gorman, "Commenting on Commentary," 105.

33 Adele Reinhartz, "Why Comment? Reflections on Bible Commentaries in General and Andrew Lincoln's *The Gospel According to Saint John* in Particular," *Journal for the Study of the New Testament* 29, no. 3 (March 2007): 334, accessed 13 January 2021, DOI: 10.1177/0142064X07076314.

34 Nash, "Exegesis or Hermeneutics," 243.

35 Gorman, "Commenting on Commentary," 118–19.

36 McClintock and Strong, "Commentary," 427.

letter, the various topics discussed, the writer's digressions, the connection between the arguments and similar enterprises are also contained in a biblical commentary. To these, the comparison of texts within the whole of the Bible and an account for the diversity on the same topic are added to the responsibility of the commentator.

Conclusion

In conclusion, a good commentator must not ignore the elements just treated above. Thus he or she must consider having an introduction, translation, history of interpretation, summary, and bibliography. Also he or she must expound the biblical author's development of argument or narration in a coherent way at a verse or paragraph level. The biblical commentator must avoid making the mistake of having a lengthy exposition of the text and representing the opinions of other scholars without presenting his or her own opinion. He or she must also not be superficial and avoid difficult passages.

A commentary is in essence a text based on a biblical text; and as a text, it is situated in a communication frame. Furthermore, commentaries have special elements belonging to their genre. These elements are important for biblical commentators, because they offer an idea of what it is that readers expect to encounter in the commentary. In a similar way, knowing and avoiding some common mistakes of commentaries is important, because readers prefer not to encounter them in the text.

In the next chapter, we will look at methodologies and exegetical approaches in commentaries. We will also analyze the purpose, audience, and language of these commentaries, together with their offered translation of the biblical text. All these should be sufficient for positioning Romanian commentaries on the popular-critical spectrum.

Chapter 5

An Evaluation of Biblical Commentaries

We have looked so far at the genre of biblical commentaries and the three aspects involved in writing them, namely, exegesis, translation and exposition. While the first chapters of this book were more theoretical and abstract in nature, the present chapter will try to balance things with a practical conversation about today's state of English and Romanian commentaries. This discussion will intentionally be narrowed down to the main English and Romanian commentaries on the book of Revelation. After researching the Romanian market, commentaries on Revelation were found to outnumber commentaries on other books of the Bible. This leads us to do a comparison study of the best commentaries on the Romanian side. In order to propose a type of Romanian commentary for today's Romanian market, we need to evaluate the existing commentaries to ascertain the current need in the Romanian context. This chapter will first present the important English commentaries, then the exclusively Romanian commentaries on Revelation (i.e., not translated from another language), and then compare these.

Preliminary Concerns

So far, the present book established that biblical commentaries vary greatly in form, methodology, purpose, and audience. With biblical commentaries, there are two opposite tendencies: to write a more popular commentary that would help apply the biblical text in daily life and ministry, or to write a more scholarly commentary in order to offer a critical assessment of the existing contributions to the understanding of the text and to contribute in its own right to this understanding.

In the following section we will take a closer look at biblical commentaries and examine them in light of the elements we identified as being part of the commentary genre. We will look at their methodology, purpose, audience, and content. All of this will be assessed in the light of the two opposite types of commentaries: critical/scholarly and popular.

This will be done by comparing only commentaries on the book of Revelation written in the English and Romanian language. English was chosen for three reasons. First, English is one of the languages that is widely used and known by Romanian commentary readers. They are more likely to have read English commentaries and to have access to English study tools. Second, English has a developed commentary market and displays a variety of approaches in terms of purpose, audience, authors, etc. Finally, to analyze German or French commentaries would have been a substantial, time-consuming process, time not available for this project. That is a project for the future.

The book of Revelation was used for this chapter's study since it is one of the books chosen by a greater number of Romanian commentators in comparison to other books of the New Testament.¹ This being the case, a comparison between commentaries on Revelation renders itself as being more fruitful and more likely to reflect the current situation of Romanian biblical commentaries.

Although the biblical commentary market in English is vast in comparison to almost all other spoken languages, the aim of this exercise is to expose the reader to the variety of commentary types. It was difficult to decide which commentaries to choose from this vast pool of English commentaries, especially given the size restrictions of this project. However, I have chosen mainly to present commentaries included in Carson's *New Testament Commentary Survey*, 6th edition, especially the ones written after 1995 with the exception of a few standard or representative for their type. Doing this, I limited the segment of commentaries available for my analysis. Even so, the number of commentaries in this segment is overwhelming, and the intent of this survey is not to offer an exhaustive analysis.

In terms of a commentary series, only two Romanian authors distinguish themselves as being the initiators of providing commentaries on more than one book of the Bible. They represent two different Christian traditions in Romania: evangelical and Orthodox. Beniamin Fărăgău is a Baptist pastor at Iris Church in Cluj-Napoca. He completed his doctoral studies at Queen's University, Belfast, and he is the author of dozens of commentaries under the umbrella of the series called *Istoria Binecuvântării* (The History of Blessing) written for Sunday School teachers in the Romanian Evangelical Churches. Cristian Bădiliță is a prolific Romanian writer and scholar who obtained his doctoral degree at the Paris-Sorbonne University. His academic projects include the coordination and contribution of a commented translation of the Septuagint completed in 2011 and a commented translation of the New Testament that currently is in process and being published in parts. Although he describes himself as a Christian anarchist, his studies were conducted in the Orthodox tradition.² Other writers produced commentaries on one of the books of the New Testament, but none of them ventured to write a commentary series. From the examples provided above, I do not wish to give the impression that writing commentaries on more than one book of the New Testament is something to be desired; nor that writing in a commentary series is. However, by writing more than one commentary, these authors provided us with a variety of commentaries on almost all of the New Testament books.

In conclusion, such Romanian Bible commentators as Fărăgău, Bădiliță, Negruț, Stancu, Bunaciu, Mihoc, Aldea, Moldoveanu, and others like Cruceru on other books of the Bible, have had an important impact in the Romanian context. Their commentaries on Revelation will be analyzed in this chapter.

---

1 For example, I have personally found ten commentaries on the whole or part of Revelation (only six of them being written by Romanian authors) and two commentaries and one passage analysis on Romans. Other books of the New Testament had only one or two commentaries represented in the Romanian market.

2 Cristian Bădiliță, accessed 10 August 2020, http://cristianbadilita.ro/index.php?page=bibliografie.

English Commentaries on Revelation

We will now proceed in analyzing some of the English commentaries on the New Testament in terms of their purpose, audience, language, contents, etc. Please note that the analysis of English, New Testament commentaries is not and cannot be exhaustive. I have chosen only a few that represent the variety provided by the English, Bible commentary market. All these commentaries were chosen mainly from Carson's list mentioned at the beginning of the chapter.

The first commentary I want to present is Isbon T. Beckwith's called *The Apocalypse of John: Studies in Introduction with a Critical and Exegetical Commentary*. From the title we realize it is closer to the scholarly or critical side of the commentary spectrum. The back cover informs us that the commentary is primarily meant for college students, seminarians, and preachers. However the author mentions the fact that he made the book available for the large number of readers that are not professional scholars.[3] To this end, he set out to offer a translation of Greek. The author offers no other details concerning methodology or information about his personal background or preparation of the material. Half of the book is about introductory matters such as apocalyptic literature, date, authorship, context, history of interpretation, and others. The other half is the verse-by-verse commentary itself.

As mentioned earlier, the *NIV Application Commentary* emphasizes the application of each biblical passage considered. The stated primary purpose of this commentary is to bring the ancient message to the modern context.[4] Nowhere in the book is mentioned the intended audience. The style of the commentary is easy to read and words or sentences in other languages are almost nonexistent, even in the footnotes. This is not to say, however, that the author in not well acquainted with Greek or other languages; he mentions from the start that he could not include in the commentary a large part of his material and documentation.[5] When it comes to its form, the commentary series has three standard sections applied to all its volumes in every passage selected; these are designed to blend exegesis with application. The first section deals with the original meaning; the second with the bridging the context; and the last with the contemporary significance. The text of the Bible has been clearly taken from the NIV as the title of the series suggest.

The NIGTC on Revelation is situated more to the scholarly side of the commentary spectrum. Nevertheless, the editors state that it is not very technical in comparison to a full-scale critical commentary. Indeed, all Greek words or phrases are accompanied by an English translation in order to facilitate the reading. In doing so, the editors of the series made sure that they address a wider audience than normally expected from a critical commentary. They identify their audience as being international. In terms of method, the forward of the book lets us know that the NIGTC's purpose is to provide a theological understanding of the biblical texts through a historical-critical-linguistic

---

3 Isbon T. Beckwith, *The Apocalypse of John: Studies in Introduction with a Critical and Exegetical Commentary* (Grand Rapids, MI: Baker Book House, 1979), ix.

4 Keener, *Revelation*, 9.

5 Keener, *Revelation*, 17.

exegesis.⁶ Further into the book the author announces that his exegesis is a verse-by-verse approach in order to trace the flow of thought within the paragraphs and from a paragraph to another, showing the larger segments of the book. A special emphasis was put on the analysis of the Old Testament use in Revelation linked to the tradition of Jewish exegesis.⁷ The commentary is divided in two parts: an introduction dealing with matters of date, authorship, purpose, theme, context, genre, symbolism, the use of the Old Testament, the grammar, structure, plan, theology, and the goal of Revelation; and the commentary itself. The author offers his own translation and sometimes refers to the text of the New American Standard Bible.

A rather interesting commentary on Revelation is that of John Newport's, entitled, *The Lion and the Lamb: A Commentary on the Book of Revelation for Today*. He is one of the commentators of Revelation who spends a great deal of space to let his readers know about himself. From this background, words like Scofield Bible, Baptist, dispensationalist, historical premillennialist, pastor, teacher, and others emerge and converge to explain his covenant-premillennial view.⁸ Taking his readers on a survey of his life circumstances is justified by the author. This acknowledges that conscious and unconscious attitudes determine the way one interprets the Bible. He admits, however, that the Holy Spirit helps in the process of bringing personal biases to the surface. This commentary is an individual contribution outside any series. This gives the author the relative freedom to choose its methodology, audience, and purpose. He explains his method as combining the historical, theological, devotional, and practical together with "newer literary, psychological and sociological approaches" in order to address "a broad variety of readers" out of which he names pastors, teachers, and those engaged in group studies. His commentary is divided into one third introduction and two thirds actual commentary sprinkled with many *excursus*. It appears that the author used the NIV text most of the time.

Robert H. Mounce wrote his commentary, *The New International Commentary of the New Testament: The Book of Revelation,* addressing the students of the New Testament, as stated on the back cover. In the revised edition, the author uses the NIV as a basis for the text according to the editorial suggestions. To this he added his own corrections for stylistic purposes. The Greek text used for this revision was the twenty-seventh edition of Nestle-Aland.

A more technical and older commentary is *Commentary on Revelation* by Henry Barclay Swete, published in 1977. This book is a reprint of the third edition of *The Apocalypse of St. John* from 1911. The language adopted in this commentary is rather technical; Greek words and sentences are inserted in the text without translation. Hebrew, Latin, Syriac and other languages are also represented in the text. This makes the reading of the commentary possible only for those with knowledge and training in biblical and classical languages. Even though the author states in his preface to the first edition that

---

6 Beale, *The Book of Revelation*, xvii.

7 Beale, *The Book of Revelation*, 3.

8 John Newport, *The Lion and the Lamb: A Commentary on the Book of Revelation for Today* (Nashville, TN: Broadman Press, 1986), 7–22.

his work is addressed to the clergy or church leaders besides students, the technical depth of the commentary makes it virtually inaccessible to the intended audience, unless one is to presume that those church leaders went to specialized seminaries.[9]

The format of the commentary is twofold. The first part deals with introductory issues and the second part with the commentary of the text of Revelation. Swete comments directly from the Greek text, making considerable remarks on textual variants. Clearly he offers his own translation to the Greek, and the majority of phrases are left without translation. Looking at the author's methodology, language, translation, and other indices, we can unmistakably say his commentary is critical and scholarly.

One key contributor in the studies of eschatology and the book of Revelation is George Eldon Ladd. His commentary on John's Revelation appeared in 1972 under the title, *A Commentary on the Revelation of John*. Although Ladd is believed to be an authority in the field, his commentary on Revelation is not presented in a scholarly way. It is hard to assess his commentary because it does not contain a preface. Thus, the motives, audience, methodology, and other details concerning the composition of the commentary are absent. In terms of language, probably for the sake of being discursive, Ladd's commentary does not present words in any language other than English, thus making his contribution accessible to the majority.

An important commentary on Revelation is the one in the ICC series. Under the title *A Critical and Exegetical Commentary on the Revelation of St. John* in two volumes, Robert Henry Charles wrote one of the standard commentaries.[10] Charles' work is thoroughly scholarly, and one needs good knowledge of the classical languages in order to profit from it. In almost three pages, the author explains his methodology for writing his commentary. He provides his own reconstruction of the Greek text and with it, his own translation. Like many other authors before and after him, he provides some introduction in the beginning and then proceeds to the commentary of the text.

The editorial preface of the WBC on David E. Aune's *Revelation* lets the reader know that the series is addressed to the "student, the working minister, and colleagues in the guild of professional scholars and teachers as well."[11] The editors commend the authors of each commentary in the series as being evangelical. They also say that what is unique about WBC is "that it is based on the biblical languages, yet it seeks to make the technical and scholarly approach to the theological understanding of the Scripture understandable." Therefore, the main text contains Greek and Hebrew words, but they always are translated immediately, resulting in a fluent text. The commentators were urged to offer their own translation and to follow the standard format of the following sections: *Bibliography* (a bibliography is offered for each paragraph), *Translation* (the translation of the commentator is offered), *Notes* (discussing the textual variants and

---

9 Henry Barclay Swete, *Commentary on Revelation: the Greek Text* (Grand Rapids, MI: Kregel Publications, 1977), xii.

10 Carson, *New Testament Commentary Survey*, 149.

11 David A. Hubbard and Glenn W. Barker, "Editorial Preface," in David E. Aune, *Word Biblical Commentary,* vol. 52A, *Revelation: 1–5*, ed. Ralph P. Martin (Dallas, TX: Word Books, 1997), 204.

translation issues), *Form/Structure/Setting* (dealing with issues like the outline of the paragraph, literary analysis, source criticism, etc.), and *Commentary* and *Explanation*. Aune's commentary on John's Revelation is clearly critical, though not at the extreme end of the spectrum.

The Letters to the Seven Churches of Asia in their Local Setting written by Colin J. Hemer is a very important contribution in the studies of the book of Revelation. This is in fact a commentary on the section of Revelation dealing with the seven churches in Asia. Not much information is given by the author about his approach, but he states his methodology as being contemporary-historical. The author starts the book with an introduction and information on the background of Patmos, and then he dedicates one chapter to each of the locations of the churches being addressed in chapters 2 to 3 of Revelation. The author's main interest is to discuss the historical and geographical settings of these chapters.

Romanian Commentaries on Revelation

In 1989 Ion Bunaciu, who was by that time the principal (or director) of the Baptist Theological Seminary in the capital of Romania, Bucharest, wrote *Gânduri exegetice asupra cărții Apocalipsa*. The then president of the Romanian Baptist Union expressed his hopes in the preface of the book that it may be of help to the church workers serving from the pulpit.[12] In the author's preface, Bunaciu explains his methodology adapted in this commentary which he calls a modest contribution.[13] He explains that he used evangelical authors (probably mostly from English commentaries, as the rest of the book reveals) out of which he selected dates and explanations. His division of verses was inspired by the 1972 edition of the *Broadman Bible Commentary*, volume 12.[14] His stated purpose was to counteract some of the wrong teachings in Romania in his day concerning the end of time and to say, "what is necessary in order to offer a better understanding" of the book of Revelation.[15] From the content of his commentary, we realize that the author used the Cornilescu translation. The book does not use technical language, and every term or word in a different language is either explained, translated, or both. The book starts with a small introduction concerning the date, authorship, apocalyptic literature, the approaches used in the interpretation of Revelation, cultural context, and the structure of the book.

A very interesting work on Revelation written by a Romanian for Romanians is Daniel Mihoc's book, *Epistolele Apocalipsei: Introducere, traducere și comentariu*.[16]

---

12 Grec Traian, "Prefață," in Ioan Bunaciu, *Gânduri exegetice asupra cărții Apocalipsa* (București, România: Editura Uniunea Comunităților Creștine Baptiste din R. S. România, 1989), 4.

13 Ioan Bunaciu, *Gânduri exegetice asupra cărții Apocalipsa* (București, România: Editura Uniunea Comunităților Creștine Baptiste din R. S. România, 1989), 6.

14 Bunaciu, *Gânduri exegetice*, 6.

15 Bunaciu, *Gânduri exegetice*, 6.

16 Daniel Mihoc, *Epistolele Apocalipsei: Introducere, traducere și comentariu* (Sibiu, Romania: Teofania, 2003).

We are not given any details about the methodology, purpose, and intended audience of this commentary. From the language of the book we can say it is a well-researched and relatively easy-to-read commentary of the second and third chapters of Revelation. This makes it accessible for the majority of readers. He begins with long bibliography and an introduction which deals with the ecclesiological and historical context of the selected chapters treated in the books of the seven churches, the literary structure of the passage, and the issue of the designated "angels." A section with the Greek text (NA27), an offered translation, a short introduction of the passage, and the commentary follow. The Greek words and phrases are accompanied each time by translations.

Pastor Dragomir Stancu had a large contribution on the Romanian evangelical studies on Revelation. His commentary came in three volumes called *Studii asupra Apocalipsei*. From a forward offered by Hușanu Mihai, we find that this commentary is in a documented study form, and that it is addressed to "pastors, their coworkers, Christians and un-Christians," and to "large masses."[17] We are also told that the author's language is "simple" and his style is "warm and attractive." From the author himself we learn that the commentaries were meant also for radio broadcasting.[18] This explains the easy-to-read style of the book. The commentary was composed by consulting a good number of good commentaries of which he mentions the following authors: Charles, Swete, Beckwith, Hort, Moffat, Simcox, Kiddle, Scott, Trench, Stott, Kepler, Newbolt, Barclay, Farrer, Hendriksen, Lenski, Milligan, Warfield, Beasley-Murray, Walvoord, and Seiss. Stancu mentions that he is using a revised version of Cornilescu, but that he consulted the ASB, KJV, NIV, RSV, NLV, James Moffat's version, Martin Luther's version, a Russian version, and the Nestle text.[19] More than 60 pages of the commentary are dedicated to the introduction to Revelation, dealing with similar issues seen in the other commentaries above. After the introduction, the commentary on the text is offered section by section, following different topics as they arise from the reading.

We will now turn our attention to three of the most recent and probably representative (if not more published) commentaries in Romania; two of them are in the Evangelical tradition, and one in the scholarly Orthodox.

Probably the most popular commentary writer in Romania is Beniamin Fărăgău who is mentioned in the beginning of this chapter. His commentary on the first three chapters of Revelation is called *Apocalipsa cap. 1-3 și Doctrina Bisericii*. The commentaries of Fărăgău were very helpful for a developing and growing Romanian church under communism. They served many local churches by providing good material for Bible studies during regular worship services. The format of the commentaries is therefore graphic and the style is pedagogical. The focus of his commentaries is on the literary analysis of the text, thus the structure of the book; the outline, the internal and external textual parallels, and the author's argument are very important elements of his commentary. In the preface of the commentary series, Fărăgău stresses that his

---

17 Dragomir Stancu, *Studii asupra Apocalipsei,* vol. 1, 2nd rev. ed. (Deva, România: Cetate Deva, 2009), 4.
18 Stancu, *Studii asupra Apocalipsei,* 7.
19 Stancu, *Studii asupra Apocalipsei,* 9.

study acknowledges that God's revelation came in book units, and that these books are mainly historical, poetical, and prophetical.[20] That is why he proposed to select books from these types of representative biblical literature in order to lay out his theology. Fărăgău starts his commentary with an introduction and continues with an analysis on a section level. The introduction is concerned with the literary structure, form, unity, themes, and with other matters like the apocalyptic and prophetic type of literature and eschatological issues. Fărăgău opted for using the Dumitru Cornilescu version as the basis for his commentaries.

A recent Romanian scholar developed two interesting projects in the last decade that deserve our attention. His audience is primarily Orthodox, though he does not address that particular religious section alone, being open to any kind of interested reader. Because the Orthodox tradition greatly values the patristic interpretation, Orthodox commentaries on the Bible in the true sense of individual contribution are not easily found. Acknowledging this fact, John Beck starts his book on Orthodox biblical interpretation by saying that "it is well known, and for some even curious, that Orthodox biblical scholars today rarely write on the books of the Bible."[21] He asserts that this is because the approach of the Orthodox leaders was a homiletic rather than an exegetical approach based on the historical-critical method. To this, the factor of not having access to research sources was added.[22] However, in spite of all that, some writers find a way to produce commentaries by writing what they call a commentated translation with introduction. This is the case of Cristian Bădiliță and his *Noul Testament: Apocalipsa lui Ioan, ediție bilingvă*. After a short introduction to the cannon and study of the New Testament, the author mentions some of the standard tools he used for his translation and commentary, like: NA27, Metzger's *A Textual Commentary on the Greek New Testament*, the *Synopsis Quattor* of Aland, Zerwick's *A Grammatical Analysis of the Greek New Testament*, the Carrez-Morel's *Dictionaire grec-françeais du Nouveau Testament*, and others. He states that his translation of the Greek text is accompanied by philological, theological, and *relaia* notes. The first part of his translation contains the Greek text on one page and the proposed Romanian translation on the next, while the second part contains the commentary of the book divided by chapters. The last part is a compilation of patristic notes and observations on the text.

A different approach on the book of Revelation is represented by Paul Negruț's book, *Cristos, biserica și vremurile de pe urmă: o abordare homiletică a cărții Apocalipsa*. Negruț is a pastor of one of the largest Romanian Baptist congregations, and he was the president of Emanuel University of Oradea. He also is past president of the Romanian Evangelical Alliance. His book is a homiletical approach to John's Revelation. Its purpose is to offer the contemporary church a practical understanding of the last book of the Bible. It is not meant to be an exegetical commentary in the usual sense, but

---

20 Beniamin Fărăgău, "Preface to the Revised and Completed Edition," in Beniamin Fărăgău, *Apocalipsa cap. 1-3 și Doctrina Bisericii* (Cluj-Napoca, România: Risoprint, 2009).

21 Beck, *Sfânta Scriptură*, 13.

22 Beck, *Sfânta Scriptură*, 13.

a homily, as is clearly indicated in the preface.[23] Accordingly, it is more a practical approach than a critical commentary. Having said this, however, it is evident that the sermons were well researched. The text is taken from Cornilescu version, and the content is dictated by the text. So, after an introduction, the book is structured around the sequence of the text of Revelation.

Scrisorile Apocalipsei: de la Patmos la Laodicea is Traian Aldea's book on the first three chapters of Revelation. This book represents the opinion of a Seventh Day Adventist acquainted with archeology. It is written from the standpoint of an actual visitor to the seven old cities. It is filled with personal impressions and geographical descriptions. The book represents a historicist's interpretation of the text of Revelation.

Nicolae Moldoveanu, who was a respected Christian song writer, also follows the same type of approach. His example of commitment to Christ during the Communist regime inspired many Christians. Moldoveanu wrote a series of what he called "spiritual meditations" on different books of the Bible. His book on Revelation is called *Apocalipsa: Hristos, descoperirea. Meditaţii duhovniceşti*. It is situated more to the popular side of the commentary spectrum. After a short introduction dealing with the authorship, date, place, purpose, audience and canonicity of the book of Revelation, he has a verse-by-verse approach to the exposition of the text.

Conclusion

An Evaluation of the Romanian Commentaries on Revelation

When we compare the Romanian commentaries with the English ones, the Romanian market is obviously deficient. The reason for this is multifaceted and primarily does not have to do with competency or lack of willingness. There is no doubt that language, circulation, finances, number of consumers or readers, academia, and other such factors play a significant role in explaining why the Romanian market seems underdeveloped in comparison to the English one. The Romanian commentaries that we have considered in this chapter are diverse in methodology, style, purpose, and structure. They represent different confessions, academic background, and even interpretative viewpoints. These commentaries on Revelation are autochthonous products in addition to the many translated commentaries on the same book of the Bible.

We can clearly see that the Romanian reader is given a choice. These commentaries can be evaluated by the average reader. However, the average Christian reader is not offered advice in relation to the various Romanian interpretations and translations of the text of Revelation. The only commentaries that discuss translation issues are those of Bădiliţă and Mihoc. While their initiative is laudable, these two commentaries, however, do not go beyond their own translation and the official Orthodox translation. Many of these Romanian commentators are most likely aware of each other, but there is little if any interaction or reference between them.

---

23 Marius D. Cruceru, "Studiu introductiv: Apocalipsa ca homilariu," in Paul Negruţ, *Cristos, biserica şi vremurile de pe urmă: o abordare homiletică a cărţii Apocalipsa* (Oradea, România: Făclia, Editura Universităţii Emanuel, 2006), 1–6.

Another conclusion from comparing the Romanian commentaries is that we do not have a good representation of the critical commentary type. The commentaries of Bădiliţă, Fărăgău, Stancu, and Mihoc can be good candidates for this type, but they lack many of its features such as dealing with the Greek text, grammatical analysis, textual criticism issues, having a good balance in methodology, etc. A further development and analysis of these commentaries is offered in the next section with final conclusions.

The Type of Commentary Proposed

Now that we have seen the important elements of a commentary, and have been introduced to the current Romanian commentaries on Revelation, we have to see what kind of biblical commentary is needed in the Romanian context. Here, many factors are considered that have not yet been discussed at length herein. One aspect is the academic context in Romania which is steadily developing and is ready for engagement into a national dialogue. Indeed, there is a dialog among schools and seminaries, publications and books, and especially blogs.

We do not have to demonstrate here the readiness of the Romanian academic environment in terms of commentaries. The simple fact that there are a good number of commentaries on Revelation, as we have seen in our analysis, is proof that a dialogue can be initiated. The dialogue I am referring to here is to be understood in terms of biblical commentaries and translations interacting with each other. A dialogue already exists, but it can be improved on multiple theologically related levels and disciplines in Romania.

The type of commentary proposed in this book is one that is critical in style but coherent for non-scholars. It must take into consideration the reception history of the biblical book, especially that of Eastern Orthodoxy. It also must offer an independent translation considering the textual variants, and then deal with the differences in other Romanian translations. It must contain an analysis at a text section level. In terms of methodology, it has to consider different levels of research like morphology, semantics, syntax, text criticism, and literary analysis as well as the historical, canonical, and theological inputs on the text.

Finally, the commentary proposed must interact especially with Romanian commentaries and writings, addressing the particular Romanian context of Orthodox heritage, tradition, and mentality. As we have seen in the survey of Romanian Bible commentaries analyzed above, there is none that approaches the biblical text in a critical way, except for the one proposed by Bădiliţă. However, even Bădiliţă's commentary is not a critical commentary in the true sense since it mostly contains patristic comments and few individual ones. The term critical in critical commentary is intended to reflect the type of commentary situated on the scholarly side of the spectrum discussed in the first chapter. This type of commentary is meant to bypass the translations and address the original language of the text. It is meant to apply a thorough historical, literal, grammatical-critical approach to the biblical text and to bring a fresh and new approach to the text. It is also intended for the leader of the church, the student of the New Testament, and the fellow scholar.

Yet, among the Romanian commentaries above, none addresses the Greek text in such a way as to bring light to the differences in the Romanian translations of the Bible. This is a crucial aspect in the present day. Romanian Christians and especially Christian leaders need to know what to make of the different available translations of the Bible. In essence, the commentary proposed in this book is a critical commentary, offering an independent translation and interacting with other Romanian translations and commentaries. Due to the unique religious context in Romania, it will interact with the Orthodox tradition by addressing the interpretations of the Greek Church fathers. Its methodology will involve the historical, grammatical, literal analysis of the text. The style of the commentary will be accessible to a non-scholarly audience by offering a translation of the other languages.

Chapter 6

A Proposed Commentary on Revelation 2:18–29

After discussing and considering the genre of Bible commentaries, the writing process, and analyzing most of the authentic Romanian commentaries on Revelation, it is now time to present a sample of the kind of commentary would best fit in the Romanian context at this time.[1] Even though the purpose is to offer a Romanian commentary for the same reasons stated above, the language will be English except for the actual translation and expressions used in the exposition.

Translation

Traducere[2]

[18]Și îngerului bisericii din Tiatira scrie-i: „Așa zice Fiul lui Dumnezeu, Cel ce are ochii ca flăcăra focului și picioarele asemenea aramei strălucitoare:[3] [19]<<Știu faptele tale și dragostea, și credința, și slujirea, și răbdarea ta, și *că* faptele tale cele depe urmă sunt mai multe[4] decât cele dintâi. [20]Dar am împotriva ta *faptul* că o îngădui[5] pe femeia aceea, Izabela, cea care se numește pe sine profetesă și învață și înșeală pe robii mei să curvească și să mănânce din carnea jertfită idolilor. [21]Și i-am dat timp ca să se pocăiască, și *tot* nu dorește să se pocăiască de curvia ei. [22]Iată o arunc în pat de boală și pe cei ce comit adulter cu ea *îi arunc* în mare necaz, dacă nu se pocăiesc de faptele ei, [23]și cu siguranță voi omorî[6] pe copiii ei și toate bisericile vor cunoaște că Eu sunt Cel ce cercetează rinichii și inima și vă voi da fiecăruia după faptele voastre. [24]Dar vă spun vouă celor rămași, celor din Tiatira, atâția câți nu ascultați de această învățătură,—*celor* care nu ați cunoscut „adâncimile Satanei", cum zic ei—nu așez peste voi o altă greutate; [25]totuși, păziți ceea ce aveți până când voi veni. [26]Și biruitorului și[7] celui ce păzește până

---

1 NB: The commentary sample below is like the form of an exegetical paper because of the formal requirements of a dissertation, the manuscript on which this book was based.

2 Translation issues such as text criticism, translation variants, and grammatical issues will be discussed with the exposition of every verse, making things easier for those interested in looking up only one verse, sentence, or expression.

3 Termenul χαλκολιβάνῳ apare numai în Apocalipsa 1:15 și 2:18 reprezentând un aliaj necunoscut de metal. Termenul (*orichalo*) din Vulgata înseamnă aramă. Se mai poate traduce prin: *bronz de Liban* (Liddle and Scott*)*, *aramă fină*, *minereu de aur* (BDAG), accentul căzând pe ideea de metal strălucitor (Louw-Nida Lexicon).

4 Sau *mai mari*.

5 Lit. *o lași (să acționeze)*.

6 Lit. *voi omorî în moarte*. Expresia poate fi tradusa și ca "voi omorî cu ciumă."

7 Aici, conjuncția coordonatoare „și" se poate înțelege prin conjuncția „adică".

la sfârșit lucrările Mele, îi voi da autoritate peste neamuri, așa cum și Eu am primit de la Tatăl Meu, ²⁷și le va conduce cu toiag de fier; ca vasele de lut le va sfărâma;⁸ ²⁸și îi voi da steaua dimineții.⁹ ²⁹Cel ce are urechi, să audă ce Duhul spune bisericilor>>".

Short Overview of the Reception History of Revelation 2:18–29 in the Church Fathers

We will not attempt here to provide a history of interpretation on the whole of Revelation but will focus on what is relevant for the reception history of this passage. For a complete understanding of the Church fathers' influence on the interpretation of Revelation, Weinrich's introduction to the *Ancient Christian Commentary on Scripture* dealing with John's Apocalypse, is highly recommended.[10] The structure of thought in the following section was inspired by this introduction.

For the Church fathers who have interpreted the book of Revelation, Revelation 2:18–29 was clearly relevant for the Christian life. The situation of the Church in Thyatira was used as a starting point for their moral teachings and homiletic advice.

For Victorinus (d. 304), this passage aligns in his general interpretation of Revelation. He saw John's book as speaking about the final days of the physical earth and the literal kingdom of Christ. His interpretation was allegorical, being probably under Origen's influence.[11] In this spirit, he interprets the promised morning star as the resurrection secured for the victorious Christian.[12] Though we have only the comments on verses 24 to 26 and 28, his interpretation of the seven letters stated elsewhere sheds light on our passage. He understands the letters addressed to the seven churches in Asia as representing seven classes of saints.[13] Therefore, this passage talks about a type of Christian who, if victorious, will "judge among the rest of the saints" and will see the resurrection or "the beginning of day." The idea of recapitulation—which says the visions of the book are not depicted in sequence but describe the "same realities that repeatedly occur throughout salvation history"—is traced back to Victorinus.[14] If this is true, the type of saint described by this passage is representative and relevant to the Church.

Tyconius (c. 370–390) differs with Victorinus' interpretation, especially of the thousand years reign. He understands Revelation not "in a carnal sense, but all in a spiritual sense."[15]

---

8 Lit. *este sfărâmat*.

9 Lit. *steaua de devreme, matinală*, referindu-se la o planetă vizibilă dimineața devreme, probabil Venus, Luceafărul-de-Dimineață.

10 William C. Weinrich, "Introduction to the Revelation of John," in *Revelation*, ed. Weinrich, 14–42.

11 Weinrich ed., *Revelation*, xxii.

12 Weinrich ed., *Revelation*, 34.

13 Weinrich, ed., *Revelation*, xxii.

14 Weinrich, ed., *Revelation*, xxii.

15 Gennadius, cited in Weinrich, ed., *Revelation*, xxiii.

Augustine and Jerome followed respectively in the line of Tyconius and Victorinus' interpretation of Revelation.[16] For this reason Victorinus and Tyconius had a great influence concerning the understanding of the book of Revelation until the Middle Ages.[17] This influence also reached Caesarius of Arles (d. 543). He is situated in the line of Tyconius-Augustine as is Primasius of Hadrumetum (d. after 553). On the other side, Apringius, Bishop of Beja in Portugal, and Bede the Venerable (d. 735) followed the tradition of Jerome's revision of Victorinus' commentary.

The first commentary on the Greek side worthy of mention is that of Oecumenius (early 6th cen.).[18] His interpretation is heavily Christocentric, and he views many of the apocalyptic visions as referring to the future coming of Christ. The Greek commentary of Andrew of Caesarea was written in the same century. This commentary became "the standard commentary on the book [of Revelation] for the later Byzantine tradition."[19] Andrew of Caesarea offered in the epilogue of his commentary his concern for the moral life of Christians, rooted in his understanding of the seven letters to the seven churches in Asia.[20] Further references to the Church fathers will be made in the following section when particular verses are expounded.

Exposition

This passage represents the message of the risen Christ to the fourth of the seven churches in Asia. After addressing the third message to the Church in Pergamum, the Lord turns to Thyatira, probably following a route that a messenger would have been able to complete from Ephesus to Laodicea.

In the Church of Thyatira, Victorinus sees a class of saints indicating "the nobility of the faithful who do good works every day and who do greater works." He sees them even though "among these the Lord shows that there are persons who too easily grant an unlawful peace and pay attention to new prophecies."[21] Apringius of Beja has suggested that the name Thyatira means "enlightened." The name has a spiritual meaning that "after the expulsion of heretical pride and after the defeat of temptations from the powers of the air, the holy church is deserving of the light of righteousness," that is, the morning star.[22] For Bede, on the other hand, "Thyatira may be translated 'for sacrifice.' For the saints present their bodies as a living sacrifice."[23] These interpretations, however, do not have support. In line with the historicist view, some see the Catholic Church in Jezebel and in the faithful remnant, the pre-Protestant reformers in Thyatira.[24]

---

16 Jerome did not, however, agree with the chiliastic view of Victorinus.
17 Weinrich, ed., *Revelation*, xxv.
18 Weinrich, ed., *Revelation*, xxvii.
19 Weinrich, ed., *Revelation*, xxix.
20 Weinrich, ed., *Revelation*, xxviii.
21 Weinrich, ed., *Revelation*, 34.
22 Weinrich, ed., *Revelation*, 10.
23 Weinrich, ed., *Revelation*, 34.
24 Traian Aldea, *Scrisorile Apocalipsei: de la Patmos la Laodicea* (Alba-Iulia, România: edura Creștină "Mateus", 1994), 108.

No matter how one understands the role of the Church in Thyatira, it was a real church known to the other six, to John, and more importantly, to Christ. The message to this church is one that must concern all Christians because of the warning at the end of the chapter. Indeed, the last verse, repeated to all seven churches, is a signal that this message is not only to this church.[25] Through these seven churches, the letters are addressed to all Christians.[26]

Fărăgău is probably the only commentator who refers to what he calls "the hermeneutical triangle." He sees the tight connection between the portrait of Christ, the warning, and the promise—three elements that are common in all seven messages. This triangle explains the situation of each church. It also refers back to the history of redemption (through different allusions) and foretells the eschatological expectations developed in chapters 4–22.[27]

The unusual and unique address to the angel of the church has been understood by the Church fathers in various ways. For example, Origen seems to take the word literally because he says, commenting on Luke 23:7,

> power has been given to man—at least to him who has the Holy Spirit—to speak even to angels. I shall give you an example from these instances, so that we might realize that angels too can be taught by human voices. It has been written in the Apocalypse of John, 'Write to the angel of the church . . .' And again . . . 'I have something against you.' Clearly it is a man who writes to angels and enjoins something.[28]

On the other hand, Oecumenius, commenting on 2:1, views the word as being used for the church. He says:

> He speaks periphrastically of the church in Ephesus as an "angel of the church in Ephesus." For the guardian angel of the church has not sinned, so that it requires the admonition to repent. He is rather most holy and for this reason exists at the right hand of the Lord, giving as proof of this the purity of his nature and flashes as of light. Moreover, what need would there be for him who is conversing with the Evangelist to say, "write to him [the angel]," since the holy angel was present and was listening to the conversation (being on the right hand of the one speaking)? And, finally, the saint himself interprets the vision seen by him and says, "He who has ears, let him hear what the Spirit is saying to the churches." He did not say "to the angels of the churches" but "to the churches." And so, also in the remaining interpretations you will find the words "write the following to the angel of the church," not that he is speaking about the angel but about the church.[29]

---

[25] In fact, the entire book was meant to address all the seven churches (see 1:11).
[26] George B. Caird, *The Revelation of St. John the Divine* (New York: Harper & Row, 1966), 15.
[27] Fărăgău, *Apocalipsa 1–3*, 171.
[28] Weinrich ed., *Revelation*, 19.
[29] Weinrich, ed., *Revelation*, 19–20.

Though this matter must be treated in 2:1, I will briefly say here that due to John's extensive use of Daniel in the first three chapters of Revelation, and due to other uses of the word elsewhere in the book, the ancient audience must have taken the word literally, as referring to an angelic being. In this case, the relationship of the angels to the respective churches needs explanation. The most probable explanation is that John wanted to draw attention to the spiritual realities surrounding the Christian communities.

Thyatira is the least important city of the seven in Asia whom the Lord addresses in chapters 2 and 3. It is situated beneath the modern city of Akhisar. Very few things are known about this city from the rare mentions in ancient literature. It became a Seleucid colony probably in 281–280 BC.[30] Thyatira was part of the Roman province of Asia, and we know that the first Macedonian convert, Lydia, was a merchant of purple from this city (Acts 16:14). It is doubtful that Lydia originated from the Church in Thyatira.[31] Ancient sources mention the dyeing guilds as being prominent in Thyatira among other guilds such as the blacksmith merchandizing. Many were "woodworkers, linen-workers, makers of outer garments, dyers, leather-workers, tanners, porters, bakers, slave-dealers and bronze-smiths" in the city. [32] Thyatira had temples dedicated to the Tyrimnaean Apollo and Artemis, and a shrine of Sambathe, but not to the Emperors. The problem of the church was not with the emperor worship, but rather with the pagan festivities associated with the trade guilds.[33]

Revelation 2:18

Aşa zice ... NTR has "acestea sunt cuvintele Celui ..." which is different than their "Aşa vorbeşte" in Jeremiah 38:2, 3 and Acts 21:11. The Orthodox translation is consistent with "Acestea zice" used in Acts 21:11. So is Bădăliță (cf. Gen. 45:9) with "Acestea le grăieşte;" and the Catholic with "Aşa spune." TLN has "Aşa zice" in Jeremiah 6, "Aşa spune" in Acts 21:11 and "Acestea le spune" in Revelation 2:18. Cornilescu has "Iată ce zice" in Acts 21:11 and Revelation 2, 3 instead of the "Aşa vorbeşte" uniformly used in the Old Testament.

This same sentence introduces the words of Christ to all seven churches. The Greek expression is used only eight times in the New Testament, seven times in Revelation 2–3 and one time in Acts 21:11. Τάδε λέγει κύριος (thus says the Lord) introduces a prophetic utterance and is a consecrated expression used by the Old Testament prophets over 250 times in the LXX. Outside the prophetic literature, the expression τάδε λέγει ὁ βασιλεύς (thus says the king) is used at least ten times, and it introduces a kingly command or decree. In Acts 21:11 we have the record of Agabus' prophecy to Paul. By using this expression, John is not only drawing attention to the prophetic character of the letters

---

30 Colin J. Hemer, *The Letters to the Seven Churches of Asia in Their Local Setting* (Grand Rapids, MI: William B. Eerdmans, 2001), 106.

31 Ellen G. White, *Tragedia veacurilor* (Bucureşti, România: edura Viață şi Sănătate, 1981), 184.

32 Robert H. Mounce, *The New International Commentary on the New Testament: The Book of Revelation*, rev. ed. (Grand Rapids, MI: William B. Eerdmans Publishing Company, 1998), 101.

33 Swete, *Commentary on Revelation*, 41.

to the churches, but he is also triggering an expectance of Old Testament allusions to his audience. So, from a translation point of view, it would be wise to utilize the same expression used in the translation of Old Testament prophecies.

In relation to Christ's appearance, the writings of the Church fathers reflect the Christological understanding of the second part of the verse. Christ's eyes like flames means "his gaze which discerns all things," and his feet signify "his unstained flesh which glows, just like bronze in a fire is bright with clarity."[34] The description of Jesus' eyes in this way indicates the terrifying threat against sinners, for Oecumenius. His feet "denote either the steadfast immutability of faith in him or the spiritual fragrance of the evangelical teaching."[35] Andrew of Caesarea also relates this description of Christ with his relationship with sinners either for salvation or damnation. Thus, his eyes "signify the illumination of the righteous and the punishment of the sinners." To this, he adds the description of his feet as symbolizing "the undivided and unmixed unity of the divinity and humanity. For this unity, as though hardened in the fire by the Holy Spirit, is incomprehensible to human reasoning." [36]

cel ce are . . . This portrait of Jesus addressed to the Church in Thyatira is in accordance with his words represented later in the paragraph, „eu sunt cel ce cercetează rinichii și inima și vă voi da fiecăruia după faptele voastre." The depiction of the fiery eyes is meant to point to the reality that nothing is hidden from his sight, not even the church's deeds. A closer observation of the Greek text reveals the unusual repetition of the word ἔργα/ ἔργων (deeds). This shows Christ's concern with their conduct. The lesson is that compromising in teaching leads to corruptness in behavior. The description of Jesus "prepares the reader for the severe tone of the utterance which follows."[37] There seems to be a connection between ὁ υἱὸς τοῦ θεοῦ (the son of God) and Psalm 2; and between ὁ ἔχων τοὺς ὀφθαλμοὺς (who has eyes) and verse 23.[38]

The title "Son of God" stands in strong opposition to local worship of Apollo and the emperor (who was said to be Apollo incarnate), both believed to be the sons of Zeus.[39] The author of Revelation changes from "son of Man" to "Son of God" in order to emphasize the importance of the message.[40] Beale agrees with Hemer as to the association of the polemic between "son of God" and the alliance Apollo-Caesar and the dead son of the emperor sitting on the globe with seven stars in the background. He thinks, however, that it is unnecessary to dissociate the allusion from Daniel. Both

---

34 Apringius of Beja, in Weinrich, ed., *Revelation*, 34.
35 Oecumenius, in Weinrich, ed., *Revelation*, 34.
36 Andrew of Caesarea, in Weinrich, ed., *Revelation*, 34.
37 Swete, *Commentary on Revelation*, 42.
38 R. H. Charles, *A Critical and Exegetical Commentary on the Revelation of St. John*, The International Critical Commentary, ed. S. R. Driver, A. Plummer, and C. A. Briggs (Edinburgh: T&T Clark, 1920), 68.
39 Mounce, *The Book of Revelation*, 102.
40 Cristian Bădiliță, *Noul Testament: Apocalipsa lui Ioan, ediție bilingvă* (București, România: Adevărul Holding, 2012), 161.

are acceptable.[41] Apparently, there was a religious alliance between emperor worship and the worship to the sun-god Apollo who is depicted "on the city's coins grasping the hand of the Roman emperor."[42]

Aramă strălucitoare is purposed to put in contrast the pagan image of the solar cult of Apollo-king with that of Christ. The apparent ambiguity of the word χαλκολίβανος (aramă strălucitoare) explains the variety in its translation. So, TLN has "arama strălucitoare;" the sinodal Orthodox "aramei strălucitoare;" the Catholic "bronzului strălucitor;" Bădiliță "bronzului de Liban;" the NTR, "bronzului încins" and Cornilescu, "arama aprinsă." Oecumenius sees both the metallic and frankincense properties of the word χαλκολίβανος. Hemer identifies the word χαλκολίβανος with a fine brass, an alloy between copper and the zinc that is obtained by distillation (thus the term λίβανος coming from the verb λείβω). He also implies indirectly that the Latin word *orichalcum* comes from the Greek ὀρείχαλκος, meaning brass. Hemer argues that the local guild in Thyatira was able to produce this alloy for military use. The author is thus able to say that the "[r]eference to the 'furnace' in 1:15 hints at local familiarity with the refining process" in which "the local lignite" was probably used.[43]

This theory is accepted by Osborne,[44] and Beale makes an interesting comment saying that "as flame of fire" and "as bronze" alludes to the furnace in which Daniel and his three friends were thrown. The author had Daniel 3 in mind because it was one like the son of God who saved them.[45] The bronze feet suggest stability, in contrast to the human fragility depicted by the feet of clay in Daniel 2.[46] In the end, the depiction of Christ is probably meant as an affective comparison, meaning that John used this kind of language in order to stir his readers' emotions for them to be able to understand his experience.[47] However one decides to translate the word, the accent must be understood to fall on the glowing of Christ's appearance; "all his being shines forth in different nuances."[48]

Revelation 2:19

Știu faptele tale . . . I know (οἶδα) is the first word of the prophetic utterance common to all seven churches, and in five of the seven uses, the object of the Lord's awareness is their deeds. Probably the new situation of persecution, coupled with the moving of the central focus of Christianity on Jerusalem, the death of the apostles, and the Jews turning against Christians, raised questions in the faith communities concerning God's

---

41 Beale, *The Book of Revelation*, 260.
42 Caird, *The Revelation of St. John*, 43.
43 Hemer, *The Letters to the Seven Churches*, 112–13, 115.
44 Grant R. Osborne, *Baker Exegetical Commentary on the New Testament: Revelation* (Grand Rapids, MI: Baker Academic, 2002), 153.
45 Beale, *The Book of Revelation*, 259.
46 Bădiliță, *Apocalipsa lui Ioan*, 130.
47 George B. Caird, *The Language and Imagery of the Bible* (Philadelphia, PA: The Westminster Press, 1980), 147.
48 Bădiliță, *Apocalipsa lui Ioan*, 129.

implication, sovereignty, and awareness of their situations. To this, Christ's message is "I know."

Dragostea, și credința, și slujirea, și răbdarea ta. . . . The praise to the church then follows after οἶδα (I know), as it does in the other messages with the exception of the ones to Sardis and Laodicea. Christ recognizes their love, faith, ministry, patience and apparent progress in conduct. The love and faith of the church were the two dynamic Christian forces that help in producing the following activities of service and patience.[49] Between love and faith, "[l]ove is characteristically placed first in a Johannine book" while "the Pauline order is the reverse."[50]

The expression "your latter deeds are greater than your former . . . shows that as they progressed, they improved in their obedience to the commandments."[51] The Greek text uses the genitive of comparison with the word πλείονα which can be translated as *more than* or *greater than*. This word seems here to be used as meaning "greater in quality."[52] This explains why Cornilescu with the majority has "mai multe," while NTR has "mai mari" and the catholic has "le întrec."

și dragostea . . . (καὶ τὴν ἀγάπην) Here καὶ (and) "introduces an explanatory description of the ἔργα (deeds)."[53]

Revelation 2:20

Dar . . . As is the case with other messages to the churches, the rebuke follows after the commendation. It is introduced by the strong adversative conjunction ἀλλὰ (but).

Femeia . . . The problem of the people of the Church in Thyatira was their permission of having the teaching and acts of a woman called Jezebel in their midst. It is important to note the use of the article accompanying the word γυναῖκα (woman). Some suggested it is a pejorative use in order to show that the church let not somebody, but a woman teach and mislead the people. So they think there are some tones of misogyny in John as hinted by the pejorative use of γυναῖκα (woman).[54] The presence of the article, however, is best explained by the fact that John is quoting the Septuagint.

The reading γυναῖκα σου (your wife) is supported by some minuscules like 1006 (11th cent.), 1841 (9–10th cen.), 1854 (11th cen.), and 2351 (10th cen.) as well as by the koine manuscript of the Majority Text. If this were to be the original reading, it would have been a support for the understanding of the ἄγγελος (angel) as the pastor of the church. Another explanation for this unlikely reading would be that the angel of the church had a wife, in which case we would have an allusion to the myth that the fallen angels had relationships with the "daughters of men."[55] However, this reading should not be

---

49 Charles, *Commentary on the Revelation of St. John*, 69.
50 Swete, *Commentary on Revelation*, 42.
51 Weinrich, *Revelation*, 35.
52 Charles, *Commentary on the Revelation of St. John*, 69.
53 Charles, *Commentary on the Revelation of St. John*, 69.
54 Bădiliță, *Apocalipsa lui Ioan*, 163.
55 Bădiliță, *Apocalipsa lui Ioan*, 162.

accepted due to the strong support by Codex Sinaiticus and other cursive manuscripts. Both Jezebel, "your wife" and "Jezebel, his wife" must be rejected.[56]

Izabela . . . For Apringius of Beja, the name Jezebel "is interpreted as 'dung heap' or a 'flowing of blood.'" He gives further clarification saying, "What else is thought to be in the filth of a dung heap or in blood, unless the evil deed and sin which is committed through fault?"[57] Charles' assessment is comical, though true: "She was a modern Jezebel, and the Church of Thyatira in tolerating her presence in the Church was no better than a modern Ahab." He sees in Jezebel a symbol of "some influential woman in the Church."[58] Oecumenius rightly thinks that the use of the name Jezebel, Ahab's wife, Christ "sees a paradigm for the wickedness of that woman who lived at that time." There may be a further parallel between the Jezebel of Thyatira and the one alluded to. Ahab, his people, and Jezebel's followers repented of their deeds (1 Kings 21:27–28), but Jezebel did not. God was ready to postpone the judgment on account of Ahab's repentance, but Jezebel was unwilling to repent.[59] There are suggestions that Jezebel was the Sibyl of the Sambathe, but it is difficult to see how this person could have gained admission to the church.[60] Others say she might have been the "patroness or hostess of one of the house churches that made up the Christian churches at Thyatira."[61] Yet, a historical reconstruction is not possible.

Se numește pe sine . . . Cornilescu's translation of the expression ἡ λέγουσα ἑαυτὴν προφῆτιν (care se numește pe sine profetesă) is "care se zice proorociță" and is unnatural for the majority of Romanians. The same is true for the Orthodox translation.

Și învață și înșeală . . . Probably "the dangers which threatened Thyatira were internal rather than external."[62] Even though we have the picture of Jezebel who taught and misguided people inside the church, the rebuke of Christ is addressed to the wrong practice in accordance to the false teaching largely accepted. The translation *să dea învățătură și să-i înșele pe robii Mei* in NTR, similar with the rendering of Cornilescu and of the catholic translation, chose the Romanian "prezent conjunctiv" mood for the Greek present indicative. They probably followed the pattern set by the Vulgate (permittis mulierem Hiezabel . . . docere et seducere). This reading takes away the force of the focus of the text on τὴν γυναῖκα Ἰεζάβελ, the one who keeps calling herself prophetess and is teaching and misleading God's servants. These translations place the accent on what was going wrong in the church, while the Greek text emphasizes the character named Jezebel. While it is true that you cannot separate the person from the deeds, the placement of the participle ἡ λέγουσα (who says) serves as an apposition for τὴν γυναῖκα Ἰεζάβελ (the woman Jezebel) even though it is in the nominative. It is known that Revelation is "full of variations (solecisms) from case-concord, especially

---

56 Beckwith, *The Apocalypse of John*, 466.
57 Weinrich, ed., *Revelation*, 36.
58 Charles, *Commentary on the Revelation of St. John*, 70.
59 Fărăgău, *Apocalipsa 1–3*, 254.
60 Swete, *Commentary on Revelation*, 43.
61 Aune, *Revelation: 1–5*, 203.
62 Charles, *Commentary on the Revelation of St. John*, 69.

in appositional clauses."[63] Therefore, it is more natural to understand the following two verbs in the present form as grouping with the previous participle (as the other Romanian translations not mentioned above correctly do), describing a repetitive act still going on in the church, namely, she is one who keeps calling herself prophetess and keeps teaching and misleading my servants. The reproach is that the church permitted her membership in the church as she was continually offering her misleading teachings. The present form of the verbs points out that "Jezebel of the Thyatiran brotherhood was still teaching when the Apocalypse was written."[64]

Some commentators believe the content of this teaching was similar to that of the Nicolaitans, while others say it was the same teaching.[65] Andrew of Caesarea links this verse to heresy, and more particular to that of the Nicolaitans saying that it "is figuratively called 'Jezebel' because of its impiety and licentiousness."[66] Others also believe that this verse can possibly refer to heretics.[67] On the other hand, the disciples of Jezebel should not be confused here with the disciples of Balaam, the heretics called the Nicolaitans.[68] That Jezebel viewed herself superior than the apostles, as Stancu suggests, is a speculation.[69] Charles identifies Jezebel's teaching as Nicolaitan.[70] However, "it is questionable whether her teaching was in any sense formal."[71] This is why we cannot identify her teachings with that of the Nicolaitans.

Să curvească și să mănânce din carnea jertfită idolilor. Another translation issue has to do with the semantic range of the verb πορνεύω (to fornicate, *a comite adulter, a săvârși un act sexual imoral*). For it, Cornilescu translated "să se dedea la curvie," while others: "să se desfrâneze" (NTR); să facă desfrânări" (Orthodox); "seducându-i la desfrânare" (Catholic); "să curvească" (TLN and Bădiliță).

Related to this verb is its interpretation. It can be understood literally or metaphorically as referring to idolatry. Oecumenius believes the reference to fornication and eating food sacrificed to idols can "refer either to physical fornication" or to "apostasy from God."[72] Bede interprets verse 20 as referring to actual fornication and idolatry, though every committing of sin is in itself idolatry.[73] We can link the reality of spiritual corruptness perpetuated by Jezebel, with James 4:4,[74] "Ye adulterers and adulteresses, know ye not

---

63 Archibald Thomas Robertson, *A Grammar of the Greek New Testament in the Light of the Historical Research* (Nashville, Tennessee: Broadman Press, 1934), 414.

64 Swete, *Commentary on Revelation*, 43.

65 Beckwith, *The Apocalypse of John*, 464.

66 Weinrich, ed., *Revelation*, 35.

67 Weinrich, ed., *Revelation*, 35.

68 Bădiliță, *Apocalipsa lui Ioan*, 163.

69 Stancu, *Studii asupra Apocalipsei*, 198.

70 Charles, *Commentary on the Revelation of St. John*, 70–71.

71 Mounce, *The Book of Revelation*, 103.

72 Weinrich, ed., *Revelation*, 35.

73 Weinrich, ed., *Revelation*, 37.

74 Nicolae Moldoveanu, *Apocalipsa-Hristos descoperirea* (Deva, România: edura Comorile Harului, 2008), 69.

that the friendship of the world is enmity with God? whosoever therefore will be a friend of the world is the enemy of God." The word for fornication means religious infidelity.[75]

Thus, it is good to conclude that πορνεύω may be understood literally, but this does not exclude its moral and spiritual implications, as is suggested by the entire message against moral corruption. Since "fornication" is mentioned first, it probably identifies "that the primary object of the prophetesses was sexual immorality."[76] The membership in the trading guild involves participating in the common meals, which were dedicated to pagan idols.[77] Pagan feasts "often led to sexual promiscuity."[78] The crisis in the Church of Thyatira was how to define their relationship with the world.[79]

Revelation 2:21

i-am dat timp ca să se pocaiască ... The subjunctive is best translated here through the Romanian "conjunctiv" with "să."[80] But this is not the problem of this verse, rather the semantic range of μετανοέω (to repent). The Catholic translation together with Bădiliță's translation chose the expression "să se convertească," instead of the "să se pocăiască" which is less understandable outside of religious circles. According to some apocryphal writings, the Apostle John has sent a letter of rebuking to Jezebel.[81]

Apringius sees in this verse the reality that the unrepentant will face great tribulation at the Day of Judgment. Primasius explains that "sinners at times do not experience the vengeance of present wrath and so neglect penance until sudden destruction comes upon them like the pain of childbirth and they are not able to escape."[82] This verse strengthens the intuition of some commentators that the practice of sexual immorality was the main teaching of Jezebel.

Revelation 2:22

O arunc ... This verse is in the same line with the one before it. In both verses, the risen Christ, the Son of God is leaving time and room for repentance. Fărăgău's observation is right that when God is deciding to punish severely the sinner, it is only after the sinner is unwilling to change.[83] He further notices dissimilarity in this message as compared to the previous one. The angel of this church is not invited to repent. Because the situation in the church is so great, Christ takes the conflict upon himself. Moreover, the number of the faithful was so small in comparison to Jezebel's adherents, and it was probably

---

75 Caird, *The Revelation of St. John*, 44.
76 Charles, *Commentary on the Revelation of St. John*, 70.
77 Charles, *Commentary on the Revelation of St. John*, 69. Beckwith disagrees that the rebuke to the church was the association with the guilds. He thinks the exhortation is to Christian fidelity and purity in the face of future temptation not necessarily connected with the unchristian society. Beckwith, *The Apocalypse of John*, 464.
78 Mounce, *The Book of Revelation*, 104.
79 Negruț, *Cristos, biserica și vremurile de pe urmă*, 55.
80 Constantin Georgescu, *Manual de greacă biblică* (București, România: Nemira, 2011), 238.
81 Negruț, *Cristos, biserica și vremurile de pe urmă*, 58.
82 Weinrich, ed., *Revelation*, 36.
83 Fărăgău, *Apocalipsa 1–3*, 255.

too late to change something.⁸⁴ Fărăgău offers a theological explanation for the quick and harsh judgment of God against Jezebel. He proposes that it is not the lack of God's patience in dealing with her (because God gave her time), but it is her unwillingness to repent which brings the judgment.⁸⁵

Arunc (βάλλω) is a Hebraism and should be translated with the future.⁸⁶ I believe Charles rightly identifies in verse 22 a Semitic parallelism in which βάλλω represents a Hebrew participle which can be translated with the future tense. Furthermore, the parallelism itself permits the translation in the future.⁸⁷

Pat de boală... Swete sees the parallelism as an explanation for the translation "bed of sickness" (cf. Θλίψης μεγάλη—great tribulation).⁸⁸ The bed is not a funeral-bier or a dining-couch as it was proposed, but a bed "of sickness and pain."⁸⁹ The Greek word κλίνη means bed (*pat* in Romanian⁹⁰). But the context here suggests it means sickbed.⁹¹ The NTR and Catholic translation has simply *pat* (bed), while the rest add *bolnavă* (sick). It is not easy to see at first why NTR's "o voi arunca la pat" is a punishment. "Pat de boală" communicates better the idea of punishment.

Instead of the word κλίνην (bed) supported by the strong testimony of Codex Sinaiticus and many other minuscules, Codex Alexandrinus has φυλακήν, the Aramaic translation mistook κλίβανον for κλίνη, the Coptic Sahidic took αν σθένειαν for κλίνη, and Primasius has *luctum*. It is probable that later Christians wanted to attribute a harsher judgment for Jezebel.⁹²

At the end of verse 22 the Majority Text tradition from Andreas of Caesarea's commentary reads αὐτῶν (their) instead of the more difficult and more probably original αὐτῆς (her). Probably many decided the scribes wrongly inserted here the word αὐτῆς from the previous verse which ends with a similar expression μετανοῆσαι ἐκ τῆς πορνείας αὐτῆς. Other manuscripts supporting αὐτῶν are Codex Alexandrinus, minuscule 1854, 2329, 2344 (all around the 10–11th century), and the Clementine Vulgate. Since the Majority Text was the Greek text available to Cornilescu, his translation has "faptele lor" instead of "faptele ei." The same reading is encountered in the Orthodox and Catholic translations.

Mihoc believes the term "great tribulation" points to the fact that the faith of Jezebel's adherents will be in common with that of the inhabitants of the earth which are opposing

---

84 Fărăgău, *Apocalipsa 1–3*, 249–50.
85 Fărăgău, *Apocalipsa 1–3*, 254.
86 Bădiliță, *Apocalipsa lui Ioan*, 163.
87 Charles, *Commentary on the Revelation of St. John*, 70.
88 Swete, *Commentary on Revelation*, 44.
89 Mounce, *The Book of Revelation*, 104.
90 Daniel Bărnuț, Emeric Hubert and Jozsef Kovacs, *Dicționar grec român pentru studiul cuvintelor Noului Testament* (Cluj-Napoca, România: edura Theologos, 1999), 117.
91 Walter Bauer, *A Greek-English Lexicon of the New Testament and Other Early Christian Literature*, ed. Frederick W. Danker, 3rd ed. (Cicago: University of Chicago Press, 2000), 549.
92 Bruce M. Metzger, *A Textual Commentary on the Greek New Testament* (London-New York: United Bible Societies, 1975), 733.

God.⁹³ However, the word θλῖψις occurs in connection to the situation of the Church in Smyrna and its future trial. This informs us not to necessarily link it to 7:14.

Revelation 2:23

cu siguranță voi omorî. . . . The unusual expression ἀποκτενῶ ἐν θανάτῳ literary means "I will kill in/by death." It is probably best explained as a Semitism. Cornilescu, NTR, TC translates it, "voi lovi cu moartea;" TLN by "cu moarte îi voi ucide;" which is similar to, but differently arranged than the Orthodox translation. Bădiliță has simply "îi voi omorî." Adding the unnecessary word in the dative, expressing the instrument or locus, strengthens the verdict. Because the expression reminds the reader of the Hebrew construction of infinitive absolute plus imperfect (used to emphasize the idea of the verb⁹⁴), it is probably best to translate it with "surely." "I will kill with death is a hyperbole used to express the determination of the speaker."⁹⁵

It is probable that this is yet another Semitism similar to Ezekiel 33:27 where we have pestilence for θάνατος (death). This will mean that we need to translate it by "I will kill them by pestilence."⁹⁶ Nevertheless, the allusion to Ezekiel is not that clear. The punishment is similar to that of Ahab's children.⁹⁷ Tyconius explains that, "the words 'I will kill' do not refer to that death that is visible but to spiritual death." He then relates the killing for God's glory with David defeating Goliath.⁹⁸ The parallel is with the death of David and Bathsheba's son.⁹⁹

Copiii ei . . . The so called children are most likely her followers. Probably it is used to contrast "the Son of God" in the introduction. The expression speaks of her disciples to Apringius and of her legacy to Tyconius. In any case, the "children" are those who have embraced Jezebel's teaching "unreservedly and unconditionally" and so their judgment is fair.¹⁰⁰ Therefore, "children" must have another meaning than the literal one, because the children of Jezebel could not have been punished by God on account of their mother's sin.¹⁰¹ There should be no distinction drawn between the children of Jezebel and those who commit adultery with her.¹⁰² The children of Jezebel are her spiritual progeny.¹⁰³

---

93 Mihoc, *Epistolele Apocalipsei*, 88.
94 Wilhelm Gesenius, *Gesenius' Hebrew Grammar*, 2nd rev. English ed., ed. E. Kautzsch and A. E. Cowley (Mineola, NY: Dover Publications, 2006), 342.
95 Bădiliță, *Apocalipsa lui Ioan*, 163.
96 Charles, *Commentary on the Revelation of St. John*, 72. See also Swete and Beckwith, *The Apocalypse of John*, 468.
97 Swete, *Commentary on Revelation*, 44.
98 Weinrich, ed., *Revelation*, 37.
99 Beckwith, *The Apocalypse of John*, 468.
100   Charles, *Commentary on the Revelation of St. John*, 72.
101   Bunaciu, *Gânduri exegetice*, 70. This is contrary to Beckwith, who says "it is better to take the word, like the other terms in the passage, literally." That is, her physical children will be smitten with death to add to her punishment. Beckwith, *The Apocalypse of John*, 467.
102   Mounce, *The Book of Revelation*, 104.
103   Swete, *Commentary on Revelation*, 44.

Toate bisericile vor cunoaște . . . This verse reminds us of the prophetic judgment utterances, where God pronounces judgment upon a city or nation. The destruction will be a sign for all the surrounding nations or cities to show that God does not let His name be taken in vain and let evil remain unpunished. The scandal in this church must have been widely known, because the surrounding churches would have been able to associate the punishment with the deed.[104]

Cel ce cercetează rinichii și inima . . . The NTR's choice to have "gânduri" for "kidneys" reflects a more functional equivalent translation at this point. Saying this, however, we must add that it is true that the word "kidneys" refers many times to emotions (i.e., the inward parts), while heart refers to the seat of thoughts.[105] This expression with the words νεφροὺς (kidneys) and καρδίας (hearts) occurring in plural is similar to Jeremiah 11:20 and 17:10.[106] Also Charles believes that "kidneys" is an independent reading of Jeremiah.[107] The image of the God who searches the kidneys and the heart oftentimes communicates the picture of a God intimately acquainted with the hidden things pertaining to men. In the expression κατὰ τὰ ἔργα (according to your deeds) reflects the fact that both reward and punishment are included, but the latter is more probably intended.[108]

Revelation 2:24

Celor rămași . . . Mihoc observes that in this passage only, Christ is no longer referring to the angel of the church, but to some of its members.[109] The rest in the church is not necessarily a minority.[110] "Celor rămași, celor din Tiatira" (τοῖς λοιποῖς τοῖς ἐν Θυατείροις) presents the image of the situation in that church. If the ones who remained faithful to Christ were a majority in the churches in Ephesus, Smyrna, and Pergamum, the condition reversed starting with this church.[111]

Însă vouă, celor rămași can be a further allusion to 1 Kings and the times of Jezebel and Ahab when God told Elijah that He had preserved a remnant of faithful people to Himself that did not worship Baal.[112]

Această învățătură . . . This expression proves that the practice spread by Jezebel was backed up by a specific teaching. As we said earlier, some commentators believe this teaching was in essence the teaching of the Nicolaitans mentioned in the message to the Church in Pergamum. However, there is no solid proof for this understanding.

---

104 Charles, *Commentary on the Revelation of St. John*, 72.
105 Charles, *Commentary on the Revelation of St. John*, 73. Charles believed the kidneys represent the will and affection, and the heart stands for thought.
106 H. Preisker, "νεφρός," in *Theological Dictionary of the New Testament*, 2nd ed., ed. Gerhard Kittel and Gerhard Friedrich, trans. Geoffrey W. Bromiley (Grand Rapids, MI: Eerdmans, 1967), 4:911.
107 Charles, *Commentary on the Revelation of St. John*, 72.
108 Beckwith, *The Apocalypse of John*, 468.
109 Mihoc, *Epistolele Apocalipsei*, 90.
110 Swete, *Commentary on Revelation*, 45.
111 Fărăgău, *Apocalipsa 1–3*, 247.
112 Moldoveanu, Apocalipsa, 67.

What is sure is that some of the members of the Church in Thyatira did not listen to this teaching and did not yield to its practices.

Adâncimile Satanei . . . For the understanding of this verse, we have two options: it is an indignant retort of the author saying that thought they claim "to know the deep things of God" (1 Cor. 2:10 and Irenaeus *Haer.* ii. 22.3) they actually know the deep things of Satan. The other option is that "the words represent the actual claim of the Gnostic element in the Church of Thyatira, as Wieseler, Spitta, Zahn," and others support.[113] This claim would mean that a Christian can live a heathen life and still remain a spiritual man, unaffected inwardly by it and thus being superior over it.[114]

Caird suggests that just as Elijah accused Israel "of lumping on two opinions, in their attempt to combine worship of Yahweh with that of Baal, and compelled them to decide which of the two was truly God, so John demands that the church shall choose between Christ and Caesar." But since there is no mention of emperor worship, this interpretation, though creative, is forced.[115] The mention of the name that some adherents of Jezebel's teaching called this doctrine, or part of it, can offer us a clue. Christ makes reference to the so called "deep things of Satan." It is uncertain whether this was meant to be taken as ironic, or that they really called it by this name. If the first case is exact, then it can be an allusion either to the deep things of God mentioned in Corinthians or to Gnostic teachings. If the latter is correct, then Jezebel's adherents must have held the teaching that you must know the deep sins and practices of Satan in order to understand and experience God's mercy. The fact that this expression was not meant as an irony, but they held to this teaching is supported by the qualifier "as they say."

Altă greutate . . . Osborn indicates that ἄλλο with πλὴν should be translated as "no other . . . than." Placing this meaning within the rest of the translation, it can be read, "they receive no other burden than to hold fast to the truths of the faith against the false teachings of Jezebel and the other Nicolaitans."[116] This expression can refer either to the apostolic creed, the traditional instructions at baptism, or no other threat of punishment. It could also point forward to "no other burden than remaining faithful to the Lord."[117] The text uses the same kind of language we encounter in the letter sent by the Church in Jerusalem to the Gentiles in Acts 15. There we have the similar words ἐπιτίθεσθαι . . . βάρος (to lay a burden). Christ does not want to add an extra weight to their current circumstances. The only different translation is that of Bădiliță's where the verb in the present, βάλλω (to cast, throw) is taken with a futuristic force. Victorinus understands the word "burden" as referring to the "observations and duties of the law," thus linking it to Acts 15.[118]

---

113   Charles, *Commentary on the Revelation of St. John*, 73.
114   Charles, *Commentary on the Revelation of St. John*, 74.
115   Caird, *The Revelation of St. John*, 45.
116   Osborne, *Revelation*, 164.
117   Osborne, *Revelation*, 163. Beckwith disagrees with the interpretation that the author had the apostolic decree in mind.
118   Weinrich, ed., *Revelation*, 34.

Revelation 2:25

Păziți ceea ce aveți până când voi veni . . . The condition for not adding an extra weight to other duties or observations of the law is to guard what they already have. Christ is here already starting to advise them on what to do until He returns. Surprisingly, they are not told to fight against Jezebel's party, but they are told to remain uncompromised. If they did not know until now the so called "deep things (or secrets) of Satan," they are to keep it that way. The accent is on the return of Christ. Since his return is taking place soon (1:1; 2:16; 3:11; 22:6, 7, 12, 20), the focus should be on holiness (22:11). We observe that "only to the church in Thyatira is made a double condition and only here and in the message to the church in Pergamum two promises are made."[119]

Fărăgău is rare among the scholars who gives an explanation for the reversed order of warning and promise. This has been seen previously within the letters of chapter 2. Fărăgău believes it is designed to give a more sober note to the last four letters.[120] It is also meant to express the spiritual decline since "starting with the church in Thyatira, evil became predominant."[121] This verse points to the two camps of the spiritual battle in the church: Christ, the angel of the church and those who did not know the depths of Satan on one side, and Jezebel with those who commit adultery with her on the other side. The first camp represents the kingdom of God, and the latter represents the kingdom of Satan.[122]

Revelation 2:26

Și celui ce biruiește, și celui ce ține. . . . Charles proposes the translation "he that overcometh—even he that keepeth."[123] This translation gives to the second conjunction an epexegetic force. Only to the Church of Thyatira is offered a further qualification of the conqueror type. The one who is continually conquering is the same one who is continually watchful on his condition and is aware of the constant reality of spiritual battle. The Church in Thyatira is the only one to which it is made plain what it means to conquer. In their case it has to do with staying uncompromised by doing Christ's works in contrast to the deeds of Jezebel. As it was mentioned above commenting on verse 20, the focus of the message to the Church in Thyatira has to do with their conduct.

Psalm 2 was interpreted as Messianic since the first century B.C.,[124] but Caird says we are compelled to view the promises "within the present order." In other words, it means that the death of the martyrs are "a personal victory over temptation," death and the world.[125] However, in the light of the promises to the other churches, it is safe

---

119 Hemer, *The Letters to the Seven Churches*, 281.
120 Fărăgău, *Apocalipsa 1–3*, 247.
121 Fărăgău, *Apocalipsa 1–3*, 248.
122 Fărăgău, *Apocalipsa 1–3*, 251.
123 Charles, *Commentary on the Revelation of St. John*, 74.
124 Charles, *Commentary on the Revelation of St. John*, 74.
125 Caird, *The Revelation of St. John*, 46.

to say that "whoever holds fast to this body will be co-heir with the Lord and he will have whatever the Son of man received, for 'he has given us all things with him.'"[126]

Beale finds overwhelming support to the notion of overcoming as being paradoxical and ironic in John. The Christians will conquer when they refuse to compromise which will cause persecution and then leads to being "overcome" by the world, just as Christ conquers by being crucified (cf. "the Lamb that was slain").[127]

The two preceding promises refer to the history of redemption in the Old Testament. These recall Genesis and the tree of life and first death (i.e., the spiritual death) hinted in the promises to the Church in Ephesus. Then it also recalls the journey through the wilderness, and the manna and Balaam episode to the Church in Pergamum. Now, the promise to the Church in Thyatira hints at the times of Ahab and Elijah, David, the psalmist, and Isaiah the prophet.[128]

The expression "așa cum și eu am primit de la tatăl meu" confuses the rest of the sentence in some Romanian translations. It is to be taken with the idea that Christ promises to the conqueror the authority over nations which he himself has received from the Father.[129] This is clear from the Greek structure, linking the dependent clause ὡς κἀγὼ εἴληφα παρὰ τοῦ πατρός μου (as even I received from my Father) with the preceding independent clause δώσω αὐτῷ ἐξουσίαν ἐπὶ τῶν ἐθνῶν (I will give him authority over the nations). It is also consistent with the reading of Psalm 2 which has been cited, where the Son of God receives the nations as a heritage from God. Some translations, however, link it with the idea that Christ will give the morning star to the conqueror as he has received it from His Father, or worse, with the sentence "he will shatter them." Thus, the sentence between the semicolons in the "triangle Bible" (TNL) does not make sense on its own: "; . . . și le va păstori cu un toiag de fier, cum sunt zdrobite vasele de lut, după cum am primit și Eu de la Tatăl Meu; . . ." Cornilescu has the same construction in a whole sentence. Bădiliță uses the dash to correctly connect the first independent clause with the dependent one.[130] The Romanian translation under the United Bible Society repeats the expression "îi voi da" to make the correct connection.[131]

Revelation 2:27

și le va conduce cu toiag de fier. . . . The promise is a quotation from Psalm 2. Even though it is not an exact quotation of the Septuagint, it offers a very close image to the Hebrew reading of the text. The problem of this verse is how to interpret the verb "to shepherd" (ποιμανεῖ). NTR and TLN have "va conduce" as do the majority of English translations. Is this the image of a shepherd shattering the pots or of an angry ruler? The exegesis of Psalm 2 leads us to believe that it is the image of a king. This one rules

---

126 Weinrich, ed., *Revelation*, 38.
127 Beale, *The Book of Revelation*, 267.
128 Fărăgău, *Apocalipsa 1–3*, 260.
129 This is why I included it in the previous verse.
130 Bădiliță, *Apocalipsa lui Ioan*, 37.
131 *Noul Testament, traducere după textele originale grecești*, TSB (București, România: edura SBIR, 2009), 374.

over the nations with sovereignty and power to break them as a potter does whatever he wishes with his handiwork (Isa. 26:16; 45:9; Jer. 18:6 and Rom. 9:21).

John had a double meaning in his mind for the word to shepherd, because he intends the same word to mean judge or destroy in 19:15.[132] John had the secondary meaning of רעע, and ποιμαίνω (to shepherd): namely to destroy, even as the Latin *pasco* took this secondary meaning.[133]

Caird wrongly assumed that "John, independently of the Septuagint, made the same mistake which the Septuagint translator has made before him . . . of supposing that, because the Hebrew חור can mean both to pasture and to destroy. Its Greek equivalent must be capable of bearing both meanings also."[134] On the contrary, Mounce, being influenced by Hemer, believes the word should be translated as "to shepherd."[135]

An interesting connection is proposed by Bunaciu. He suggests that the breaking of clay pots is associated with an Egyptian and Mesopotamian custom. When a king was crowned, pots with the names of the enemies that were engraved on them were shattered.[136]

Apringius is sure that this promise "refers to the apostate angels who abandoned their own dominion, for they are going to be judged by the saints on the Day of Judgment and damned and thrown into eternal destruction, as the apostle says."[137] On the other hand, Andrew of Caesarea believes the promise refers to the judgment of the unfaithful, "through which the deceived will be crushed, as though beaten with a rod of iron, and will be judged by those who believed in Christ."[138] He adds that, "The words 'as I, myself, received from the Father' refer to his human nature, which he assumed through the flesh."

Revelation 2:28
îi voi da steaua dimineții . . . Mihoc wrongly attaches the subordinate clause introduced by ὡς (as) to the second promise.[139] In support for our translation, the subordinate "as I received from my father" is put in connection with the power in the previous verse also by Beckwith.[140] Morning star is messianic.[141] This promise means "when thou hast won through the strife I will be thine."[142]

The morning star is taken figuratively by Tyconius to "represent both Christ and the first resurrection, because his appearance scatters the darkness of error and the worldly

---

132   Beale, *The Book of Revelation*, 267.
133   Charles, *Commentary on the Revelation of St. John*, 74.
134   Caird, *The Revelation of St. John*, 45–46.
135   Mounce, *The Book of Revelation*, 104.
136   Bunaciu, *Gânduri exegetice*, 71.
137   Weinrich, ed., *Revelation*, 38.
138   Weinrich, *Revelation*, 38.
139   Mihoc, *Epistolele Apocalipsei*, 81.
140   Beckwith, *The Apocalypse of John*, 471.
141   Beale, *The Book of Revelation*, 267.
142   Charles, *Commentary on the Revelation of St. John*, 77.

shadows of the night are put to flight by the approaching resurrection."[143] Apringius also takes the morning star to mean the first resurrection. He also says that this shows Christ "is the eternal light." On the opposite view, Oecumenius affirms that the star "speaks of the Assyrian, namely, of Satan, of whom the prophet speaks." This means Christ "will make Satan to be subject" to Christians, because the apostle Paul "also made a similar statement: 'God will trample Satan quickly under your feet.'"[144] Andrew of Caesarea gives the two options of the star representing Satan or Christ, just as the lion represents the lion of Judah and the lion of Bashan, the antichrist.[145] Another suggestion is that the promise of the morning star means the conqueror is to possess Christ.[146]

Bădiliţă seems to incline to the theological reversal of the morning star in Isaiah. In his opinion, the message does not talk about the coming of the Messiah, but about the renewal of the world at the second coming of Christ when even the bad associated morning star will be transformed into a star of salvation and not of damnation.[147] My conclusion is that the promise of the morning star is probably connected to the apocalyptic saying that in the messianic kingdom, the righteous will shine like the star; and the morning star is specified because it is the brightest.[148]

Revelation 2:29
Cel ce are urechi, să audă ce spune Duhul bisericilor. . . . This is the final warning for the faith community in Thyatira. These are the exact same words addressed to all the seven churches. The difference is that it comes after the promise. This will be the pattern for the rest of the messages in chapter 3. The hearing formula has its source in Isaiah 6:9–10 and the Synoptic Gospels and is meant to enlighten some, but blind others.[149]

Summary
The message to the Church in Thyatira is the fourth of the seven churches in Asia Christ is addressing, and it is part of the literary unit from chapter 1 to chapter 4. Christ's message seems to be more sober in spite of her spiritual progress. The situation of this church is revealed by the three sections in the paragraph: the depiction of Christ, the rebuke, and the promise. The Church in Thyatira was struggling in the area of moral conduct. More precisely, moral compromise was embraced by the majority of the believers because of the influence of a particular teaching of a woman called Jezebel. Christ's admonition to the church is to conquer this situation by doing His works, in order to receive the reward of co-regality with the Messiah.

---

143   Weinrich, ed., *Revelation*, 38.
144   Weinrich, ed., *Revelation*, 38.
145   Weinrich, ed., *Revelation*, 39.
146   Swete, *Commentary on Revelation*, 47. Stancu associates the star with Christ, who is a light in death. Stancu, *Studii asupra apocalipsei*, 208.
147   Bădiliţă, *Apocalipsa lui Ioan*, 166.
148   Beckwith, *The Apocalypse of John*, 471.
149   Beale, *The Book of Revelation*, 238.

Conclusion

This sample commentary from Revelation 2:18–29 was intended to better illustrate the type of biblical commentary needed in the Romanian context. As we have seen from this sample, a critical type of commentary should provide deep research and exegesis of the biblical text. It also offers a translation of the biblical text that can function as a bridge between exegesis and exposition, presenting a good beginning to the discussion about the meaning or interpretation of the passage. Starting from the translation offered in this commentary, it was easy to interact and understand other Bible translations. For example, we have observed where Cornilescu was different than the Orthodox Synodal translation or the Catholic one as well as the reasons behind such differences. Another trait of this commentary is the reception history and history of interpretation. Particularly, such Church fathers as Victorinus, Tyconius, Andrew of Caesarea, or Oecumenius played an important role in facilitating a dialogue with the Orthodox tradition and interpretation. Finally, the interaction with other Romanian commentaries and interpretations that originated from diverse traditions and approaches were important characteristics of this commentary. Its benefit comes from pointing to textual issues of exegesis, text criticism, or interpretation that caused such divergences. It consists in exposing the causes rather than the symptoms. This could only be done by exegeting the Greek text of the Scripture.

Final Conclusions

This book proposed to analyze the genre of New Testament commentary and to compare the existing Romanian commentaries in order to advance the case for the current need for Romanian exegetical Bible commentaries. There can be many other types proposed here or in other academic papers, but there needs to be a starting point. Many would agree the exegetical or critical type of commentary is a good basic tool and can function as a foundation for other academic or clerical works. Not only can church leaders and workers greatly benefit from such a commentary, but virtually any student of the New Testament or church member can benefit as well. It can function as a standard tool for teaching, preaching, pastoring, or Christian counseling ministries.

A study in the genre of biblical commentaries is both a risky and a complex enterprise. It is risky because so few articles or chapters and even fewer books deal with the genre of biblical commentary. It is a complex enterprise because one has to bring to the discussion the key points of a good commentary which are worthy subjects of study in and of themselves. These main points are: interpretation, exegesis, history of reception, translation, and exposition; and they come from the two faces of the commentary genre: its research and its expositional process.

As we discussed the genre of biblical commentary, certain conclusions became clear. One of them was that commentaries entail a twofold process seen in their exegesis and exposition, and some commentaries also offer an individual translation meant as a bridge between the two. The entire outline of this book was molded by this fact. Another conclusion was that the methodology of interpretation, the audience, the purpose, the language, the presuppositions of the commentator, and the entire communication (presupposed by the literary work nature) of the commentary will guide the whole outcome of that commentary in terms of type. Yet another conclusion from comparing Romanian Bible commentaries was reached: none of them included satisfactory interaction with the variety of Romanian translations, or with the variety of Romanian commentaries and related articles. Overall, there is also little engagement with the Greek text and with the history of interpretation, especially on the Orthodox side, considering the Romanian religious context. All these conclusions lead to propose the writing of a critical or exegetical commentary that would offer a fresh translation of the text; would interact with other Romanian translations, commentaries, and articles in a revealing way; and would include the discussion of the Greek text and its reception history in such a way as to be relevant to the Romanian context.

The kind of biblical commentary proposed and exemplified in this book will create a cultural event by opening and facilitating an inter-confessional dialogue on the text of the Bible. This will not only take place in Romanian academia, but also among the different parochial communities.

Considering the existence of various translations of the Bible in Romanian, the commentary suggested here will offer a basis for the understanding, analysis, and critique of different renderings of the sacred text. In this way the faithful reader of the Bible and the church minister will be offered with an understanding of the translation phenomenon and in the end an enriched understanding of the text. Furthermore, the text criticism that comes with the translation of the text will also explain the differences in translations and will bridge the seeming discrepancy between different confessional translations.

This kind of commentary will aim to create a cultural event by addressing the peculiarities of cultural and religious circumstances through interacting specifically with the existing Romanian commentaries and resources.

Through the decision of adopting a short section with a presentation of the reception history of the biblical passage, a commentary of the kind suggested in this book will create a connection between different religious Romanian affiliations by exposing the common theological understanding among the Church fathers. It can also create an awareness of the engrained Orthodox mentality of many Romanians.

Combining these aforementioned features, the biblical commentary suggested in this book will be a trustworthy tool in the hands of Christian leaders and members. The last chapter of this book was useful for the demonstration of these conclusions and of the argument of this entire work.

Bibliography of Works Cited

Abelson, Raziel. "Definition." In *The Encyclopedia of Philosophy*. 2nd ed. Edited by Donald M. Borchert, 2:664–77. Farmington Hills, MI: Macmillan Reference USA, 2006.

Adler, Mortimer J. and Charles van Doren, *How to Read a Book: The Classic Guide to Intelligent Reading.* New York: Simon and Schuster, Inc., 1972.

Aland, Kurt, and Barbara Aland. *The Text of the New Testament: An Introduction to the Critical Editions and to the Theory and Practice of Modern Textual Criticism.* Grand Rapids, MI: W. B. Eerdmans, 1989.

Aldea, Traian. *Scrisorile Apocalipsei: de la Patmos la Laodicea.* Alba-Iulia, România: Editura Creștină "Mateus," 1994.

Aune, David E. *Word Biblical Commentary.* Vol 52A, *Revelation: 1–5*. Edited by Ralph P. Martin. Dallas, TX: Word Books, 1997.

Baban, Octavian. "Reflecții asupra locului Bibliei și a traducerilor ei în mărturia și viața Bisericii Baptiste." *Jurnal Teologic*, 5 (2006): 130–40.

———. *Curs de hermeneutica biblica,* unpublished notes. București, România, 2009. Accessed, 23 December 2012. http://obinfonet.ro/docs/herm/herm_c.pdf.

Bădiliță, Cristian. Accessed 10 August 2020. http://cristianbadilita.ro/index.php?page=bibliografie.

———. *Noul Testament: Apocalipsa lui Ioan, ediție bilingvă*. București, România: Adevărul Holding, 2012.

Baird, William. "Biblical Criticism." In *The Anchor Bible Dictionary*, vol.1. Edited by D. N. Freedman, 726–36. New York: Doubleday, 1992.

Bărnuț, Daniel Emeric Hubert and Jozsef Kovacs. *Dicționar grec român pentru studiul cuvintelor Noului Testament.* Cluj-Napoca, România: Editura Theologos, 1999.

Beckwith, Isbon T. *The Apocalypse of John: Studies in Introduction with a Critical and Exegetical Commentary.* Grand Rapids, MI: Baker Book House, 1979.

Bauer, Walter. *A Greek-English Lexicon of the New Testament and Other Early Christian Literature*. Edited by Frederick W. Danker. 3rd ed. Chicago: University of Chicago Press, 2000.

Beale, Gregory K. *The Book of Revelation: A Commentary on the Greek Text*. New International Greek Testament Commentary. Grand Rapids, MI: William B. Eerdmans Publishing Company, 1999.

Beck, John. *Sfânta Scriptură în Tradiția Bisericii.* Translated by Ioana Tămăian. Cluj-Napoca, Romania: Patmos, 2008.

Broderick, Robert C. "Biblical Commentaries." In *The Catholic Encyclopedia, Revised and Updates Edition.* Edited by Robert Broderick, 125–27. Nashville, TN: Thomas Nelson Publishers, 1987.

Borgen, Peder, "Philo of Alexandria." In *Anchor Bible Dictionary*. Vol. 5. Edited by David Noel Freedman, 333–42. New York: Doubleday, 1992.

Bruce, Frederick Fyvie. "Exegesis and Hermeneutics, Biblical." *The New Encyclopaedia Britannica*. 15th ed. Chicago: Encyclopaedia Britannica, Inc., 1978.

———. "Criticism." *International Standard Bible Encyclopedia*. Edited by Geoffrey W. Bromiley, 1:676–85. Grand Rapids, MI: William B. Eerdmans Publishing Company, 1979.

Bunaciu, Ioan. *Gânduri exegetice asupra cărții Apocalipsa*. București, România:Editura Uniunea Comunităților Creștine Baptiste din R. S. România, 1989.

Burke, David G. "Interpret." In *International Standard Bible Encyclopedia:* Edited by Geoffrey W. Bromiley, 3:861–63. Grand Rapids, MI: Eerdmans Pub. Co., 1979.

Caird, George B. *The Revelation of St. John the Divine*. New York: Harper & Row, 1966.

———. *The Language and Imagery of the Bible*. Philadelphia, PA: The Westminster Press, 1980.

Carson, Donald Arthur. *New Testament Commentary Survey*. 6th ed. Grand Rapids, MI: Baker Academic, 2007.

———. *Exegetical Fallacies*. 2nd ed. Carlisle, England: Paternoster, 1996.

———. "The Limits of Functional Equivalence Translation—and other Limits, too." In *The Challenge of Bible Translation: Communicating God's Word to the World*. Edited by Glen G. Scorgie, Mark L. Strauss, and Steven M. Voth, 65–114. Grand Rapids, MI: Zondervan, 2003.

Charles, R. H. *A Critical and Exegetical Commentary on the Revelation of St. John*. The International Critical Commentary. Edited by S. R. Driver, A. Plummer and C. A. Briggs. Edinburgh: T&T Clark, 1920.

Charlesworth, James H. *The Pesharim and Qumran History: Chaos or Consesus?* Grand Rapids, MI: William B. Eerdmans, 2002.

Collins, John Joseph. "Introduction: Towards the Morphology of a Genre. *Semeia* 14 (1979). Accessed 11 January 2021. *ATLA Religion Database with ATLASerials*, EBSCO*host*.

Comfort, Philip W. *Essential Guide to Bible Versions*. Wheaton, IL: Tyndale House Publishers, 2000.

Comunicat de presa. Accessed 10 August 2020. http://www.recensamantromania.ro/wp-content/uploads/2012/08/Comunicat-presa_Rezultate-preliminare.pdf.

Conzelmann, Hans and Andreas Lindemann. *Interpreting the New Testament: An Introduction to the Principles and Methods of N.T. Exegesis*. Peabody, MA: Hendrickson Publishers, 1999.

Cruceru, Marius David. "'Cornilescu' față de alte traduceri ale Sfintelor Scripturi în limba Română. Propunere de system de grille analitice pentru ediții ale Bibliei după 1989, în cadrul mișcării evanghelice din România." *Creștinul Azi*, vol. 4, 1/2004.

Dupont-Sommer, André. *The Essene Writings from Qumram*. Translated by G. Vermes. Cleveland, OH: World Publishing Company, 1961.

Dunn, James D. G. *Word Biblical Commentary*. Volume 38A, *Romans 1–8*, edited by Ralph P. Martin. Dallas, TX: Word Books, 1988.

Fee, Gordon D. *New Testament Exegesis: a Handbook for Students and Pastors*. 3rd ed. Louisville, KY: Westminster John Knox Press, 2002.

Fărăgău, Beniamin. *Apocalipsa cap. 1—3 și Doctrina Bisericii.* Cluj-Napoca, România: Risoprint, 2009.

———. "Preface to the Revised and Completed Edition." *Apocalipsa cap. 1–3 și Doctrina Bisericii.* Cluj-Napoca, România: Risoprint, 2009.

Fee, Gordon. "Reflections on Commentary Writing." *Theology Today* 46, no. 4 (1990): 387–92. Accessed 13 January 2021. *ATLA Religion Database with ATLASerials*, EBSCO*host*.

Fee, Gordon D. and Mark L. Strauss. *How to Choose a Translation for All It's Worth: A Guide to Understanding and Using Bible Versions.* Grand Rapids, MI: Zondervan, 2007.

Fishbane, Michael A. *Biblical Interpretation in Ancient Israel.* Oxford: Clarendon Press, 1988.

Gadamer, Hans-Georg. *Truth and Method.* 2nd rev. ed. Translated by Joel Weinsheimer and Donald G. Marshall. New York: Continuum, 2004.

Georgescu, Constantin. *Manual de greacă biblică.* București, România: Nemira, 2011.

Gesenius, Wilhelm. *Gesenius' Hebrew Grammar.* 2nd rev. English ed. Edited by E. Kautzsch and A. E. Cowley. Mineola, NY: Dover Publications, 2006.

Gorman, Frank H. Jr. "Commenting on Commentary: Reflections on a Genre." In *Relating to the Text: Interdisciplinary and Form-Critical Insights on the Bible.* Edited by Timothy J. Sandoval and Carleen R. Mandolfo editors, 100–19. London: T&T Clark International, 2003.

Gorman, Michael J. *Elements of Biblical Exegesis: A Basic Guide for Students and Ministers* Peabody. MA: Hendrickson Publishers, 2001.

Grant, Robert M. and David Tracy. *A Short History of the Interpretation of the Bible.* 2nd rev. ed. Philadelphia: Fortress Press, 1984.

Grassmick, John D. *Principles and Practice of Greek Exegesis: a Classroom Manual.* Dallas, TX: Dallas Theological Seminary, 1976.

Green, Joel B. "Commentary." In *Dictionary for Theological Interpretation of the Bible.* Edited by Kevin J. Vanhoozer, 123–27. Grand Rapids, MI: Baker Academic, 2005.

Grobel, Kendrick. "Commentary." *The Interpreter's Dictionary of the Bible: An Illustrated Encyclopedia.* Vol. 1. Edited by George Arthur Buttrich, 663. Nashville, TN: Abingdon Press, 1962.

Hayes, John H. and Carl R. Holladay. *Biblical Exegesis: A Beginner's Handbook.* Atlanta: John Knox Press, 1982.

Hartman, Lars. "A Commentary: A Communication about a Communication." *Novum Testamentum* 5 (2009): 389–400. Accessed 10 October, 2012. *ATLA Religion Database with ATLASerials*, EBSCO*host*.

Hawthorne, G. F. "Translate." In *International Standard Bible Encyclopedia.* Edited by Geoffrey W. Bromiley, 4:890. Grand Rapids, MI: William B. Eerdmans publishing Company, 1979.

Hemer, Colin J. *The Letters to the Seven Churches of Asia in Their Local Setting.* Grand Rapids, MI: William B. Eerdmans, 2001.

Hubbard, David A. and Glenn W. Barker, "Editorial Preface." In David E. Aune, *Word Biblical Commentary*. Vol. 52A, *Revelation: 1–5*. Edited by Ralph P. Martin, x–xi. Dallas, TX: Word Books, 1997.

Keener, Craig S. *Revelation*; *The NIV Application Commentary.* Grand Rapids, MI: Zondervan, 2000.

Kaiser, Walter C., Jr., and Moisés Silva. *Introduction to Biblical Hermeneutics: The Search for Meaning.* Rev. and exp. ed. Grand Rapids, MI: Zondervan, 2007.

Lattimore, Richmond. Cited in Eugene Nida. *Towards a Science of Translation: With Special Reference to Principles and Procedures Involved in Bible Translating.* Leiden, Netherlands: E. J. Brill, 1969.

Levițchi, Leon D. *Îndrumar pentru traducătorii din limba engleză in limba româna.* Bucharest, Romania: Editura Științifică și Enciclopedică, 1975.

Manea, Dragoș Ștefăniță. "A Short Exploration on the Importance of Greek Language Study for the Romanian Evangelical Church." MET thesis, Tyndale Theological Seminary Badhoevedorp The Netherlands, 2010.

March, Francis Andrew and Francis Andrew March, Jr. *A Thesaurus Dictionary of the English Language.* Philadelphia, PA: Historical Publishing Company, 1913.

Marshall, I. Howard. *New Testament Interpretation: Essays on Principles and Methods.* Grand Rapids, MI: William B. Eerdmans Pub. Co., 1979.

McClintock, John and James Strong. "Commentary." In *Cyclopedia of Biblical, Theological, and Ecclesiastical Literature*. Vol. 2. Edited by J. McClintock and J. Strong, 427–37. Grand Rapids, MI.: Baker Book House, 1981.

McKechnie, Jean L., ed. *Webster's New Twentieth Century Dictionary of the English Language, Unabridged: Based Upon the Broad Foundations Laid Down by Noah Webster.* 2nd ed. Grand Rapids, MI: Collins World, 1979.

McKnight, Scot, editor. *Introducing New Testament Interpretation (Guides to New Testament Exegesis).* Louisville, KY: Baker Academic, 1990.

Metzger, Bruce Maning. *The Bible in Translation: Ancient and English Versions.* Grand Rapids, MI: Baker Academic, 2001.

———. *A Textual Commentary on the Greek New Testament.* London: United Bible Societies, 1975.

Metzger, Bruce Maning and Bart D. Ehrman. *The Text of the New Testament: Its Transmission, Corruption, and Restoration.* 4th ed. New York: Oxford University Press, 2005.

Mihoc, Daniel. *Epistolele Apocalipsei: Introducere, traducere și comentariu.* Sibiu, Romania: Teofania, 2003.

Moldoveanu, Nicolae. *Apocalipsa-Hristos descoperirea.* Deva, România: Editura Comorile Harului, 2008.

Mounce, Robert H. *The New International Commentary on the New Testament: The Book of Revelation.* Rev. ed. Grand Rapids, MI: William B. Eerdmans Publishing Company, 1998.

Nash, Henry S. "Exegesis or Hermeneutics." In *The New Schaff-Herzong Encyclopedia of Religious Knowledge*. Vol. 4. Edited by Samuel Macauley Jackson, 237–47. Grand Rapids, MI: Baker Book House, 1949–50.

Negruț, Paul. Cristos, *Biserica și vremurile de pe urmă: o abordare homiletică a cărții Apocalipsa*. Oradea, România: Făclia/Editura Universității Emanuel, 2006.

Neusner, Jacob. "Talmud." *International Standard Bible Encyclopedia*. Edited by Geoffrey W. Bromley, 4:717–24. Grand Rapids, MI: William B. Eerdmans Publishing Company, 1979.

Newport, John. *The Lion and the Lamb: A Commentary on the Book of Revelation for Today.* Nashville, TN: Broadman Press, 1986.

Nida, Eugene A. *Signs, Sense, Translation.* Cape Town, South Africa: Bible Society of South Africa, 1984.

———. *Toward a Science of Translating: With Special Reference to Principles and Procedures Involved in Bible Translating.* Leiden, Netherlands: E. J. Brill, 1969.

Nida, Eugene A., and Charles R. Taber. *The Theory and Practice of Translation* Reprint, Leiden, Netherlands: E. J. Brill for UBS, 1982.

Nolland, John. "The Purpose and Value of Commentaries." *Journal for the Study of the New Testament* 29, no. 3 (March 2007): 306–11. Accessed 13 January 2021. DOI: 10.1177/0142064X07076311.

O'Donnell, Matthew Brook. "Translation and the Exegetical Process, Using Mark 5.1-10,'The Bidding of the Strongman', as a Test Case." In *Translating the Bible: Problems and Prospects.* Edited by Stanley E. Porter and Richard S. Hess, 162–88. London: T&T Clark International, 2004.

Orr, James and Frederic W. Danker. "Commentaries." *International Standard Bible Encyclopedia*. Edited by Geoffrey W. Bromley, 1:737–43. Grand Rapids, MI: William B. Eerdmans Publishing Company, 1979.

Osborne, Grant R. *Baker Exegetical Commentary on the New Testament: Revelation.* Grand Rapids, MI: Baker Academic, 2002.

Porter, Stanley E. and Richards S. Hess editors. *Translating the Bible: Problems and Prospects*. London: T&T Clark International, 2004.

Preisker, H. νεφρός. In *Theological Dictionary of the New Testament*. Vol. 4. 2nd ed. Edited by Gerhard Kittel and Gerhard Friedrich. Translated by Geoffrey W. Bromiley, 911. Grand Rapids, MI: Eerdmans, 1967.

Reinhartz, Adele. "Why Comment? Reflections on Bible Commentaries in General and Andrew Lincoln's *The Gospel According to Saint John* in Particular." *Journal for the Study of the New Testament* 29, no. 3 (March, 2007): 333–42. Accessed 13 January 2021. *ATLA Religion Database with ATLASerials*, EBSCO*host*.

Repphun, Eric, Deane Galbraith, Will Sweetman and James Harding. "Beyond Christianity, the Bible and the Text: Urgent Tasks and New Orientations for Reception History," *Relegere: Studies in Religion and Reception* 1, no.1 (2011): 1–12. Accessed, 11 January 2021. http://www.relegere.org/index.php/relegere/article/viewFile/391/494.

Ryken, Leland. *The Word of God in English: Criteria for Excellence in Bible Translation.* Wheaton, IL: Crossway Books, 2002.

Roberts, Jonathan and Christopher Rowland. Review of *Encyclopedia of the Bible and Its Reception. Relegere: Studies in Religion and Reception* 1, no. 2 (2011):

351–58. Accessed 11 January 2021. http://www.relegere.org/index.php/relegere/article/viewFile/473/556.

Sailhamer, John H. *Introduction to Old Testament Theology: A Canonical Approach.* Grand Rapids, MI: Zondervan Publishing House, 1999.

Scorgie, Glen G., Mark L. Strauss, and Steven M. Voth, eds. *The Challenge of Bible Translation: Communicating God's Word to the World.* Grand Rapids, MI: Zondervan, 2003.

Sheppard, Gerald T. and Anthony C. Thiselton. "Biblical Interpretation in Europe in the Twentieth Century." *Dictionary of Major Biblical Interpreters.* Edited by Donald K. McKim, 67–87. Nottingham, England: Inter-Varsity Press, 2007.

Smith, Wilbur M. "Commentaries." *The Zondervan Pictorial Encyclopedia of the Bible.* Vol.1. Edited by Merrill C. Tenney, 920. Grand Rapids, MI: Zondervan Publishing House, 1976.

Spurgeon, Charles H. *Lectures to My Students.* Vol. 4, *Commenting and Commentaries.* Peabody, MA: Hendrickson Publishers, 2010.

Stancu, Dragomir. *Studii asupra Apocalipsei,volumul 1.* Arad, România: Candela, 1995.

Steiner, George. *After Babel: Aspects of Language and Translation.* Oxford: Oxford University Press, 1998.

Stewart, Roy A. "Commentaries, Hebrew." *International Standard Bible Encyclopedia.* Edited by Geoffrey W. Bromley, 1:743–47. Grand Rapids, MI: William B. Eerdmans Publishing Company.

Stenger, Werner. *Introduction to New Testament Exegesis.* Douglas W. Stott translator. Grand Rapids, MI: William B. Eerdmans Publishing Company, 1993.

Swete, Henry Barclay. *Commentary on Revelation: The Greek Text.* Grand Rapids, MI: Kregel Publications, 1977.

Thomas, Robert L. "Dynamic Equivalence: A Method of Translation or System of Hermeneutics." *The Master's Seminary Journal* 1, no. 2 (Fall 1990): 149–69. Accessed 13 January 2021. http://www.tms.edu/tmsj/tmsj1g.pdf.

Thomas, Robertson Archibald. *A Grammar of the Greek New Testament in the Light of the Historical Research.* Nashville, TN: Broadman Press, 1934.

Traian, Grec. "Prefață." *Gânduri exegetice asupra cărții Apocalipsa.* Editat de Ioan Bunaciu, 4. București, România: Editura Uniunea Comunităților Creștine Baptiste din R. S. România, 1989.

Weinrich, William C., ed. *Ancient Christian Commentary on Scripture, New Testament.* Vol. 12, *Revelation.* Downers Grove, IL: InterVarsity Press, 2005.

White, Ellen G. *Tragedia veacurilor.* București, România: Editura Viață și Sănătate, 1981.

Wiles, M. F. "Origen as Biblical Scholar." In *The Cambridge History of the Bible.* Vol. 1, *From the Beginnings to Jerome.* Edited by P. R. Ackroyd and C. F. Evans, 454-89. Cambridge: Cambridge University Press, 1975.

———. "Theodore of Mopsuestia as Representative of the Antiochene School." In *The Cambridge History of the Bible.* Vol. 1, *From the Beginnings to Jerome.* Edited by P. R. Ackroyd and C. F. Evans, 489–510. Cambridge: Cambridge University Press, 1975.

Williams, D. H. *Evangelicals and Tradition: The Formative Influence of the Early Church*. Grand Rapids, MI: Baker Academic, 2005.

Online Resources

Webster's Online Dictionary with Multilingual Thesaurus Translation, Accessed 24 July 2012. http://www.websters-online-dictionary.org/definitions/exegesis.

United Bible Societies, Accessed 5 August 2012. http://www.unitedbiblesocieties.org/sample-page/bible-translation.

Cultele Neoprotestante (Evanghelice): Baptist, Adventist de Ziua a Şaptea, Penticostal, Creştin după Evanghelie, Biserica Evanghelică Română), Accessed 16 January 2021. http://web.archive.org/web/20120130012119/http://www.culte.ro/DocumenteHtml.aspx?id=1738

Bible Translations

Apocalipsa Sfântului Ioan Teologul în limbile română, greacă şi latină. Traducere Bratolomeu Valeriu Anania. Bucureşti, România: Editura Paralela 45, 2001.

Biblia sau Sfânta Scriptură a Vechiului şi Noului Testament cu trimiteri. Translated by Dumitru Cornilescu. Belarus: Romanian Bible Society, 2006.

Biblia sau Sfânta Scriptură a Vechiului şi Noului Testament: traducere literară nouă. Bucureşti, România/Dilenburg. Germany: GBV, 2001.

Biblia, Noua traducere în limba română (NTR). International Bible Society, 2007.

Noul Testament, traducere după textile originale greceşti. Bucureşti, România: SBIR, 2009.

Noul Testament, ediţia a II-a, traducere Alois Bulai şi Anton Budău. Iaşi, România: Sapientia, 2008.

Noul Testament cu Psalmi, traducere Bartilomeu Anania. Bucureşti, România: IBMBOR, 2006.

BOOK 2

Translation of σῴζω in the Romanian Orthodox Bible and Its Implications for Soteriology

Alexandru Costea

Novum Testamentum Graece (Nestle-Aland), 28. Edition,
© Deutsche Bibelgesellschaft, Stuttgart 2012.

Scripture quotations are from the SBL Greek New Testament. Copyright
© 2010 Society of Biblical Literature and Logos Bible Software.

Abstract

The aim of this study is to analyze the translation of the verb σῴζω [sōzō] in the Romanian Orthodox Bible and its implication for theology, as σῴζω in the passive/middle voice is translated with a reflexive nuance. It begins with the history of the Romanian Orthodox Bible translation and several principles for translation that one must have in mind. This process will reveal the methodology of these translations as well as pointing to the importance of grammar and context. Throughout the book, it will be shown that the Greek middle voice cannot be understood primarily reflexive, as there are different ways of translating it. Moreover, a case by case study through the canonical gospels will make it clear that the context also does not support a reflexive understanding. The danger in translating σῴζω as reflexive is that it communicates a type of salvation outside "by grace, through faith." However, it will be advocated that this was not the interpretation of the Eastern Church Fathers either. Finally, a proposed revision for the examples given from the canonical gospels is presented in order to better illustrate the grammatical understanding of the voice—as well as the context in which is used—and the Eastern Church Fathers understanding of it.

Dedication

With thanks to Dr. H. H. Drake Williams III who encouraged me and guided me through the thesis process upon which this book is based.

Contents

Acronyms and Abbreviations 117
Introduction 119
    Objectives   121
    Delimitations   121
    Methodology   121

Chapter 1 123
    History of the Translation of the Romanian Bible and Bible Translation Principles
    History of the Translation of the Romanian Bible   124
        Noul Testament de la Bălgrad (1648)   124
        Biblia de la București (1688)   125
        Biblia Sinodală (1914)   125
        Biblia Galaction-Radu (1938)   126
        Biblia Anania (2001)   126
        The Interdenominational Bible Society of Romania   127
        The Protestant Translations of the Bible   127
        Biblia Cornilescu   128
        Noua Traducere Românească   130
    Historical Perspective on the Translation of σῴζω   130
        Biblia de la București (1688)   130
        Biblia Sinodală (1914)   130
        Biblia Galaction-Radu (1939)   131
        Biblia Anania (2001)   131
        Dumitru Cornilescu (1924)   131
        Noua Traducere (2007) and *Societatea Biblică Interconfesională din România* (2013)   131
    Principles for Translation   131
        Formal equivalence/correspondence   132
        Dynamic equivalence   133

Chapter 2 135
    An Analysis of the Greek Voice
    Voice   135
    Voice System in the Romanian Language   135
    Voice System in Koine Greek   137
        The active voice   138
        The passive voice   138
        The middle voice   140
    Conclusion   151

Chapter 3 153
   Σώζω in the Canonical Gospels
      Case by Case Study of the Verb σώζω in the Canonical Gospels   153
      Conclusion   163

Chapter 4 165
   Soteriology in the Eastern Church Fathers
      John Chrysostom   167
          His Commentaries on the Gospel Passages   168
      Cyril of Alexandria   170
      The Translation of σώζω in Regard to Soteriology   172
      Conclusion   174

Conclusion and Recommendations 177

Bibliography of Works Cited 183

Acronyms and Abbreviations

BBS	British Bible Society
BDAG	W. Bauer, F. W. Danker, W. F. Arndt, F. W. Gingrich, *A Greek English Lexicon of the New Testament*, 3rd ed.
IBSR-SBIR	Interdenominational Bible Society of Romania
NTLR	*Noua Traducere în Limba Română*

Introduction

Romania is considered to be more than eighty percent Christian. This number has to do with the long tradition of the Orthodox Church in Romania, the religion that influenced the inhabitant people of the country throughout history. In a country that sees itself as being Orthodox, the obvious outcome is that the Bible which is the most read by the people is the Romanian Orthodox translation of the Bible. Yet, translation of the Bible is not an easy task since it requires in-depth grammatical knowledge of the biblical languages. No matter what one thinks about it, translation involves interpretation and is bound to encounter all the challenges that appear in this field. One of these challenges is the theological conviction that one might bring to a translated text. In certain cases the Orthodox translations can be critiqued.

One area that needs greater attention is the translation of the Greek middle voice. Providing the translation equivalent of the voice is not easy to do since one must pay attention to a large number of nuances. For instance, while describing a modern understanding of the Greek middle voice, Dana and Mantey admit that this is "one of the most distinctive and peculiar phenomena of the Greek language. It is impossible to describe it, adequately or accurately, in terms of English idiom, for English knows no approximate parallel."[1] An especially hard task is distinguishing the middle voice from the passive since in the Greek language; only the future and aorist tenses have separate forms for the middle and passive voices. The forms for passive and middle voice are the same in the present, imperfect, perfect, and pluperfect, and one should decide each case individually by analysis.[2]

One of the problems in understanding the middle voice is encountered when defining it as primarily reflexive. This struggle with the understanding of the Greek voice can be seen in the Romanian Orthodox translation where both the passive voice and the middle voice are understood to have a reflexive nuance. An examination of a few instances of the verb "to save" used in the middle/passive voice reveal that the Orthodox translation of it favors the reflexive voice. Thus, in Matthew 10:22 the following verse is found: καὶ ἔσεσθε μισούμενοι ὑπὸ πάντων διὰ τὸ ὄνομά μου· ὁ δὲ ὑπομείνας εἰς τέλος οὗτος σωθήσεται. The verb "to save" in this verse could be interpreted as being either middle or passive voice from its parsing. The Orthodox translation has chosen to translate it as a middle, and then also viewed it to be reflexive: "Şi veţi fi urîţi de toţi pentru Numele Meu; iară cela ce va răbda pînă în sfîrşit, acela *se va mântui*" (And you will be hated by all for

---

1 Dana H. E. and Julius R. Mantey, *A Manual Grammar of the Greek New Testament* (New York: The Macmillan Company, 1957), 156.

2 Daniel B. Wallace, *Greek Grammar Beyond the Basics: An Exegetical Syntax of the New Testament* (Grand Rapids, MI: Zondervan, 1996), 410.

my sake's name; but the one who will endure to the end, that one *will save himself*).³ This translation communicates a reflexive reading of the verb.

The same situation is in οἱ σῳζόμενοι found in Luke 13:23–24: "Şi I-a zis cineva: Doamne, puțini sunt, oare, cei ce *se mântuiesc?* Iar El le-a zis: Siliți-vă să intrați prin poarta cea strâmtă." In this case, the translation provided is: "And someone said to him: 'Lord, are they few those who *save themselves*?' And he said to them: 'Strive to enter through the narrow door.'" In this verse, the present participle is understood to have a reflexive aspect: "the ones who save themselves".

This book will argue that the Romanian Orthodox translation of the Greek passive and middle voice as reflexive in the New Testament has not taken into account a more recent and better understanding of the Greek voice. This will be shown through a grammatical analysis of the two voices in which all the nuances will be discussed.

The implications of this study have significant theological and practical implications for soteriology. The Romanian Orthodox Church claims that salvation is by faith in Christ, but added to the faith are the works done by a Christian and the sacraments of the Church. For the Orthodox, salvation is not a onetime experience in the life of the Christian, but is a process that continues throughout the life of the Christian. Thus, the Orthodox Church understands that the ultimate goal of an Orthodox Christian is *theosis*, defined as the union with God. In this understanding, "God became man so that man might become god." As a result, the process through which Christians become united with Christ is more emphasized in the Orthodox Church. In contrast, the Reformed understanding of salvation is that *theosis* can be what is called sanctification, but sanctification is a result of salvation and not a way of saving oneself. While the Orthodox understanding emphasizes God's initiative in this process, salvation is explained as a process that has at its foundation a divine-human cooperation.⁴ Thus, in Christ "true humanity is kept and brought back to its original form," and deification is understood to happen through grace.⁵

Unlike the Orthodox view, the position which will be argued is that salvation is not a process. When one talks about unity with Christ, a process has already taken place in which one becomes more conformed to the image of Christ (Rom. 5:1). Also, men are saved only by grace through faith as Ephesians 2:8–9 states so succinctly: "For by grace you have been saved through faith. And this is not your own doing; it is the gift of God, not a result of works, so that no one may boast."⁶ Moreover, salvation is both about justification, a past event that happened once you believed in Christ and you were declared righteous, and sanctification, a lifelong process of being made holy

---

3 This translation appears first in *Biblia Sinodală* 1914.

4 D. Stăniloae, *Sinteză Eclesiologică: Biserica, Organ al Mîntuirii și Sfințirii*, accessed January 9, 2020, http://faculty.go.ro/text/text-pdf/Dumitru%20Stanilaoe%20-%20Sinteza%20 eclesiologica.%20Biserica,%20sfintire%20si%20mantuire.pdf, 1.

5 Stăniloae, *Sinteză Eclesiologică*, 1.

6 Ephesians 2:8–9 (The ESV® Bible (The Holy Bible, English Standard Version®), copyright © 2001 by Crossway, a publishing ministry of Good News Publishers. Used by permission. All rights reserved.)

after justification. In contrast, the Orthodox hold justification and sanctification to be aspects of one continuous process.[7]

Objectives

In light of the discussion above, the objectives of the present work are the following:

1. To provide a grammatical analysis of the Greek middle voice in the light of the more recent reference grammars.
2. To analyze the Romanian Orthodox translation of the Greek middle voice, which is rendered as reflexive.
3. To show the correlation between the Orthodox translation and its theological and practical implications in soteriology.
4. To suggest a revision of the translation based on grammatical points proven in the paper.
5. To supply a study case where the verb σῴζω and its appearance in the middle voice is analyzed.

Delimitations

The following work will not examine all of the verbs in the Greek New Testament that appear in the middle/passive form, but the emphasis will be on the passages in the Gospels where the verb "to save" is used. Moreover, this work will not attempt to make an exhaustive case on the soteriological discussion in which justification by faith and salvation through deeds are at stake.

Methodology

This work will follow the traditional approach to Greek grammar; in other words, it will not use a function-based approach to language. This traditional approach will be made by consulting the most recent reference grammars as well as several articles that provide advance studies in the middle voice. To present the soteriological implications, a case-by-case approach will be followed in order to distinguish the middle voice from the passive voice.

Chapter one deals with the introductory matters that need to be addressed. In the beginning of the chapter, the problem will be introduced to show the preference of the Romanian Orthodox Church's translation for the reflexive nuance regarding the verb σῴζω. As discussed above, the verb σῴζω that appears in both the passive and the middle/passive verbs in the Synoptic Gospels is translated by the Orthodox Church as "save yourself," a translation that carries important implications for soteriology. A brief presentation of the available Romanian Orthodox translations will be provided in the next section, starting with the first translation of the Bible in Romanian (*Biblia de la București*) and finishing with the latest editions in the Orthodox Church. Furthermore,

---

[7] Fr. Jack Norman Sparks, ed., "Justification by Faith," in *The Orthodox Study Bible* (Nashville, TN: Thomas Nelson, 2008); see also Victor E. Klimenko, "The Orthodox Teaching on Personal Salvation," Orthodox Christianity, accessed July 29, 2020, http://orthochristian.com/46463.html.

since the main argument of this study concerns translation, a few introductory matters on the field of translation will be presented.

Chapter two will deal with the analysis of the Greek passive and middle voice. It will examine the current discussion, drawing attention to the important characteristics of the Greek voice that will help in arguing against the reflexive understanding of the middle voice. A brief introduction of the voice in the English, Greek, and Romanian languages will be presented. Of note here is the reflexive active, a construction that is similar to the direct middle, the Orthodox understanding of the middle voice. Since one argument in favor of the reflexive understanding is that the middle voice has been historically understood to be reflexive in nature, the main difficulties in understanding the middle voice will be discussed: the middle; the middle-passive endings for verbs and how one can differentiate between them; and the primarily reflexive understanding of the Greek middle voice. The latter is treated more extensively; both proponents and critics of the view will be presented in order to provide an introduction to the problem.

Chapter three will be a case by case study of the verb σῴζω in the canonical gospels, looking at several translations of the Romanian Orthodox Church in these passages alongside the Protestant translation of the same verses. The main critique of the translation will derive from the understanding of grammar from chapter two. Furthermore, since this work deals with the interpretation of the text, an exegetical approach to the selected texts also will be provided.

Chapter four will continue the examination of the Orthodox Church's translation of the verb "to save," but the approach will be a more historical one. The chapter will look at some writings of the Eastern Church Fathers and their understanding of the passages considered earlier. Since salvation is mostly explained in the Orthodox Church through theosis or deification, an overall understanding of this doctrine in the Eastern Church Fathers also will be discussed.

The last chapter of this work will bring together all the discussed topics in order to provide the best translation of the verb σῴζω. Additionally, a proposed revision for the translation of the verb "to save" will be addressed in this last chapter.

CHAPTER 1

History of the Translation of the Romanian Bible and Bible Translation Principles

The verb σῴζω appears in the New Testament more than one hundred times and is found in all three voices.[1] In the Romanian Orthodox Bible, it is translated in a number of ways: a tămădui (to heal), a se spăşi (archaic word for to repent), a salva (to save).[2] While the meaning does not bring major problems for its use in the New Testament, there is a tendency in the Romanian Orthodox Bible for the verb to be expressed in a reflexive way, particularly the translation of the verb in both the passive and the middle voice. In the passive voice, the verb is found in the Romanian Bible and is translated as "to save oneself." The grammatical analysis in the next chapter will help explain why this reading is not very well supported or recommended. As will be seen, two things are to be taken into consideration here. First, the Romanian language has a less common way of expressing the passive which is the reflexive-passive. In this construction, the verb has the characteristics of the passive but is expressed through the use of the reflexive pronoun "se."[3] Second, the context of the verses in which σῴζω appears are to be taken in consideration. Furthermore, the verb "to save" in the middle voice is also translated as reflexive. This translation may be justified through the historical interpretation of the middle voice as mainly reflexive and one of its categories. Thus, a careful analysis of the verb "to save" will be needed in order to provide the best translation for the passive and the middle voice.

This work will examine the appearances of σῴζω in the canonical gospels. Almost half of the appearances of the verb are in the canonical gospels, while the vast majority of the other books make use of the verb less than ten times. Another good reason to consider σῴζω in the canonical Gospels is that the word appears in all of the different voices of the verb. Lastly, the relation between the canonical gospels provides a solid foundation in which different uses of the verb in the same stories can be analyzed grammatically and in context.

---

1 W. F. Moulton and A. S. Geden, *A Concordance to the Greek Testament* (Edinburgh, T&T Clark, 1978), 928–29.

2 Dexonline, "18 Definiţii pentru Mântui," accessed April 20, 2017, https://dexonline.ro/definitie/m%C3%A2ntui.

3 Luminiţa Hoarţă Cărăuşu, "Un Aspect al Morfosintaxei Textelor Religioase din Secolul al XVI-lea: Construcţia Pasivă," in *Text şi Discurs Religios*, 2nd ed. (Iaşi, RO: Editura Universităţii „Alexandru Ioan Cuza," 2010), 271–74, accessed February 7, 2017, http://www.cntdr.ro/sites/default/files/c2009/c2009a27.pdf.

This chapter will proceed in the following manner. The chapter will begin with a survey of the history of the translation of the Romanian Bible. This will provide a context for understanding a history of translation. Following this, the historical perspective on the translation of σῴζω in the Romanian Bible will be discussed briefly as well as some general principles for the translation of the Bible.

History of the Translation of the Romanian Bible

One cannot talk about the translation of the word σῴζω in the Romanian Bible without taking into consideration the history of the translation of the Romanian Bible. Accordingly, this section will look at the most important and popular translations of the Orthodox Church and the Protestant communities in Romania. This survey introduces those translations that will be analyzed in the third chapter and reveal the translators' methodology in the process.

The history of Bible translation in Romania is different than the surrounding countries for several reasons. As Constantin Jinga states in his article about the historical retrospective of the Bible translations, Romania was the only country "in the Orthodox world that did not have anything in common with the languages used in the Orthodox Churches across Europe: the Slavic language and Greek."[4] Thus, there was a great impetus for translation into the vernacular language. Also, some important manuscripts such as *Tetraevangelul grecoslav* (1429), *Evangheliarul*, *Tetraevanghelul* (1561), or *Palia de la Orăştie* (1582) can be traced in the history of the Romanian translation of the Bible.[5] All these were prior to the first major translation of the New Testament, *Noul Testament de la Bălgrad*.

Noul Testament de la Bălgrad (1648)

This translation happened relatively late, over one century later than the publishing of the New Testament in other European languages.[6] The translation occured in Transilvania, a region influenced by the West and by the Calvinistic theology. The first translation of the New Testament was attempted under Gheorghe Rákóczi I, the promoter of the Reformation in the Orthodox churches, the translation itself being an attempt to facilitate this Reformation.[7] Thus, during the reign of Gheorghe Rákóczi I, Noul Testament de la Bălgrad was written as supervised by the steward Simion Ştefan.

---

4 Constanting Jinga, "Biblia cea mai tradusă carte: O retrospectivă istorică a traducerilor Sfintei Scripturii, *Ortho-logia* (2000), accessed November 21, 2016, http://ortho-logia.com/Romanian/Articole/Trad_Istorica.htm.

5 Dragoş-Ştefăniţă Manea, "A Short Exploration on the Importance of Greek Language Study for the Romanian Evangelical Church," MET thesis, Tyndale Theological Seminary, 2010.

6 Emanuel Conţac, *Dilemele Fidelităţii: Condiţionări Culturale şi Teologice în Traducerea Bibliei* (Cluj-Napoca: Logos, 2011), 28.

7 Conţac, *Dilemele Fidelităţii*, 28–29.

Biblia de la București (1688)

All these translations prepared the way for *Biblia de la București*, in its original title *Biblia, adecă Dumnezeiasca Scriptură a Legei Vechi și Acelei Noauă Lege*, the first integral Bible translation in the Romanian language, the work of the High Steward Constantin Cantacuzino and Șerban and Radu Greceanu. Also known as *Biblia de la 1688*, this translation made use of the Greek text for both the Old (Septuagint) and the New Testament, the Latin Vulgate, and the previous Romanian translations. This 1688 translation is seen as one of the reference translations by the Orthodox Church and is considered to be "for the Romanian language what Martin Luther's Bible is for the German language."[8] N. I. Nicolaescu, in his short history of the main translations of the Bible in the Romanian Orthodox Church, calls this edition to be "from all points of view, one of the most valuable translations." "Even though in many places the translation is too literal and has too many Slavic words, the construction of phrases sometimes follows the Greek language, and there are many problems of translation that do not have the best answer. The translation proves not only perseverance and careful attention to the text, but also proves a deep understanding of both the Greek and Romanian languages."[9]

Biblia Sinodală (1914)

Several important editions followed after *Biblia de la 1688*, some more praised than others. Among these are *Biblia de la Blaj* (1875), a translation based on the Septuagint, *Biblia de la Petersburg* (1819), *Biblia de la Sibiu* (1856–1858), also based on the Septuagint, and *Biblia de la Budapesta* (1873). In 1914 the *Biblia Sinodală* appeared, a highly regarded translation used even today. It is called "sinodală" because during its preparation for publishing, more members of the Holy Synod of the Romanian Orthodox Church worked on it. The revision of the Bible translation started in 1908, but because of different difficulties, the Old Testament revision began in 1911 and took three years before it was ready for publication.[10] The New Testament was not as heavily revised, and an older revision of it was used. The revision process of the Old Testament took into account the text of *Biblia de la 1688*, but also Samuil Micu's translation (1795) and the "daughters-edition" (Petersburg, Buzău, Sibiu).[11] Of special significance is that the *Biblia Sinodală* is the last official edition that consistently used the text of the Septuagint while the preceding versions also consulted *veritas hebraica*.[12] Several editions have followed, such as *Biblia Sinodală* 1936, *Biblia Sinodală* 1944, the work of Nicodim Munteanu, *Biblia Sinodală* 1968,[13] and *Biblia Sinodală* 1982.

---

8 Conțac, *Dilemele Fidelității*, 40–41.

9 N. I. Nicolaescu, "Scurt Istoric al Traducerii Sfintei Scripturi. Principalele Ediții ale Bibliei în Biserica Ortodoxă Română," *Studii și Articole* 26, no. 7–8 (September-October 1974): 500, accessed January 5, 2017, http://forum.teologie.net/download/file.php?id=419.

10 Conțac, *Dilemele Fidelității*, 62.

11 Conțac, *Dilemele Fidelității*, 62.

12 Conțac, *Dilemele Fidelității*, 62.

13 This was heavily criticized by Galaction as containing his New Testament. Conțac, *Dilemele Fidelității*, 62.

Biblia Galaction-Radu (1938)

Another important translation of the Bible is the work of Gala Galaction whose activity of translation spanned almost twenty years.[14] According to Conțac, even though Galaction felt the need for a new version starting with 1918, what pushed him to work on a new translation was the goal of seeing the Protestant New Testament translated by Dumitru Cornilescu. Galaction received this translation with mixed emotions.[15] After encountering difficulties with funding, Galaction started the translation of the New Testament and was finished within five years; it was published by Editura Institutului Biblic Ortodox. Galaction considered his translation as "too ingenious and to literal" and expected it to be welcomed with protests. This happened later on when Mitropolitul Athanasie Mironescu cataloged his New Testament as superior to the Cornilescu version but not surpassing some of the old translations of the Orthodox Church. The criticisms were mainly stylistic and lexical.[16] In 1935, he started working on the Old Testament, and with the help of Vasile Radu they finished their work in 1937. The translation was received positively, but some criticisms were also made regarding the work on the Old Testament.[17]

Biblia Anania (2001)

After the Bible translation of Gala Galaction, three Synodal translations followed in a period of forty years. *Biblia Sinodală* 1944 was the first one, the work of Hierarch Nicodim Munteanu. His translation of the New Testament did not become too well known but was instead criticized for its literal approach. As a response, Munteanu stated that "a translation which is muter is more faithful to the original."[18] The second Synodal translation was made at the direction of the Synod of the Orthodox Church and was a revision of the New Testament from 1951 and Galaction 1927. In this translation, the largest changes were made in the lexicon as a consultation of the 1914 Synodal translation. The last Synodal Bible was published in 1982 when recent translations were consulted and problems in vocabulary and expressions were corrected.[19]

The last Bible produced under the auspices of the Romanian Orthodox Church which will be discussed is *Biblia Anania* 2001, a well-received translation by the Orthodox community. This revision of the Orthodox Bible started as the initiative of the Father Dumitru Fecioru. He told Valeriu Anania that "the present version of the Bible is completely outdated by the evolution of the Romanian language, but also by the new critical editions of the Septuagint."[20] Thus, by the end of 1990, Anania started the revision of the Bible, a work that lasted for eleven years. In between 1993 and 2000 he worked on the New Testament (two editions, 1993 and 1995), the Pentateuch (1997)

---

14 Conțac, *Dilemele Fidelității*, 63. Gala Galaction's real name was Grigore Pișculescu,
15 Conțac, *Dilemele Fidelității*, 63.
16 Conțac, *Dilemele Fidelității*, 65–66.
17 Conțac, *Dilemele Fidelității*, 68.
18 Conțac, *Dilemele Fidelității*, 69.
19 Conțac, *Dilemele Fidelității*, 74.
20 Conțac, *Dilemele Fidelității*, 74.

and Poetry of the Old Testament (2000).²¹ These works received positive reviews, and thus the approval of the Holy Synod was sought for permission to print the whole Bible. Soon afterwards, the Bible version of Anania was adopted as the official text of the Romanian Orthodox Church. The improvements brought by this version are his notes on the pages of the Bible where he explains the choice of terms and the preferred translations. As the author himself stated, his work was mostly on four levels: lexical, syntactical, orthographical, and stylistic.²²

The Interdenominational Bible Society of Romania
A new translation of the Bible was produced by the Interdenominational Bible Society of Romania (IBSR-SBIR). Founded in 1992 by the churches in Romania, this Christian organization has the mission of translating, publishing, and distributing the Bible and other Christian materials.²³ The translation of the Bible was published in 2010, and it used "the original texts to produce a Holy Bible, which without replacing the Holy Scripture used by different Churches, minimized the differences produced by Church history. This initiative is the most important project of the Interdenominational Bible Society of Romania (IBSR)."²⁴ The translation team had theologians from different denominations, two Roman-Catholic translators, two Orthodox translators and two Protestant translators.

The Protestant Translations of the Bible
The Protestant translations of the Bible in Romania received more attention in the nineteenth century. The first popular translation was the *Biblia de la Iași*, published in 1874. Soon enough, this Bible became the Bible of the evangelical community in Romania. The translation started as an activity of the British Bible Society (BBS), Simon Mayers being the coordinator of BBS in Romania at that time. Yet, once Alexander Thomson took his place, the British Bible Society finished the Pentateuch by comparing the translation with the Masoretic text of the Old Testament, one which was prefered over the Septuagint.²⁵ From the beginning, the work of BBS was not like the Orthodox Church. One of the points of interest was the use of the Masoretic text. In his article on the short history of the Bible translation in the Romanian Orthodox Church, N. I. Nicolaescu talked about the translations made by the BBS. Many of the translators were not even named because they did not have the approval of the Orthodox Church, and some were exposed to "canonical sanctions."²⁶ The translators for whom

---

21 Conțac, *Dilemele Fidelității*, 75.
22 Conțac, *Dilemele Fidelității*, 77.
23 IBSR, "About us," accessed January 27, 2020, http://web.archive.org/web/20170512054431/http://societateabiblica.org/about-us/.
24 Bible.com, "Romanian Interdenominational New Testament Translation," accessed April 21, 2017, https://www.bible.com/versions/1506-bint09-romana-noul-testament-interconfesional-2009.
25 Conțac, *Dilemele Fidelității*, 79.
26 Nicolaescu, "Scurt Istoric al Traducerii Sfintei Scripturi," 33–34.

an exception was made, according to the Orthodox Church, were N. Nitzulescu and Dumitru Cornilescu. Nitzulescu, a Romanian theologian and professor in the University of Orthodox Theology, became known for his translation of the New Testament, using different Greek manuscript traditions for it. His New Testament was published in five editions with the first under the title "Noul Așezământ."[27] Nitzulescu's translations were also not well received by the Orthodox since his use of biblical languages and lexicons were too innovative for that time. Nicolaescu considered the translation a correct one overall but still not a new one as he believes that he borrowed from *Biblia de la Buzău*.[28]

Biblia Cornilescu

The British Bible Society published one more revised edition of the Bible in 1911 with the New Testament written by Nitzulescu and the Old Testament based on *Biblia de la Iași*. After that, the translator that worked solely on a new translation was Dumitru Cornilescu. No translator had a greater influence at the beginning of the twentieth century in Romania than Cornilescu. His translation made available for the Romanians a Bible that in that time was much harder to read because of its Cyrillic characters and Slavic influence.[29] Cornilescu was an Orthodox theologian who studied at Seminarul Central starting in 1904, a time when Iuliu Scriban, a translator contacted by the British Bible Society, became the president of the seminary. Cornilescu caught the attention of Scriban early in his studies since he occupied first place in the president's hierarchy due to his talent in foreign languages.[30] In this time young Cornilescu started to read theological books outside of Romania and became influenced by them and attracted by what he read. He writes:

> I started to order these books and read them. While I was reading them, I found out that all were speaking about a special Christian life, completely different than the religious life in our country. The idea of this sort of life gave me a passion and I was telling myself all the time: 'This is going to be my ministry when I will become a priest: to make known this life to our people.' But how?[31]

Due to these influences, Cornilescu went to the University of Theology during which he worked on translating Christian books and started his own translation of the Bible, finishing only the Gospel of Matthew. In 1916, he intended again to translate the Bible. This time he had the full support of Princess Ralu Callimachi, who also supported the translation of the Bible a few decades before meeting Cornilescu.[32] During the work of

---

27 Nicolaescu, "Scurt Istoric al Traducerii Sfintei Scripturi," 34.

28 Nicolaescu, "Scurt Istoric al Traducerii Sfintei Scripturi," 34.

29 Manea, "A Short Exploration on the Importance of Greek Language Study for the Romanian Evangelical Church," 33.

30 Emanuel Conțac, *Cornilescu: Din Culisele Publicării celei mai Citite Traduceri a Sfintei Scripturi* (Cluj-Napoca: Logos, 2014), 48.

31 Dumitru Cornilescu, *Cum m-am întors la Dumnezeu,* accessed January 10, 2017, http://www.resursecrestine.ro/eseuri/10402/cum-m-am-intors-la-dumnezeu.

32 Conțac, *Cornilescu*, 53.

translation, Cornilescu entered the monastic life, and then he experienced a conversion to Christ through the translation and study of the epistle to the Romans. He must have finished translating the New Testament by then, but his conversion led Cornilescu to reconsider his translation since that was the work of the "old man." Now he was a "new man" and needed a new translation.[33]

In 1921, with the financial support of Princess Callimachi, Dumitru Cornilescu managed to finish the translation of the Bible, working with the Hebrew and Greek languages. The translation was well received in the beginning, but soon afterwards it was considered a heretical version and not sufficiently in agreement with the traditional Orthodox translations. Galaction resisted it saying: "Although he had minimal literary sense, Cornilescu managed to offer us a fluid and understandable translation . . . But unfortunately, Cornilescu's work is tendentious and heretical. He sought to introduce in the translation his Protestant theories and conceptions."[34] Cornilescu's translation though became popular among the evangelical circles in Romania. Since the Orthodox Church was wary of him, Cornilescu left the country, and the Orthodox forbade the use of the Bible by both lay people and clerics. Two more editions of *Biblia Cornilescu* were published after that, one in 1924 and another one in 1931. The 1924 version appeared as a discussion between Cornilescu and BBS because they wanted to publish his Bible on a bigger scale. The 1931 edition is more a revision of his unpublished translation from 1911.[35]

As stated earlier, Cornilescu's Bible was embraced as the Bible of the Protestants in Romania. Even though it is criticized in the present day, it is still the most popular version. Yet, the Orthodox Christians in Romania still find Cornilescu's translations encouraging what they consider to be Protestant heresies. For example, Nicolaescu writes: "The reluctant attitude of the Orthodox and Catholics towards these Bibles is due to the assurance that what the Protestants call Bible is actually an incomplete Bible, a Bible broken from the old Christian tradition."[36] The difference between the Orthodox Bible and Cornilescu's Bible is understood by Cristian Stavriu, an Orthodox priest and professor, as teaching two different ways of salvation:

A major problem is the way in which Cornilescu translates verses related to the salvation of Christians (Matt. 24:13; John 10:9; Acts 2:40, etc.). While in the Orthodox translation "salvation" has a sense that implies being watchful, a struggle throughout the whole life, in Cornilescu's translation we read about Christians who "are saved" or "are already on the salvation path," in the spirit of the neoprotestant teaching where the salvation already occurred at a particular time in the past and that is secure.[37]

---

33 Conțac, *Cornilescu*, 62.

34 Gala Galaction, *Piatra din Capul Unghiului. Scrisori Teologice* (București: Tipografiile Române Unite, 1926) as cited in Contac, *Dilemele Fidelității*, 87.

35 Conțac, *Dilemele Fidelității*, 87–91.

36 Nicolaescu, "Scurt Istoric al Traducerii Sfintei Scripturi," 35.

37 Cristian Stavriu, "*Biblia Cornilescu*: Un Fals, o Înșelare, o Modalitate de Îndreptățire a Ereziilor," *Catehetica* (October, 2011), accessed January 19, 2017, http://www.catehetica.ro/biblia-cornilescu-un-fals-o-inselare-o-modalitate-de-indreptatire-a-ereziilor.

Nonetheless, Cornilescu's work influenced many other Bible editions that followed.[38]

Noua Traducere Românească

While *Biblia Cornilescu* still remains the most popular among the evangelical Christians in Romania, one recent translation has gained popularity in the last decade. *Noua Traducere Românească* (NTR) is the product of a project that started back in 1994. With the help of three consecutive coordinators it saw the light in 2007. It started as the Romanian equivalent of the *Living Bible* (1984, rev. 1991). Once it was published by the International Bible Society (IBS), they started a project in Romania where the translation moved from a dynamic equivalent rendering to more an ESV rendition.[39] After years of working on the translation and consulting different translators for both the Old and the New Testament, NTR was published in 2007. The version has modern terminology and a rich number of side notes that explain the text or gives alternative translations.[40]

Historical Perspective on the Translation of σῴζω

As the Bible was translated throuhout the years in Romania, the translation of σῴζω underwent different translation values. This survey will be useful in the third chapter, where the translation of σῴζω will be analyzed in the canonical gospels. In this section the translation of the verb in Matthew 9:21, Matthew 10:22, and Luke 13:23 will be examined, three usages of σῴζω that differ both in terms of range of meaning and the voice used by the authors.

Biblia de la București (1688)

In the first published translation of both the Old and the New Testament, σῴζω is translated either as "mântui," or "spăşi." In Matthew 9:21, the words used for the translation of σῴζω are "a mântui," (infinitive) while in Matthew 10:22 and Luke 13:23 they are "a spăşi." (infinitive). While the verb "a mântui" can be understood as "to save," "to heal," or "to finish," the verb "a spăşi" has a wider range of meaning such as "to suffer," "to pay," "to redeem," "to repent," or "to save."[41] The latter verb was more common in the 17th century.

Biblia Sinodală (1914)

The first Synodal translation of the Romanian Orthodox Church changes the verb "a spăşi" for the more familiar "a mântui," as this is the verb used in all three passages, while the voice remains reflexive. This shift in the biblical lexicology is explained by Eugen Munteanu who, talking about the changes or innovations in the church language,

---

38 As Dragoş Manea, citing Marius Cruceru, showed in his study. Manea, "A Short Exploration on the Importance of Greek Language Study for the Romanian Evangelical Church," 36–37.
39 Contac, *Dilemele Fidelității*, 91.
40 Contac, *Dilemele Fidelității*, 92–93.
41 Dexonline, "A spăşi," accessed April 21, 2017, https://dexonline.ro/definitie/spasi.

he mentions that the verb "a spăşi," originary from the Slavic languages and used predominantly in the 16th and 17th century, was slowly replaced by "a mântui."[42]

Biblia Galaction-Radu (1939)
Biblia Galaction-Radu that was published in 1939 provides a revision to the translation of σώζω in Matthew 9:21. While *Biblia de la Bucureşti* 1688 and *Biblia Sinodală* 1914 translated as "a spăşi" or "a mântui," the offered translation here is "a fi sănătoasă," which is to be understood as "to be healthy." This is understood to be an interpretation on the meaning range of the word σώζω. However, in Matthew 10:22 and Luke 13:23 the word is translated as in *Biblia Sinodală* 1914, "a mântui."

Biblia Anania (2001)
One of the most used translations in the Romanian Orthodox Church is *Biblia Anania*, published in 2001. While this translation has brought many changes as compared to the previous translations, the word used by the author in the three passages mentioned above is also "a mântui."

Dumitru Cornilescu (1924)
In Dumitru Cornilescu's translation of the Bible, there are few changes in the translation of σώζω. First, in Matthew 9:21, the verb is translated as "a tămădui," a Romanian word of Hungarian origin meaning "to heal" and an interpretation of the verb "to save." However, in Matthew 10:22 and Luke 13:23, Cornilescu also goes with the verb "a mântui."

Noua Traducere (2007) and Societatea Biblică Interconfesională din România (2013)
Worth mentioning here is the Protestant translation *Noua Traducere* (NTR) and the interconfessional translation of the *Societatea Biblică Interconfesională din România* (IBSR). The NTR translation from 2007 reads in Matthew 9:21 "a vindeca," a word originated from Latin which means "to heal." Thus, while using the Latin word, the NTR nonetheless follows Cornilescu in interpreting σώζω. However, in Matthew 10:22 and Luke 13:23 the translation of σώζω remains "a mântui." The IBSR translation published in 2013 has the same translation as NTR in all three passages.

Principles for Translation
One cannot talk about how a word or idea should be translated from one language to another without bringing justification for his choice of translation. Certain principles ought to be made clear regarding what is the best translation value for each verse. In the above survey, the authors' methodology has been seen in the process of translation. While the first translation of both the Old and the New Testament interacted with the Greek language for both Testaments, the translations that followed dealt with the revision, comparison, and adaptation of the language for the present day. Since my

---

42 Eugen Munteanu, *Lexicologie Biblică Românească* (Bucureşti: Humanitas, 2008), 467.

conclusion will suggest different revisions to the Orthodox translation of σῴζω, the following section serves the purpose of discussing those principles for translation that need to be taken into consideration.

Bible translation is a complex work, but several principles can be made in order to provide a better understanding of the verb "to save" in the canonical gospels. First, as Y.C. Whang discusses, there are at least four factors that need to be taken in consideration: the translator's work is personal, the translator's competency in the source and receptor language, the translator's professionalism, and the translator's cultural gap.[43] This in a sense is what Nida refers to when he talks about "new attitudes" concerning both the receptor and source language. With respect to the language, Nida believes that each language has its own genius, unique phrases, and vocabulary, and one must respect these. In the same way, Nida talks about form and content in the receptor language, and for him "anything that can be said in one language can be said in another, unless the form is an essential element of the message," but also if the content is held on to, then "the forms must be altered."[44] In the same way, the source language should be understood as "subject to the same limitations as any other natural language," while also having in mind that the biblical writers were expecting to be understood. Thus the translator has the responsibility of "reproducing the meaning of a passage as understood by the writer."[45]

Once one has taken basic matters into consideration, one must ask what is the aim of the translation? At its basic level every translator that is faithful to his job knows that the author's intent has to be sought carefully as well as how that intent can be translated into the receptor language as smoothly and readably as possible.[46] Authorial intent has been a main issue in translators' debates for the past decades. How does the traditional understanding intersect with the "new" way of translating the Bible? The traditional way is called by Nida "formal equivalence/correspondence," while the new approach is called "dynamic/functional equivalence."

Formal equivalence/correspondence
The term "formal equivalence" in Nida's work refers to that method which "focuses attention on the message itself, in both form and content."[47] In this method, the translator tries to reproduce the form and content of the source language as literally as possible. Thus, one translator finds delight in reproducing as closely as possible different stylistic

---

[43] Y.C. Whang, "To Whom is a Translator Responsible—Reader or Author?" in *Translating the Bible: Problems and Prospects*, ed. Stanley E. Porter and Richard S. Hess (London: T&T Clark International, 2004), 47.

[44] Eugene A. Nida and Charles R. Taber, *The Theory and Practice of Translation* (Leiden: Brill, 1982), 3–6.

[45] Nida and Taber, *The Theory and Practice of Translation*, 7–8.

[46] Whang, "To Whom is a Translator Responsible," 49.

[47] Eugene A. Nida, *Toward a Science of Translating with Special Reference to Principles and Procedures involved in Bible Translating* (Leiden: Brill, 1964), 159, as cited by Whang, "To Whom is a Translator Responsible," 50.

features such as rhythms, rhymes, and plays on word; through these he allows the reader to identify himself and understand the context of the source language. However, according to Nida and Taber, this method of translation reproduces the message mechanically, and also "formal correspondence distorts the grammatical and stylistic patterns of the receptor language, and hence distorts the message, so as to cause the receptor to misunderstand or to labor unduly hard."[48]

Dynamic equivalence
In contrast to formal equivalence, Nida discusses the method called dynamic equivalence. Nida defines dynamic equivalence as that

> quality of a translation in which the message of the original text has been so transported into the receptor language that the *response* of the *receptor* is essentially like that of the original receptors. Frequently, the form of the original text is changed; but as long as the change follows the rules of back transformation in the source language, of contextual consistency in the transfer, and of transformation in the receptor language, the message is preserved and the translation is faithful.[49]

Thus, this method of translation is one that focuses more on the receptors and not on the forms. The translator should look more for the impact of the message translated rather than for words translated literally or the grammatical construction of the sentence.[50] Dynamic equivalence stresses what is corresponding instead of what is word for identical. In this method, the translator will not try to conserve the form of what is said but emphasizes the overall message. While not word for word like formal equivalency, the closest equivalent wording should be sought while priority is given to the meaning and the content of what is communicated. Priority should also be given to the translation of words in their context and not to "a fixed system of verbal consistency": "it is inevitable that the choice of the right word in the receptor language to translate a word in the source-language text depends more on the context than upon a fixed system of verbal consistency."[51] This is nonetheless an argument to take in consideration, having in mind that the verb σῴζω has different meanings based on the text in which is used. Thus, in the Gospels one of the most frequent uses of σῴζω is in talking about the sick being healed by Jesus, even though the verb itself means "to save." The same word can mean rescue from a disaster, saving from sin, or a future eternal salvation, all fitting the meaning of σῴζω depending on the context.

The case for the translation of the verb "to save," however, is more a matter of grammar, and thus a grammatical analysis and translation principles related to it should be taken into consideration as well. When talking about grammatical analysis, Nida starts by pointing to two different systems for translating: (a) one that "consists in setting

---

48 Nida and Taber, *The Theory and Practice of Translation*, 201.
49 Nida and Taber, *The Theory and Practice of Translation*, 200.
50 Nida and Taber, *The Theory and Practice of Translation*, 22.
51 Nida and Taber, *The Theory and Practice of Translation*, 15.

up a series of rules which are intended to be applied strictly in order and are designed to specify exactly what should be done with each item or combination of items in the source language so as to select the appropriate corresponding form in the receptor language," and (b) one that

> consists of a more elaborate procedure comprising three stages: (1) analysis, in which the surface structure (the message as given in language A) is analyzed in terms of the grammatical relationships and the meanings of the words and combinations of words, (2) transfer, in which the analyzed material is transferred in the mind of the translator from language A to language B, and (3) restructuring, in which the transferred material is restructured in order to make the final message fully acceptable in the receptor language.[52]

Having in mind that a procedure like the first which comprises one stage is not the case for grammar, Nida goes on in giving some basic principles of grammatical analysis. First, grammar is not just about rules, but it has meaning, even though one grammatical construction may have a different meaning. In this case, context becomes crucial—and not only the immediate context but the wider context becomes especially crucial—in understanding what the overall message is being communicated by the author.[53]

When it comes to the Orthodox translation of σώζω and the meaning of voice (especially passive voice), Katharine Barnwell also believes that context becomes important: "when translating a passive form in the source text, consider why in that particular context the passive was used. There will be ways of achieving the same effect in the translation. This may be by using some quite different grammatical form in the receptor language."[54] There may be times when the passive must be re-expressed since some languages express passive through constructions such as "they did something," or "one did something," where "they" or "one" simply means the subject is indefinite. Thus, she urges the translator to "observe natural texts to find out how the passive is used, and use it in the same way. Do not just put a passive wherever there is a passive in English without considering carefully."[55]

---

52 Nida and Taber, *The Theory and Practice of Translation*, 33.
53 Nida and Taber, *The Theory and Practice of Translation*, 46.
54 Katharine Barnwell, *Bible Translation: An Introductory Course in Translation Principles*, 3rd ed. (Dallas, TX: Summer Institute of Linguistics, 1986), 134.
55 Barnwell, *Bible Translation*, 134.

CHAPTER 2

An Analysis of the Greek Voice

The voice is one aspect of Greek grammar that can create problems in understanding Greek sentences. The first consideration that will be used to discuss the Romanian Orthodox translation of the voice with respect to the verb "to save" in the canonical Gospels is the Koine Greek grammar. In the Orthodox translation, the verb "to save" is translated as "s-a salvat" ("he saved himself") for both the passive and middle/passive verbs. The middle voice is particularly difficult to translate due to the lack of equivalence in languages such as English or Romanian. However, the middle voice is a much more complex topic than this understanding such that grammar has to be addressed in order to provide the best understanding.

This chapter will consider the voice in the English, Greek, and Romanian languages. The main difficulties in defining the passive and middle voice also will be addressed, and the best definitions provided. The grammatical questions addressed in this chapter will serve later as the main arguments for the chapter which follows after.

Voice

Voice is one of the grammatical categories heavily discussed by the grammarians, and one about which recent discussions are taking place. In Romanian, this grammatical category is called "diateza," a word that comes from the Greek "diathesis" and is a more agreeable word than the English "voice." It is understood to carry "a variety of meanings such as arrangement, condition, state, force, function."[1] A general definition of the voice is "that property of the verbal idea which indicates how the subject is related to the action."[2] This is different than the notion of transitiveness, which is easy to confuse with voice. While voice describes the action of a verb to its subject, transitiveness describes the action of a verb to an object. In the Greek language, there are three categories that show this relationship between the subject and the action. Before discussing Greek voice, however, the voice should first be discussed as expressed in the Romanian language.

Voice System in the Romanian Language

The Romanian language has three voices to show the relation between the grammatical subject and the action that it expresses: active, passive, and reflexive. The middle voice is not present in the language as one can see.

---

1 Suzane Kemmer, *Typological Studies in Language*, vol. 23, *The Middle Voice* (Amsterdam: John Benjamins Pub. Co., 1993), 4.
2 Dana and Mantey, *A Manual Grammar of the Greek New Testament*, 155.

The active voice, just as in English, shows that the action is done by the grammatical subject, a subject who can be expressed or not expressed.

E.g.: Copiii merg la biserică.
The children go to the church.
Ai alergat atâția kilometri cât ți-ai propus.
You ran as many kilometers as you decided for yourself.

The passive voice shows that the grammatical subject (also expressed or not) receives the action which is made by someone else. According to *Gramatica Limbii Române* (*The Grammar of the Romanian Language*), the passive construction is characterized by three features: a) the subject from the active construction is moved into a postverbal position of prepositional complement of the verb, the so-called agency; b) the direct complement from the active construction is externalized as subject, changing its syntactic hierarchy, and c) the previous features has as effect the intransitiveness of the verb.[3]

The passive voice is constructed in Romanian language in two ways:

1) by using an auxiliary verb and the participle of the conjugated verb. This is the most common way of expressing the passive in the Romanian language. In most cases it is followed by a complement of agent that shows who does the action.

E.g.: Vei fi primit de director în câteva ore.
You will be received by the director in a few hours' time.
Părinții trebuie să fie iubiți de către copii.
Parents should be loved by (their) children.

2) by using the reflexive pronouns in the accusative case, in which case the passive is called reflexive passive.

E.g.: *Casa a fost construită într-un scurt timp* (the passive with the auxiliar verb) thus becomes *Casa s-a construit într-un scurt timp* (the reflexive passive expressed with the reflexive pronoun *se*).

Even though both of the sentences are in the passive and are translated in the same way (The house was built shortly), the second sentence is more ambiguous since it uses the reflexive pronoun and can be confused with the reflexive voice.[4] This is the case with the construction "a se salva," where one might argue that the reflexive passive is communicated and not the reflexive voice. However there are some characteristics of

---

[3] These three features are described in *Gramatica Limbii Române* as cited in Cărăușu, "Construcția Pasivă," 270.

[4] Cărăușu, "Construcția Pasivă," 270.

the reflexive passive that will be considered and also serve as a test for the appearances analyzed in chapter three.[5]

a) the reflexive passive always uses the reflexive pronoun *se* and is limited to the third person, not the first and second person.
b) it is more often used in a construction where the agency is not expressed, thus it is more often used in sentences like *Cererea se va semna mâine* (The application will be signed tomorrow) instead of *Cererea se va semna de către manager* (The request will be signed by the manager).
c) the passive reflexive construction is prefered in cases where the passive subject is to be read as "non-individual": *Se caută menajeră* (They are looking for a housekeeper) simply communicates that a house-keeper is sought while the more common passive with the auxiliar verb is used when there is a more "individual" reading: *În acest magazin a fost vândut deja romanul lui Eliade* (In this shop Eliade's novel was already sold). Moreover, the reflexive passive is preferred in constructions where the impersonal aspect is sought: *Se știe rezultatul* (The result is known).

The reflexive voice is that voice which shows that the action is done by the subject but is also suffered by the same subject. The conjugated verb is always followed by reflexive pronouns or unaccented personal pronouns that are used as a reflexive pronoun. These do not have a syntactical function, but are just grammatical signs used to indicate the reflexive voice.[6]

E.g.: Te-ai tăiat cu cuțitul până la os (You cut yourself with the knife to the bone).

An interesting fact about the reflexive pronoun in Romanian is that not every verb that is followed by one is in the reflexive voice, but when the reflexive voice has its own syntactical function, the verb is in the pronominal active voice.[7] One way of recognizing this is by seeing if the reflexive pronoun can be replaced with a personal pronoun.

Voice System in Koine Greek

Koine Greek has three voices: the active, the passive, and the middle voice. All three of them will be discussed with special emphasis on the passive and the middle voices, since the Romanian Orthodox translation of the Bible attributes to these two voices the reflexive aspect.

---

5 The following characteristics are from Cărăușu, "Construcția Pasivă," 270.
6 Constantin Georgescu, *Manual de Greaca Biblică* (București: Nemira, 2011), 104.
7 Gramatica limbii române, "Gramatica limbii române pe înțelesul tuturor," accessed August 10, 2016, https://gramaticalimbiiromane.ro/morfologia/parti-vorbire-flexibile/verbul/diatezele-verbelor/.

The active voice
The active voice represents "the subject performing the action of the verb, producing or experiencing the action, or existing in the state expressed by the verb."[8] There are three main categories of the active voice: simple active, causative active, and reflexive active.

a) Simple Active
The simple active is the most common use and also the most basic use of the active voice. In this category, the subject performs the action of the verb directly. For instance, in the sentence "Christ redeemed us," the subject is Christ who directly performs the action, action also focused toward an object.

b) Causative Active
In this category, "the subject is not necessarily performing the action but is the source or cause behind it."[9] For example, in Matthew 5:45, it is written: "He causes his sun to rise on the evil and the good and sends rain on the righteous and the unrighteous." Noticeable in this example is that the subject (God) is not directly performing the action, but he causes the sun to rise and the rain to fall. According to Dana and Mantey, the best way of understanding this category is by thinking of such expressions in English as "to blow a horn," to shine a light," or "to run a horse."[10]

c) Reflexive Active
In the reflexive active the subject performs the action on himself. It is a category understood by some grammarians as similar to the middle voice, and for this reason this category will be analyzed in more detail in the upcoming chapters. The construction of the category is the active voice of a verb, followed by a reflexive pronoun.

Examples:
- 1 Timothy 4:7 Γύμναζε σεαυτὸν πρὸς εὐσέβειαν (Train yourself in godliness).
- Mark 15:30 σῶσον σεαυτὸν (Save yourself). This example is worth noticing as it will serve as one of the arguments in the next chapter.

The passive voice
The passive voice is the opposite of the active voice. The subject is not performing the action, but the subject receives the action. The one performing the action is normally implied or referenced using another grammatical constructional, usually a prepositional phrase (ὑπό + genitive).

---

8 Wallace, *Greek Grammar*, 410.
9 Andreas J. Köstenberger, Benjamin L. Merkle, and Robert L. Plummer, *Going Deeper With New Testament Greek: An Intermediate Study of the Grammar and Syntax of the New Testament* (Nashville, TN: B&H Academic), 193.
10 Dana and Mantey, *Greek New Testament*, 156.

The passive in the Koine Greek can be constructed in two ways: first, it can be constructed with and without expressed agency, and second, it can be constructed with an accusative object.[11]

a) With and without expressed agency

According to Wallace, in Koine Greek the passive can be constructed with and without expressed agency (or means), but "the presence or absence of an agent is not an intrinsic part of the passive's meaning, it belongs to the force of the clausal construction in which the passive is used," while the agency discussion for Wallace helps to illuminate "an author's overall meaning."[12]

If the agency is expressed, it can be ultimate agency, intermediate agency, or impersonal means. Matthew 1:22 is seen a good example of the first two types of agency: "What was spoken by the Lord through the prophet." In this verse, "by the Lord" is the ultimate agent "because prophecy ultimately comes from God," while "through the prophet" is the intermediate agent, "because prophets are those who communicate God's Word to the people."[13] The third category is constructed usually with ἐν + dative, but the meaning is that "usually there is an implied agent who uses the noun in the dative as his or her instrument."[14] Thus, in James 2:22 the phrase "faith was perfected *by works*" communicates that the works were the means through which faith was perfected. If the agency is not expressed, it is for reasons such as the agent expressed in the context, rhetorical effect, emphasis on the subject, or the divine passive, where God is "the obvious agent."[15]

b) With an accusative object

The passive constructed with an accusative object is not common in the English language, but in Greek a passive verb can be used with an accusative: "in this instance, the *accusative of thing* in a double accusative person-thing construction with an active verb *retains its case* when the verb is put in the *passive*."[16] Such an example in the New Testament is 1 Corinthians 12:13 where Paul writes: καὶ πάντες ἓν πνεῦμα ἐποτίσθημεν. (and all were made to drink [of] one Spirit). In this example, πάντες is the person, in the nominative with the passive verb, and the accusative of thing ἓν πνεῦμα is retained.[17]

Seeing how the passive is constructed, the three main categories for the passive voice will be considered:[18]

---

11 Wallace, *Greek Grammar*, 431–39.
12 Wallace, *Greek Grammar*, 431.
13 Köstenberger, *Going Deeper*, 198.
14 Wallace, *Greek Grammar*, 435.
15 Wallace, *Greek Grammar*, 438.
16 Wallace, *Greek Grammar*, 438–39.
17 Wallace, *Greek Grammar*, 439.
18 The following categories are from Köstenberger, *Going Deeper*, 196.

a) Simple passive
The simple passive is the most common use and indicates the subject who receives the action. One of the reasons for which New Testament writers might use the passive voice is for "thematizing the subject," as Paul does in Romans 1:17 where he writes, "For in it the righteousness of God is revealed".[19]

b) Permissive passive
Like in the case of the permissive middle, it indicates permission of the action (or cause, as some grammarians have these two categories combined). The example given by Köstenberger is Ephesians 5:18, which seems to be an oxymoron: "Don't get drunk with wine . . . but be filled with the Spirit." In this verse, Paul gives a command, but the verb is translated as passive. The explanation is that "the Christians are commanded to be filled with the Spirit, but the filling itself is not something that the Christian does but something that is done to him when he submits himself to God's will."[20]

c) Deponent passive
This category will be considered in the section below which treats the middle voice.

The middle voice
Besides the active and the passive voice, the New Testament Greek has a third voice, called the middle voice. Often the middle voice is understood to be that voice that is neither active nor passive, but standing in the middle, as Daniel Wallace rightly states it in his grammar:

> For Koine Greek, the term middle has become a misnomer, because it inherently describes that voice that stands halfway between the active and the passive. Only the direct middle truly does this (in that the subject is both the agent and receiver of the action). Since the direct middle is phasing out in Hellenistic Greek, the term is hardly descriptive of the voice as a whole.[21]

No matter how one calls this particular Greek voice, it is asserted that the Greek middle voice is "one of the most distinctive and peculiar phenomena of the Greek language. It is impossible to describe it, adequately or accurately, in terms of English idiom, for English knows no approximate parallel."[22]

In explaining this peculiar voice, Carl Conrad talks about English constructions that are neither active nor passive. While the English grammar does not have any

---

19 Köstenberger, *Going Deeper*, 198–99.
20 Köstenberger, *Going Deeper*, 199.
21 Wallace, *Greek Grammar*, 415.
22 Dana and Mantey, *Greek New Testament*, 156.

other grammatical voice, Conrad gives an example of "other relationship between the grammatical subject and the action or state/condition indicated by the verb:"[23]

a. "The boy is having his hair cut" or "The boy has his hair cut"
b. "The boy gets up every morning at 7 a.m."
c. "The boy will undergo baptism tomorrow."

Of special attention in these examples is letter c., where "will undergo" is

> a transitive verb and 'baptism' is its direct object. Upon further reflection, however, we can see that what is meant is that the boy is going to be baptized by some person credentialed to perform the ritual; that is to say, the expression seems implicitly to be passive, although it is formulated in such a way as to indicate the boy's willing participation in the upcoming baptism.[24]

The verb in this case will have the form βαπτισθήσεται. Thus, for Conrad, while the sentence may be understood as "The boy will be baptized," in this case it might be translated as "The boy will have himself baptized tomorrow," and this is what one might call the "middle voice."

Yet even so, the middle voice presents difficulties in explaining what the exact relationship is between the subject doing the action and the subject being involved as well as how it can be defined.

Difficulties in defining the middle voice
The Greek middle voice, as has been seen, is a rather peculiar phenomenon in the Greek grammar which does not have a direct equivalent in other languages such as the English or Romanian languages. For this reason, there are some difficulties that have been encountered in defining the middle voice. The most important challenges that occur when one defines it are the following: is the middle voice truly a voice or just a disposition, what are the middle-passive verbs, and is the middle voice primarily reflexive in meaning?

a) Middle voice—voice or disposition?
One of the difficulties encountered in a discussion about the middle voice is that most of the languages have only two voices, active and non-active. As Alexiadou Doron stated, "most theoretical studies recognize, in addition to the active voice, a single non-active voice, *passive*. Since there is no direct equivalent in most of the languages, the term *middle* is not used to denote voice; rather, it is usually restricted to a form of

---

23 Carl W. Conrad, "New Observations on Voice in the Ancient Greek Verb": 2–3, unpublished paper, 2002, https://pages.wustl.edu/files/pages/imce/cwconrad/newobsancgrkvc.pdf. The examples below are also given by Conrad in his paper.
24 Conrad, "New Observations on Voice," 2–3.

the verb denoting *disposition,* as in *the bread cuts easily.*"[25] But, going with the active and non-active voice system, Doron argues for the split of the non-active voice in two other voices: the middle voice and the passive voice. These two voices, even though they are part of the non-active voice and "prevent the insertion of an external argument, they have different properties."[26] Moreover, in explaining this, he talks about five voice markings of the non-active verbs:[27]

1. anticausatives (i.e., spontaneous events like break, open)
2. reflexives which are mostly limited to verbs of body care (*wash, comb*) and naturally reciprocal events (*meet, kiss*)
3. dispositional middles (*This book sells well*)
4. medio-passives
5. passives

Giving examples for all of them, Doron reaches the conclusion that the first four are designated for a different voice than what is known commonly as passive, therefore that voice is the middle voice.

b) The middle-passive verbs

Another difficulty related to the middle voice is its differentiation from the passive voice. This is due to the Greek language sharing the same endings for these two voices in the present, perfect, and pluperfect tenses, with only the future and aorist tenses having distinct forms.[28] Alexandriou Doron has addressed how to make a distinction between the middle-passive verbs and the passive verbs. In his explanation, Doron talks about the five voice markings discussed above, and he makes the statement that, unlike the passives, these ones can have an anticausative reading, allow non-agentive by-phrases (the passive verbs allow only agentive or instrumental by-phrases), and can have a dispositional reading.[29]

However, one of the linguists who closely studied the middle voice, Carl Conrad, believes that the middle-passive verbs are both "ambivalent and flexible" and require a careful analysis in relation to the character of each verb:

> The middle-passive morphoparadigms must be interpreted each in accordance with the character of the verb in question and the contextual indicators of the instance under examination. The usage of the middle-passive morphoparadigms is unquestionably one of the most difficult features of ancient Greek for a learner to appreciate; while one may develop some facility with reading Greek middle-passive forms and understanding

---

[25] Alexiadou, Artemis and Edit Doron, "The Syntactic Construction of Two Non-Active Voices: Passive and Middle," *J Linguistics* 48 (2012): 1, accessed October 25, 2022, doi:10.1017/S0022226711000338.

[26] Artemis and Doron, "Passive and Middle," 1.

[27] The following classification is taken from Artemis and Doron, "Passive and Middle," 3.

[28] Wallace, *Greek Grammar*, 410.

[29] Artemis and Doron, "Passive and Middle," 10–11.

their meaning, it will be much more difficult to formulate the proper Greek verb-forms corresponding to one's native English verbs. If ever there was a feature of ancient Greek hindering word-to-word equivalent expressions, this is certainly one such feature.[30]

c) Middle as primarily reflexive

Another common problem in relation to the middle voice is its description by some grammarians as primarily reflexive. In the reflexive sense, the main definition is that "the action is directly referred back to the subject," or the subject is the one who does the action and is patient of it as well.[31] This position is taken by the Romanian Orthodox Church, which translates the middle or medio-passive verbs as reflexive. In one of the grammars used by the Orthodox seminaries, the middle voice is defined as that voice "which shows that the subject does the action not upon a separated 'object,' but upon itself, even in a direct way or an indirect way. Thus, the action is suffered by the subject, as in the example 'elevul îşi învaţă/ elevul se învaţă' (subject = agent and patient)."[32] Moreover, the translation rule given by the grammar is that "for the middle voice they are used assigns of the reflexivity from the Romanian language (λύομαι "îmi/ mă dezleg"), while the deponent verbs are translated active or reflexive (e.g. λογίζομαι "socotesc; mă gândesc").[33] Thus, in Luke 13:23 Εἶπεν δέ τις αὐτῷ· κύριε, εἰ ὀλίγοι οἱ σῳζόμενοι; ("Şi I-a zis cineva: Doamne, puţini sunt, oare, cei ce se mântuiesc?") the translation provided is: "And someone said to him: 'Lord, are they few those who save themselves?" In this verse, the present participle, middle voice, οἱ σῳζόμενοι translated in the Orthodox versions in a reflexive way, "the ones who save themselves." The same principle is applied in many other verses that contain the verb "to save," but the discussion of this type of translation represents the core of the present study and it will be extensively analyzed in the next chapter. For the moment, a general introduction on the problem is worth having.

The middle voice as primarily reflexive is also the position of some other grammarians. One of them is William Jelf who, even though he divides the middle in two categories, reciprocal and reflexive, considers reflexive as the primary usage of the middle:

> The essential sense which runs throughout the middle reflexive verb is Self—the action of the verb has immediate reference to self. This is the proper notion of all middle verbs, and the particular sense of each middle verb must be determined by discovering the relation in which that notion of self stands to the notion of the verb.[34]

---

30 Carl W. Conrad, "Active, Middle and Passive: Understanding Ancient Greek Voice," accessed August 18, 2016, http://www.cultus.hk/latin_lessons/deponens/GreekDeponens.pdf.

31 George J. Cline, "The Significance of the Middle Voice in the New Testament" (master's thesis, Grace Theological Seminary, 1983), 14, accessed January 9, 2020, https://faculty.gordon.edu/hu/bi/ted_hildebrandt/new_testament_greek/text/cline-middlevoice/cline-middlevoice.pdf.

32 Georgescu, *Manual de Greaca Biblică*, 104.

33 Georgescu, *Manual de Greaca Biblică*, 106.

34 William E. Jelf, *A Grammar of the Greek Language*, 2nd ed., 2 vols. (Oxford: James Wright, 1851), 14.

Other grammarians assert that the notion of the middle is not only reflexive, but is the primary one. For them, reflexive is not limited only to a "directly reflexive sense," but sometimes there is also a notion of "reciprocity, indirectness, and self-interest."[35]

On the opposite side, there are grammarians such as Jay who hold to the position that in the New Testament the middle voice does not have a reflexive usage in a direct sense: "The beginner is apt to jump to the conclusion that the Greek Middle Voice is reflexive. This is not so. It denotes that the subject performs the action for himself, but not to himself."[36] However, some of the examples in the New Testament show that the reflexive translation of the middle would be appropriate by the context in which it is used. For example, in John 18:18 the Greek wording is: ὅτι ψῦχος ἦν, καὶ ἐθερμαίνοντο· ἦν δὲ καὶ ὁ Πέτρος μετ' αὐτῶν ἑστὼς καὶ θερμαινόμενος. Translated in English: "Because it was cold and they were warming themselves; And Peter also was with them standing and warming himself." In this example the two participles in the middle voice carry a direct reflexive sense, where the action is done by the subject upon himself.

However, these examples do not prove (as in the case of the first grammarians cited above) that the Greek middle is exclusively reflexive. After analyzing the evidence in the New Testament, Moulton states that the middle voice is "quite inaccurately described as reflexive."[37] Talking about the middle voice as being primarily reflexive, Moule also states that "whether or not this is true for certain periods, it is manifestly not true of the New Testament usage."[38] Stanley Porter's conclusion seems to fit this brief discussion the best on the matter:

> Grammarians are undecided how exactly to characterize the Greek middle voice, but most are agreed that a reflexive middle sense ('he washed himself'), in which the agent (subject) and recipient (object) of the action are the same, is not the predominant one in the Hellenistic period. . . . [The middle voice] could be reflexive in some contexts (these are probably best confined to intransitive uses), or it could simply draw attention to the subject.[39]

Definitions and understanding of the middle voice

While most grammarians have difficulties in defining the middle voice, there is one common criterion for describing it. This is the special attention that is given to the subject. One of the first significant grammarians of the New Testament Greek, James Moulton, attests that the middle voice in its origins meant "a word for another and for oneself respectively. . . . The essence of the middle therefore lies in its calling attention

---

35 Cline, "The Significance of the Middle Voice", 13.

36 Eric G. Jay, *New Testament Greek: An Introductory Grammar* (London: SPCK, 1958), 14.

37 James Hope Moulton, *A Grammar of New Testament Greek* (Edinburgh: T&T Clark, 1908), 155.

38 C. F. D. Moule, *An Idiom Book of New Testament Greek* (Cambridge: Cambridge University Press, 1986), 24.

39 Stanley Porter, *Idioms of the Greek New Testament*, 2nd ed. (Sheffield: JSOT, 1992), 67.

to the agent as in some way closely concerned with the action."[40] Yet, according to Moulton, if one presently were to see the middle voice in this manner, it would not be understandable since it has lost all distinction of meaning and now one only could guess. Soon after him, A. T. Robertson agreed with Moulton that the middle voice has its origin in Sanskrit, and in the beginning there was only the active and the middle voice with the passive voice developing later. While agreeing with the idea that "middle" is a good term since it stands between the active and the passive, Robertson states that the middle was before the passive and the passive "arose out of the middle."[41] Nonetheless, for Robertson "the middle calls especial attention to the subject" and "the subject is acting in relation to himself somehow."[42] Dana and Mantey agree with Robertson on the definition, that the middle voice describes "the subject as participating in the results of the action," but the definition is less certain since it is asserted that "just how the action is thus related is not indicated by the middle voice, but must be detected from the context or the character of the verbal idea."[43]

However, new studies on the middle voice have also taken the task of defining the middle voice. Referencing E. J. W. Barber, Rutger J. Allan provides a modern definition concerning the middle voice:

> a marker of *subject-affectedness*, taken in the broad sense. This comprises, on the one hand, affectedness in which the subject is very much like a patient (as in the passive, reflexive and reciprocal middle), and, on the other hand, affectedness in which the subject is similar to an indirect object (as in the indirect middle).[44]

Classification

The definition of the middle voice is best understood in the classification of the voice where the subject involved somehow is seen in the action event as described in the categories below. Moreover, the classification of the middle voice will serve as a main argument in refuting the primarily reflexive understanding of it.

a) Direct middle
In the direct middle, "the subject acts *on* himself or herself."[45] In this category, the direct object is the self. According to Herbert Weir Smyth, the direct middle has "verbs

---

40 Moulton, *Grammar of New Testament Greek*, 15.
41 A. T. Robertson, *A Grammar of the Greek New Testament in the Light of Historical Research* (Nashville, TN: Broadman Press, 1934), 803.
42 Robertson, *Grammar of the Greek New Testament*, 804.
43 Dana and Mantey, *Greek New Testament*, 157.
44 Rutger J. Allan, "The Middle Voice in Ancient Greek: A study in Polysemy" (PhD diss., University of Amsterdam, 2002), 12, http://dare.uva.nl/record/108528.
45 Wallace, *Greek Grammar,* 416.

expressing external and natural acts, as the verbs of washing: ἀλείφεσθαι ("anoint oneself"), or λοῦσθαι ("wash oneself").[46]

There are several examples in the New Testament where one can see the direct middle. One of the clear examples as agreed by most of grammarians is found in Matthew 27:5, where the verb ἀπήγξατο is translated as "he hanged himself." Moulton considers this example to be the clearest in the New Testament and "a survival from classical Greek." However, even then Moulton questions this example because "he choked" may be a "truer parallel than the reflexive *hang oneself*."[47] Yet, Wallace suggests that ἀπάγχω is the verb used more for "to choke" and it became "a stereotyped idiom by the Koine era."[48]

Other examples considered by Wallace as being clear reflexive middles:

Mark 14:54 ἦν . . . θερμαινόμενος πρὸς τὸ φῶς ("he was warming himself by the fire")
Acts 12:21 ὁ Ἡρῴδης ἐνδυσάμενος ἐσθῆτα βασιλικὴν ("Herod clothed himself with royal clothing")

According to Wallace, this category of the middle voice is where one can see "the genius of the middle," but nonnative speakers were not familiar with its subtlety. For this reason it was replaced with other forms.[49] One of the more familiar forms of employing the reflexive meaning is discussed by Smyth in his grammar: "Instead of the direct middle the active voice with the reflexive pronoun is usually employed; often of difficult and unnatural actions (especially with αὐτός ἑαυτόν)."[50] This form of constructing the reflexive is described as the active reflexive, a category understood by Wallace as being used in the Koine Greek. He writes: "Due to the Koine tendency toward greater explicitness and the concomitant erosion of subtleties, the active voice with a reflexive pronoun has increasingly replaced the (direct) reflexive middle."[51] There are several examples in the New Testament that support this construction. One of these is the crucifixion passage in the Synoptic Gospels, where one can find the active reflexive σῶσον σεαυτόν ("save yourself"). Due to the importance of these passages and the importance of the construction for the argument, the (direct) reflexive middle will be analyzed in the next chapter.

b) Indirect middle

The indirect middle, or also called the "special interest middle," is the most common use of the middle voice in the New Testament apart from the deponent. It shows that "the subject performs something *for* himself (i.e., for his own interest)."[52] For Zerwick,

---

46 Herbert Weir Smyth, *A Greek Grammar for Colleges* (New York: American Book Company, 1920), 390.
47 Moulton, *A Grammar of New Testament Greek*, 155.
48 Wallace, *Greek Grammar*, 417.
49 Wallace, *Greek Grammar*, 416.
50 Smyth, *Greek Grammar*, 389.
51 Wallace, *Greek Grammar*, 414.
52 Köstenberger, *Going Deeper*, 195.

this nuance is what shows that the biblical writers "have retained a feeling for even the finer distinctions between the sense of active and middle forms." As examples, Zerwick notes the use of Romans 3:9, where it could "be understood as excelling *by one's virtues* or in that of proffering an excuse or a defense of *oneself*." He further notes the same can be found in Acts 9:39, where "the widows bewailing their benefactress Tabitha are described as to Peter the garments she has made, the middle voice indicating as it were how they so showed the garments they were actually wearing."[53]

However, grammarians such as Moulton or Dana and Mantey caution us with regard to this usage. The indirect middle, or the "dynamic" middle as Moulton calls it, is defined as being hard to interpret since "this category will include a number of verbs in which it is useless to exercise our ingenuity on interpreting the middle, for the development never progressed beyond the rudimentary stage."[54] Furthermore, Dana and Mantey call it "the most extensive use of the middle, and a use which requires and rewards the closest study," since any fixed definition or distinction is hard to make with regard to this nuance.[55] Nevertheless, differences in the interpretation of the indirect middle can be seen in comparison with other categories earlier discussed.

c) Permissive (Causative) Middle

Another classification of the middle voice is with regard to the permissive and the causative middle. Thus, in the permissive middle "the subject *allows* something to be done *for* or *to* himself or herself," while in the causative middle "the subject *has* something done *for* or *to* himself or herself."[56] The traditional grammarians of the New Testament Greek, such as Blass, Robertson, Moulton, treat them as one category. In BDF, this middle is "in the sense of to let oneself be,"[57] while for Robertson the middle is not distinguished "from the active and occurs both with the direct and the indirect use of the middle."[58] Whether one makes a distinction between the causative and the middle, all the grammarians agree that they are very close to each other, and some of the examples could belong to either category. For Wallace, the causative "implies ultimate source and often volition, while the permissive suggests that the prompting lay elsewhere and only that consent or permission or toleration was wrung from the subject."[59] Yet, the permissive is differentiated like a passive where the subject receives

---

53 Maximilian Zerwick, *Scripta Pontificii Instituti Biblici,* English ed., vol. 114, *Biblical Greek* (Rome: Iura Editionis et Versionis Reservantur, 1963), 75.

54 Moulton, Greek Grammar, 158.

55 Dana and Mantey, *Greek New Testament*, 159–60.

56 Wallace, *Greek Grammar*, 423–25.

57 F. Blass and A. Debrunner, *A Greek Grammar of the New Testament and Other Early Christian Literature*, rev. ed., trans. and ed. Robert W. Funk (Chicago: University of Chicago Press, 1961), 166.

58 Robertson, *Grammar of the Greek New Testament*, 808.

59 Wallace, *Greek Grammar*, 425.

the action, but unlike it since "the middle always implies acknowledgment, consent, toleration, or permission of the action of the verb."[60]

- Acts 22:16 ἀναστὰς βάπτισαι καὶ ἀπόλουσαι τὰς ἁμαρτίας σου (Get up and be baptized and wash away your sins)
The two imperatives (βάπτισαι and ἀπόλουσαι) are in the middle voice, understood as being permissive (or causative) middles since the idea of someone baptizing himself or washing away his sins does not correspond to what the Bible represents in other places.[61] The two middles imply that Paul is to "permit himself to be baptized and allow God to wash away his sins."[62]

- 1 Corinthians 10:2 καὶ πάντες εἰς τὸν Μωϋσῆν ἐβαπτίσαντο (And all were baptized into Moses)
According to Wallace, "the force of the middle here is close to a passive, but it adds the element of cognition of the action and permission or voluntary cause.... A translation that might bring out the force of the middle would be, 'and all allowed themselves to be baptized into Moses' (permissive) or 'and all had themselves baptized into Moses' (causative)."[63] However, many manuscripts have this verse with the passive ἐβαπτίσθησαν, with NA27 and BDF supporting this reading.[64]

- Acts 1:18 ἐκτήσατο χωρίον (he purchased a field)
The middle here should be read as a causative one, since a reading in which Judas purchased the field would not fit the gospel of Matthew since the chief priest purchased it. Thus, the middle indicates "that ultimately Judas purchased the field, in that it was purchased with his blood money."[65]

d) Reciprocal Middle
This nuance of the middle voice is used sometimes with a "plural subject to represent interaction among themselves."[66] It is not frequently found in the New Testament, and some of the examples are disputed. The reciprocal middle, however, is a category accepted by most grammarians.

Examples:
- Matthew 26:4 καὶ συνεβουλεύσαντο ἵνα τὸν Ἰησοῦν ... κρατήσωσιν (They resolved together that they should arrest Jesus)

---

60 Wallace, *Greek Grammar*, 426.
61 Köstenberger, *Going Deeper*, 195.
62 Köstenberger, *Going Deeper*, 195.
63 Wallace, *Greek Grammar*, 427.
64 Blass and Debrunner, *Greek Grammar*, 166.
65 Wallace, *Greek Grammar*, 424–25.
66 Wallace, *Greek Grammar*, 42

In this example, the verb συνεβουλεύσαντο in the middle voice implies that the subjects of the action interacted with one another in order to arrest Jesus.

- John 9:22 ἤδη συνετέθειντο οἱ Ἰουδαῖοι (The Jews had already agreed with one another). The verb here is also understood to be a reciprocal middle, but the line of classification in the middle voice is so unclear that only "a wide study of the context that the Jews were holding recurrent conferences in their effort to suppress the work of Jesus" makes one interpret it as carrying the idea of reciprocity.[67]

e) Redundant Middle
In this category, the middle voice is used with the reflexive pronoun, but "the effect is artificial" and thus can be more defined as a subcategory.[68] However, Gildersleeve believes that the use of the pronoun shows even clearer the reflexive force of the middle.[69]

Examples:
- John 19:24 διεμερίσαντο τὰ ἱμάτιά μου ἑαυτοῖς (They divided my garments among them). In this example, the reflexive pronoun follows the middle voice.
- Romans 6:11 λογίζεσθε ἑαυτοὺς [εἶναι] νεκροὺς μὲν τῇ ἁμαρτίᾳ (Consider yourselves to be dead to sin)

The middle voice and deponency

One of the main debates in relation to the middle voice has been with regard to deponency. More than seventy-five percent of the middle verbs in the New Testament could be classified as deponents, thus it is relevant for this discussion. The traditional understanding of deponency is that of a middle voice verb that has no active form but is active in meaning. The term "deponency" comes from the Latin *deponere*, which means "to lay aside." Thus, the deponent verbs were treated by grammarians as verbs that laid aside their original meaning and borrowed the active meaning instead.

Moulton discusses deponency in his grammar, stating that the verbs which "are found with active only or middle only forms" should be called with the "unsatisfactory name deponent": Discussing these verbs, Moulton makes the distinction where the former "denotes an action, an occurrence, or a state," while the latter even though the same are "prevailingly such as take place in the sphere of their subject, the whole subject being concerned in the action."[70] Nevertheless, for Moulton the line is fine, and there is a danger in forcing to find a distinction between them.

After Moulton, A. T. Robertson also dealt with the term deponency in his grammar, and while he agrees with Moulton that the term should be applied to all three voices, he

---

67 Dana and Mantey, *Greek New Testament*, 155.
68 Robertson, *Grammar of the Greek New Testament*, 811.
69 Basil L. Gildersleeve, *Syntax of Classical Greek from Homer to Demosthenes* (New York: American Book Company, 1900), 1:68.
70 Moulton, Grammar of New Testament Greek, 153.

immediately states that the term should not be used at all. The reason why "deponency" should not be used as in relation to these verbs is that Robertson considers them defective and not deponent, since it is hard to see in them the distinctive force of the voice.[71] For Robertson, however, the best solution is that each verb should be examined individually in order to see what it is communicating.

Besides the classical grammarians, new studies in the field have discussed the deponency problem. One of the first was Neva Miller, who pointed out that the problem stays in two assumptions: "(1) in the earlier stages of the development of the language, every Greek verb had an active form; and (2) in later developments of the language some verbs lost their active forms and thus became "defective.""[72] Miller agrees with none of these assumptions since the conclusion drawn is that these "so-called" deponent verbs are not active in meaning, but "express personal interest, self-involvement, or interaction of the subject with himself or with others in some way."[73] Starting from this definition, Miller talks about seven classes that mirror the above definition, classes that also are helpful in the category topic of the middle verbs:[74]

1. Reciprocity—some verbs involve situations where two parties are involved and where the removal of one party would render the verb meaningless and no action possible. It can be a positive interaction (δέχομαι—welcome), negative interaction (μάχομαι—fight), or a positive and negative communication (ἀποκρίνομαι—answer; ψεύδομαι—lie to).
2. Reflexivity—the action turns back or is reflected back on the subject (ἐγκρατεύομαι—abstain/control oneself). Some reflexive verbs express the notion of moving oneself in one direction or another (ἐπανέρχομαι—return).
3. Self-involvement—some verbs intimately involve the self in the processes going on within the action. These have to do with thinking, feeling, deciding—processes that the subject alone can experience for himself (λογίζομαι—reckon).
4. Self-Interest—verbs occasionally show the subject acting in his own interest (κτάομαι—get, acquire).
5. Receptivity—sometimes the subject is the center of emphasis, the receiver of sensory perception (θεάομαι—see, behold).
6. Passivity—if verbs show a passive subject, the verbal concept alludes to involuntary experiences. The subject is viewed as unable to avoid the experience depicted in the verb (γίνομαι—be born, come into being).

---

71 Robertson, Grammar of the Greek New Testament, 811–12.
72 Neva F. Miller, Appendix 2, "A Theory of Deponent Verbs," in *Analytical Lexicon of the Greek New Testament*, Barbara Friberg, Timothy Friberd, and Neva F. Miller (Grand Rapids, MI: Baker, 2000), 426.
73 Miller, "Theory of Deponent Verbs," 426.
74 All the seven classes presented are from Miller, "Theory of Deponent Verbs," 427–29.

7. State, condition—the subject is the center of gravity (δύναμαι — be able, powerful).

While admitting that this classification does not settle the issue, Miller draws the conclusion that

> if the verbs in the above classes are understood as true middles—and if active forms could not have expressed such concepts—then it may be that categorizing such verbs as deponent is no longer relevant . . . [the conclusion thus is] to look for the enriched meaning being communicated by this category of verbs by letting each middle or passive "deponent" verb speak with its own voice.[75]

Conclusion

The passive voice in the Romanian translation can be expressed in two ways: the more common way is by using the auxiliary verb, which is similar to the way the English language constructs the passive. The less common way of constructing it is by using the reflexive pronoun *se,* called the reflexive passive. Whether the verb "to save" in the Romanian Orthodox Bible is understood to be a reflexive passive depends on several arguments such as the immediate context of the surrounding verses and the use of the voice in that context. These will be discussed more on the next chapter. However, it is worth noticing that the middle voice is understood by grammarians to be more ambiguous since it can be easily confused with the reflexive voice.

Furthermore, the middle voice is a complex concept in the Greek grammar, with different nuances that need to be addressed. This chapter has posited that the term "subject-affectedness" is the best term assigned for the middle voice. This shows the involvement of the subject in different ways. These different ways can be seen in the categories discussed above, where the main conclusion is that the reflexive understanding of the middle is one of the functions but not the only one. In the next chapter, a number of texts in the canonical gospels will be examined individually to see whether the primarily reflexive understanding or another means of translating the middle and passive voices is preferred.

---

75 Miller, "Theory of Deponent Verbs," 430.

CHAPTER 3

σῴζω in the Canonical Gospels

One aspect about translation issues that was raised in chapter one was the importance of the context in Bible translation. Context is important according to Nida in grammar analysis and in determining the structural role of elements. Context is also important in understanding how the voice functions in a given language. The following chapter will be looking at a case by case study of the verb σῴζω in the canonical gospels. Since translation principles and also the voice in context is important, how the authors of the canonical gospels used the verb σῴζω will be analyzed and, more importantly, if an understanding of the verb as referring to *theosis* is in accordance with its immediate and wider context.

A good starting point for the examination of the word σῴζω is the lexicon, *A Greek-English Lexicon of the New Testament and Other Early Christian Literature* (BDAG). According to BDAG, the verb can be grouped into three large categories. First, the verb signifies "to preserve or rescue from natural dangers and afflictions, save, keep from harm, preserve, rescue."[1] In this category a number of different possibilities exist, such as to save from death, or as is the case in most of the occurrences in the gospel, to save someone from disease. Second, the verb may refer to saving someone "or preserve from transcendent danger or destruction, *save/preserve from eternal death*, from judgment, and from all that might lead to such death, e.g. sin, also in a positive sense bring Messianic *salvation, bring to salvation*."[2] In this category the verb is in the active where God and Christ, or "a mediator of divine salvation" does the action, but the largest category is in the passive voice with the meaning "be saved, attain salvation." This is the category in which most of the canonical gospels' appearances fall.[3] The last category of the verb contains those appearances where the verb refers to both the first and second category. For instance, Mark 8:35 can be taken as both referring to salvation from death but also salvation from eternal death.

Case by Case Study of the Verb σῴζω in the Canonical Gospels
A. Matthew 9:21—ἔλεγεν γὰρ ἐν ἑαυτῇ· ἐὰν μόνον ἅψωμαι τοῦ ἱματίου αὐτοῦ σωθήσομαι. Even though σῴζω in this verse is not in the middle voice, yet in the Orthodox translation there are instances where the passive voice is also translated as reflexive. The verb used here is future passive ("I will be saved"), but in the *Biblia de la Bucureşti* 1688 (also known as *Biblia de la 1688*), the translation provided is in the reflexive voice: "Că zicea

---

1 BDAG, 3rd ed., s.v. "σῴζω."
2 BDAG, 3rd ed., s.v. "σῴζω."
3 BDAG, 3rd ed., s.v. "σῴζω."

întru sine: Macară numai de m-aș atinge de veșmîntul Lui, *mă voiu mîntui*" ("For she was saying to herself: If I only touch his garment, I will save myself"). One example in which the passive voice has a reflexive nuance to it is the causative or permissive passive, a category that "implies consent, permission, or cause of the action of the verb on the part of the subject."[4] In the Gala Galaction translation, the Anania translation, and the IBSR-SBIR translation as well, the construction is kept, but σώζω is translated "to heal" ("mă voi vindeca") or "to be healthy" ("mă voi face sănătoasă"). Of note is that the Gala Galaction translation is the translation provided by Dumitru Cornilescu as well ("mă voi tămădui"), with the reflexive pronoun *mă*. The passive voice is however used by *Noua Traducere în Limba Română* (NTLR): "voi fi vindecată."

One such example is 1 Corinthians 6:7, where both verbs are in the passive voice, but the translation may be "why not allow yourselves to be wronged (ἀδικεῖσθε). Why not allow yourselves to be defrauded (ἀποστερεῖσθε). "This usage, however, is rare, and not all passive imperatives as in this case make sense as a causative/permissive passive."[5]

Mark 5:23—καὶ παρακαλεῖ αὐτὸν πολλὰ λέγων ὅτι τὸ θυγάτριόν μου ἐσχάτως ἔχει, ἵνα ἐλθὼν ἐπιθῇς τὰς χεῖρας αὐτῇ ἵνα σωθῇ καὶ ζήσῃ.

A similar interpretation is also found in Mark 5:23. In this verse, the verb σώζω appears in the form of aorist passive subjunctive, but the translation provided by *Biblia de la 1688* is reflexive: "Și rugă pre El mult, zicînd că fiica mea spre moarte iaste, ca, viind, să pui mînile preste ea, ca să să mîntuiască și să trăiască" ("and implored him earnestly, saying 'my daughter is at the point of death, that, coming, you may but your hands on her in order that she might save herself and live"). It may be suggested that verse thirty-four sees the woman as the subject for σώζω, or more specifically her faith. Thus this shows an active participation in the verb: "Your faith has saved you." In the light of the meaning of σώζω in verse twenty-eight, the verb here should be understood as "to be healed" or "to be made well."[6] She has been healed through her faith, which was "to reach out from the crowd and touch Jesus, and then at his behest to stand forth and be identified."[7] However, Jesus tells her "go in peace," which is "not simply a word of dismissal. The Hebrew term for peace that forms the background for the New Testament concept of peace is *shalom*. It covers wholeness, well-being, prosperity, security, friendship, and salvation."[8]

b. Matthew 10:22—καὶ ἔσεσθε μισούμενοι ὑπὸ πάντων διὰ τὸ ὄνομά μου· ὁ δὲ ὑπομείνας εἰς τέλος οὗτος σωθήσεται.

---

4 Wallace, *Greek Grammar*, 440.

5 Wallace, *Greek Grammar*, 440.

6 Robert G. Hamerton-Kelly, *The Gospel and the Sacred Poetics of Violence in Mark* (Minneapolis: Fortress, 1994), 94.

7 Robert G. Hamerton-Kelly, *The Gospel and the Sacred Poetics of Violence in Mark*, 94.

8 David E. Garland, *Mark*, The NIV Application Commentary (Grand Rapids, MI: Zondervan,1996), 221–22.

In this verse the same use of σῴζω is found (future passive) with the same translation provided by *Biblia de la 1688*: "Şi veţ fi urîţi de toţi pentru Numele Mieu; iară cela ce va răbda pînă în sfîrşit, acela *să va spăşi*" ("And you will be hated by all for my name's sake; but the one who will endures to the end, that one will repent"). In this translation is found the verb "a spăşi," preferred in the 17th century but later changed with "a mântui."[9] The reflexive pronoun *se* is used here (in Romanian language it is a reflexive understanding, since one repents for himself), but "to save" is either understood as "to repent," or "to save." While "a spăşi" can have different meanings, the modern translation and Gala Galaction's translation sheds some light as the translation is "to save," since the voice is reflexive: "se va mântui" ("he will save himself"). Dumitru Cornilescu, NTLR, and the IBSR-SBIR version translate it as "va fi mântuit" (he will be saved). If the passive reading is the recommended translation, it is worth mentioning that BDAG also categorizes this usage in Matthew 10:22 under the passive "be saved, or attain salvation."[10] Unlike the previous verses, this verse is of great importance since σῴζω here has a different connotation. The first usage of the verb in the Gospel of Matthew (1:21) talks about salvation from sins, while sometimes it is used in saving your life by losing it. In the same way here, "Jesus is talking not about the preservation of physical life, but the ultimate well-being which is compatible with the loss of physical life. In the face of persecution and possible martyrdom, disciples must remain true to their loyalty to Jesus. If they do so 'to the end,' they will be 'saved,' even though they may be executed."[11]

c. Matthew 19:25—ἀκούσαντες δὲ οἱ μαθηταὶ ἐξεπλήσσοντο σφόδρα λέγοντες· τίς ἄρα δύναται σωθῆναι;
For this verse, *Biblia de la 1688* provides the following translation: "Şi auzind ucenicii Lui, să mirară foarte zicînd: Dară cine să va putea spăşi?" ("And his disciples hearing, they were greatly astonished saying: But who will be able to save himself?"). In the more modern translation, the reflexive nuance is kept: "Dar cine poate să se mântuiască?" ("But who can save himself?"). Just as in the previous verse that was discussed, the voice of the verb is passive (σωθῆναι), and the voice is preserved in the Protestant translation: "Cine poate atunci să fie mântuit?" ("Who then can be saved?"). Moreover, the context of the passage supports a passive understanding of the verb. In this passage, Jesus had an encounter with the rich young man who eventually went away sorrowful since he could not sell his possessions, for he was rich. As a response Jesus states the famous words: "it is easier for a camel to go through the eye of a needle than for a rich person to enter the kingdom of God." Hearing these words, the disciples then say: "Who then can be saved?" Through this statement the disciples set in parallel entering the kingdom

---

9 E. Munteanu, in his book, draws to attention the change in the church language from the slavic word "a spăşi" to the word "a mântui," hungarian at origins. For further explanations see Munteanu, *Lexicologie Biblică Românească*, 467.

10 BDAG, 3rd ed. s.v. "σῴζω."

11 R. T. France, *The Gospel of Matthew*, The New International Commentary on the New Testament (Grand Rapids, MI: Eerdmans, 2007), 395.

of God with being saved, and as a result, they became astonished. In his comments on this verse, Keener concludes that probably they were shocked because

> many of their contemporaries viewed wealth as a mark of God's blessing (e.g., *Ep. Arist.* 204-5; *m. 'Abot* 4:9; *Qidd.* 4:14), the disciples may have assumed that Jesus' standard for people who were not rich was even stricter: [If not the rich], who then can be saved?" Yet because God alone is good (19:17), salvation by merely human means is impossible for anyone; only with God is salvation possible.[12]

Therefore, such a statement sees salvation as depending on who is more worthy of entering God's kingdom, but Jesus' answer debunks the human-worthiness presuppositions. While it is not explicitly stated in this passage (and all is said is that with God everything is possible), Jesus' words are in line with Paul's teaching of salvation by grace, through faith (Eph. 2:8).

Mark 10:26—οἱ δὲ περισσῶς ἐξεπλήσσοντο λέγοντες πρὸς ἑαυτούς· καὶ τίς δύναται σωθῆναι; As in the story from Matthew, the disciples were amazed by Jesus' sayings, thus leading to the response: "Then who can be saved?" In Biblia de la 1688, the passive voice of σῴζω is translated as reflexive once again: "Iară ei mai mult să mirară, zicînd întru eiș: Cine poate să să spăsească?" ("But they even more were amazed, saying to themselves: Who can save himself?"). The reflexive nuance is kept in the Bartolomeu edition, and other more modern translations: "And who can save himself?" This translation is not the recommended one since it does not follow the passive voice of the verb. The translation also does not fit the context because Jesus makes it clear that neither wealth nor your own worthiness saves you, but with God all things are possible.

Luke 18:26 is the parallel verse of Matthew and Mark: εἶπαν δὲ οἱ ἀκούσαντες· καὶ τίς δύναται σωθῆναι; in the Synoptic Gospels, σῴζω is an aorist passive infinitive. Like in the previous instances, the Orthodox Bible translates it as reflexive: "Şi cine poate să se mântuiască?" ("And who is able to save himself?").

d. Matthew 24:13; 22. ὁ δὲ ὑπομείνας εἰς τέλος οὗτος σωθήσεται. καὶ εἰ μὴ ἐκολοβώθησαν αἱ ἡμέραι ἐκεῖναι, οὐκ ἂν ἐσώθη πᾶσα σάρξ·
In the Olivet Discourse, the verb σῴζω is found two times, in verses thirteen and twenty-two. In both instances the verb is found in the passive voice, but the translation in the Orthodox Bible is still reflexive. In *Biblia de la 1688*, as well as in the Bartolomeu edition the given translation for verse thirteen is the following: "Iară cela ce va răbda pînă în sfîrşit, acela să va spăşi" ("But the one who will endure to the end, that one will save himself"). Verse twenty-two has the verb translated in the reflexive voice as well: "Şi de nu s-ar fi micşorat zilele acelea, nu s-ar fi mîntuit tot trupul." (And if those days had not been cut short, nobody would save himself"). In the modern translation of

---

12 Craig S. Keener, *A Commentary on the Gospel of Matthew* (Grand Rapids, MI: Eerdmans, 1999), 477–78.

the Orthodox Bible and the Bartolomeu edition, ἐσώθη is translated as "nobody would escape" with σώζω meaning "to escape" and the verb in the active voice. This meaning is the same as the one provided by Cornilescu ("no one would escape"), but the NTLR, which aims for the same meaning, provides the passive voice found in the Greek text: "nici un om n-ar fi scăpat" ("no man would be allowed to escape"). This meaning of "to escape" is the suggested translation of BDAG, where it means "to preserve or rescue from natural dangers and afflictions, *save, keep from harm, preserve, rescue*," or in our case "to save from death."[13] It has been suggested that the "salvation" provided here is related to being saved from the eternal death, but the verb in the context is best understood to refer to "physical safety."[14] Therefore, while the passage itself is not crucial in relation to the doctrine of salvation, *Biblia de la 1688*, the modern Orthodox translation and Cornilescu have not represented the passive voice of the verb.

Mark 13:13—καὶ ἔσεσθε μισούμενοι ὑπὸ πάντων διὰ τὸ ὄνομά μου. ὁ δὲ ὑπομείνας εἰς τέλος οὗτος σωθήσεται.
As in Matthew, in a context of persecution, Jesus says to the disciples that whoever will endure to the end will be saved. As a passive verb, the Orthodox Bible again renders it reflexive: "Și de toți veți fi urâți din pricina numelui Meu; dar cel ce va răbda până la sfârșit, acela se va mântui" ("And will be hated by all because of my name; but the one who will endure to the end, that one will save himself"). The Protestant translations, Cornilescu, and the NTLR, provide the best translation: "that one will be saved." It is possible that the end in the discussion is not the end of the present age, but more likely refers "to one's own end in case of martyrdom."[15] The verse, however, is theologically important since the reflexive voice shows human involvement in it, but σωθήσεται "contains a divine passive: God will grant eternal salvation to the martyr."[16]

Mark 13:20a—καὶ εἰ μὴ ἐκολόβωσεν κύριος τὰς ἡμέρας, οὐκ ἂν ἐσώθη πᾶσα σάρξ·
This verse is the same as the one in Matthew, with the same translation provided: "Și dacă Domnul n-ar fi scurtat zilele acelea, nici un trup n-ar mai scăpa" ("And if the Lord had not cut short those days, nobody would escape"). In this passage, Jesus talks about the abomination of the desolation, a time when there will be a great tribulation and the end is near. However, God's mercy is manifested in that he cuts short the days for the sake of the elect, and if it were not for God cutting short the days, no one "will be saved." Thus in this context, the meaning of ἐσώθη is understood as escaping from the tribulation.[17]

---

13 BDAG, 3rd ed. s.v. "σώζω."
14 Donald A. Hagner, *Word Biblical Commentary*, vol. 33B, *Matthew 14–28* (Dallas, TX: Word Books, 1995), 703.
15 Robert H. Gundry, *Mark: A Commentary on His Apology for the Cross*, vol. 2 (9–16) (Grand Rapids, MI: Eerdmans, 1993), 740–41.
16 Gundry, *Mark*, 740–41.
17 Garland, *Mark*, 496.

e. Matthew 27:40, 42—καὶ λέγοντες· ὁ καταλύων τὸν ναὸν καὶ ἐν τρισὶν ἡμέραις οἰκοδομῶν, σῶσον σεαυτόν, εἰ υἱὸς εἶ τοῦ θεοῦ, [καὶ] κατάβηθι ἀπὸ τοῦ σταυροῦ.
ἄλλους ἔσωσεν, ἑαυτὸν οὐ δύναται σῶσαι· βασιλεὺς Ἰσραήλ ἐστιν, καταβάτω νῦν ἀπὸ τοῦ σταυροῦ καὶ πιστεύσομεν ἐπ' αὐτόν.

The crucifixion passages in the canonical gospels raise a special interest in terms of the construction chosen by the authors. As one can see, the construction in Matthew 27:40, 42 provides the verb (in the active voice) and reflexive pronoun to form the reflexive nuance of the verse. Biblia de la 1688, as well as the Bartolomeu edition and the modern translations, render the verses as following: "mântuieşte-te pe tine însuţi" (save yourself) (verse 40), "dar pe sine nu poate să se mântuiască" (But he himself cannot save [himself]) (verse 42). While discussing this topic as in relation to the understanding of the middle voice as being primarily reflexive, Daniel Wallace writes the following:

> [In the reflexive active] the subject acts upon himself or herself. In such cases naturally the *reflexive pronoun* is employed as the direct object, while the corresponding reflexive middle omits the pronoun. This usage is relatively common. In classical Greek, this idea would have often been expressed by the middle voice. However, due to the Koine tendency toward greater explicitness and the concomitant erosion of subtleties, the active voice with a reflexive pronoun has increasingly replaced the (direct) reflexive middle.[18]

Mark 15:30, 31b—σῶσον σεαυτὸν καταβὰς ἀπὸ τοῦ σταυροῦ. ἄλλους ἔσωσεν, ἑαυτὸν οὐ δύναται σῶσαι.

The reflexive active in the crucifixion passages appears in Mark's Gospel as well, the context being the same as in Matthew 27:40, 42. As already has been seen, the grammarians Wallace and Smyth make the claim that the reflexive idea was more often communicated through the reflexive active and not the direct middle or the passive voice.

Luke 23:35, 37, 39—ἄλλους ἔσωσεν, σωσάτω ἑαυτόν, εἰ οὗτός ἐστιν ὁ χριστὸς τοῦ θεοῦ ὁ ἐκλεκτός. εἰ σὺ εἶ ὁ βασιλεὺς τῶν Ἰουδαίων, σῶσον σεαυτόν. οὐχὶ σὺ εἶ ὁ χριστός; σῶσον σεαυτὸν καὶ ἡμᾶς.

In chapter twenty-three of Luke's Gospel, three instances of the reflexive active are found, all being taunts directed to Jesus when he was on the cross: the leaders mock him, the soldiers mock him, and even one of the two criminals mock him by telling him to save himself. These instances are translated in the Orthodox Bible as reflexive, with an emphasis on the reflexive pronoun since it appears in the original text: "mântuieşte-Te pe Tine Însuţi" (save yourself). These constructions are similar to the reflexive active seen in Mark 15:31 and Matthew 27:40, 42, also appearing in the crucifixion passages.

f. Mark 6:56—καὶ ὅπου ἂν εἰσεπορεύετο εἰς κώμας ἢ εἰς πόλεις ἢ εἰς ἀγρούς, ἐν ταῖς ἀγοραῖς ἐτίθεσαν τοὺς ἀσθενοῦντας καὶ παρεκάλουν αὐτὸν ἵνα κἂν τοῦ κρασπέδου τοῦ ἱματίου αὐτοῦ ἅψωνται· καὶ ὅσοι ἂν ἥψαντο αὐτοῦ ἐσῴζοντο.

---

18 Wallace, *Greek Grammar*, 413–14.

In this verse, the verb appears in a form that has identical form in the middle and passive voices. The Orthodox translations render the passage with the middle voice, with a direct middle nuance. In *Biblia de la 1688* the following is found: "Și cîți să atingea de El să vindeca" ("And as many were touching by him were healed"). The Bartolomeu translation as well as some more modern translations follows the same interpretation: "se vindecau."

g. Luke 8:12—οἱ δὲ παρὰ τὴν ὁδόν εἰσιν οἱ ἀκούσαντες, εἶτα ἔρχεται ὁ διάβολος καὶ αἴρει τὸν λόγον ἀπὸ τῆς καρδίας αὐτῶν, ἵνα μὴ πιστεύσαντες σωθῶσιν.
In this verse, the voice of the verb is again passive, however the translation provided throughout the editions of the Orthodox Church is reflexive. Moreover, this is unique to Luke. In *Biblia de la 1688*, the verse is translated as following: "Iară cei de lîngă cale sînt ceia ce aud, după aceaea vine diavolul și ia cuvîntul de la inima lor, să nu cumva, crezînd, să să spăsască" ("But the ones along the path are those who heard, then the devil comes and takes the word from their heart so that, believing, they may not save themselves"). *Ediția Sinodală 1914*, as well as the Bartolomeu Anania translation, follows the reflexive understanding: "să se mântuiască."

Exegetically speaking, an understanding of a person who is actively involved in the process could be made based on the context of the verse. In chapter eight, Jesus is explaining the Parable of the Sower, and the first place where the seed falls notes what is stolen by the devil and never gets the chance to germinate. While all these types of responses may be seen as "saved," Bock rightly believes that this is "often over interpreted": "Jesus is not communicating the minimum response required to receive blessing. Rather, he is instructing the disciples on fruitfulness by pointing out obstacles that prevent such a response."[19] Bock concludes by adding that the responses require reflection from the side of the person, thinking about "What single type of response to the word have I given?"[20] Such a response would encourage the consideration of a person who is also active in salvation; however, one cannot ignore that the verb is in the passive voice.

h. Luke 8:36—ἀπήγγειλαν δὲ αὐτοῖς οἱ ἰδόντες πῶς ἐσώθη ὁ δαιμονισθείς.
This verse is one example of a verse which got revised and corrected in the modern translation of the Orthodox Bible. Once again, it is unique to Luke. In the first translation of both the Old Testament and the New Testament, *Biblia de la 1688*, ἐσώθη is translated as reflexive: "Și spusără lor și văzînd cum s-au mîntuit cel îndrăcit" (And those who had seen it told them how the demon-possessed man saved himself"). In *Ediția Sinodală 1914*, the same translation is provided: "cum s-a mântuit cel îndrăcit" ("how the demon-possessed man saved himself"). However, the modern translation of Bartolomeu Anania brings a different translation of the passage: "Și cei care văzuseră le-au spus cum a fost izbăvit demonizatul" ("And the ones who had seen it told them how the demon-

---

[19] Darrell L. Bock, *Luke*, vol. 1, *1:1– 9:50*, Baker Exegetical Commentary on the New Testament (Grand Rapids, MI: Baker Books, 1994), 733-34.

[20] Bock, *Luke. 1:1–9:50*, 734.

possessed man was delivered").²¹ The main Protestant translations, Cornilescu and NTR, also translate the verb as passive, but with different nuances. The Cornilescu version translates it to mean "be healed," while NTR does not attempt to interpret it but simply translates it "to be saved."

i. Luke 8:50—ὁ δὲ Ἰησοῦς ἀκούσας ἀπεκρίθη αὐτῷ· μὴ φοβοῦ, μόνον πίστευσον, καὶ σωθήσεται.

A few verses later, σώζω in the passive voice is translated again as reflexive in both the traditional and modern translation of the Orthodox Bible. This is also unique material to Luke. In *Biblia de la 1688* the verse is translated as following: "Iară Iisus auzind, răspunse lui, grăind: Nu te teame, numai creade și să va mîntui" ("But Jesus hearing, answers to him: Do not fear, only believe, and she will save herself"). *Ediția Sinodală 1914*, and also the more modern translation of Anania, has the verb in the reflexive voice this time: "se va mântui" (will save himself). However, comparing this verse with the previous one, there are more similarities than differences. In both instances, Jesus performs a miracle on the persons. In the first case it is on a demon-possessed man, and in the second case on Jairus's daughter. In both instances, the verb σώζω is used in the context of a healing, thus leading to the translation of the verb as "to be healed" or "to be well." In both verses the verb is in the passive voice with the only thing that differs being the tense. In Luke 8:36 the verb is an aorist passive indicative, while in Luke 8:50 it is a future passive indicative. Nevertheless, in Luke 8:36 the modern translation translates it as passive, while in this verse it is the reflexive nuance that predominates once again. In Cornilescu and NTR, the verb is in the passive voice, with σώζω translated as "to be healed."

j. Luke 13:23—Εἶπεν δέ τις αὐτῷ· κύριε, εἰ ὀλίγοι οἱ σῳζόμενοι;

In this verse, οἱ σῳζόμενοι is the disputed word in terms of its translation. This is unique Lukan tradition although there is a similar story in Matthew. οἱ σῳζόμενοι is a participle that can be taken morphologically as middle or passive. The Orthodox translations take it as middle, with a reflexive understanding: "Și i-a zis cineva: Doamne, puțini sunt oare cei care se mântuiesc?" (And someone said to him: Lord, are they few the ones who save themselves?") This is the translation provided in all the major editions, such as *Biblia de la 1688*, *Ediția Sinodală 1914*, *Gala Galaction*, or *Anania*. However, the Protestant translations, Cornilescu and NTR, understand the participle as being passive: "those who are saved."

According to Carl Conrad, how one differentiates whether a verb is in the middle or passive is "unquestionably one of the most difficult features of ancient Greek."²² There are not easy ways of choosing between the middle or passive voice, and the best answer is a case-by-case basis related to the context in which the verb is used. However, one

---

21 According to the Explanatory Dictionary of the Romanian Language, the verb "a izbăvi" means to be delivered from something, to escape or made someone escape from a danger or disease, as well as to save or save himself.

22 Carl W. Conrad, "Active, Middle, and Passive," 4.

point that may help decide which voice is being used can be seen by the surrounding Greek words. The Greek grammarian Zerwick notes, "the Hellenistic tendency to greater explicitness often results indeed in the use of the active voice with a pronoun (reflexive or not in form) or the addition of such a pronoun to the middle verb."[23] Thus, it is probable that the author would have chosen to express the reflexive nuance by using a form followed by ἑαυτοὺς, "since this fits the general trend of preferring the active voice in Koine Greek."[24]

When words that would determine the voice one way or another are not present, the best answer for the verse is the context in which appears. In this passage, Jesus talks about the narrow door in the light of the question of the number of the saved ones. Jesus' answer to this question is indeed a middle imperative, where the subject is directly involved by having to strive in order to enter through the narrow door. By the narrow door, "like the narrow way, it is pictured the way of righteousness or entry into God's presence and blessing."[25] Thus, a subject involved in the previous verse is made possible through the understanding of the participle as middle. However, Jesus' words do not end here. In a discussion where he stresses that the door is opened for a short period of time, the main argument given by Jesus to strive to enter the narrow door is that many will not be able. He declares this to be true, mainly because "the master of the house" does not know them. T. W. Manson explains this the best as he points to both God's role in salvation and man's striving:

> The reply of Jesus begins by asserting that the way of salvation is a door which God opens and man enters. The entry cannot be made without God. The gate of heaven opens only from the inside. But also man has to make his own way in, once the door is opened. And this is not easy. The entrance is narrow, and it is a case of struggling through rather than strolling in. If men fail to enter, it is not that God is unwilling to admit them, but that they will not enter on the only terms on which entrance is possible.[26]

Thus, from the context, the participle should not be understood as reflexive, where a person works his way of righteousness to God. It is rather that one has "to labor hard at listening and responding to his message."[27]

k. John 3:17—οὐ γὰρ ἀπέστειλεν ὁ θεὸς τὸν υἱὸν εἰς τὸν κόσμον ἵνα κρίνῃ τὸν κόσμον, ἀλλ' ἵνα σωθῇ ὁ κόσμος δι' αὐτοῦ.

---

23 Zerwick, *Biblical Greek*, 233.

24 Esther Yue L. Ng, "ἦσαν τεταγμένοι in Acts 13:48: Middle Voice or Passive Voice? Implications for the Doctrine of Divine Election," *CGST Journal 50* (January 2011): 189–90, accessed January 9, 2020, http://tci.ncl.edu.tw/cgi- https://drive.google.com/file/d/0B58X1TJ3bk7FZ3UwQ1kxa3hpdlk/view.

25 Darrell L. Bock, *Luke*, vol. 2, *9:51–24:53*, Baker Exegetical Commentary on the New Testament (Grand Rapids, MI: Baker Books, 1996), 1234–35.

26 T. W. Manson, *The Sayings of Jesus as Recorded in the Gospels According to St. Matthew and St. Luke* (London: SCM Press LTD, 1949), 125.

27 Bock, *9:51– 24:53*, 1234.

Biblia de la 1688 translates this verse as following: "Pentru că n-au trimis Dumnezău pre Fiiul Lui în lume ca să judece lumea, ce ca să să mîntuiască lumea pren El" ("For God did not send his Son in the world to judge the world, but that the world might save itself through Him"). *Ediția Sinodală 1914* and Anania's translation follow the same reflexive understanding: "ci pentru ca lumea *să se mântuiască* printr-Însul." Cornilescu and NTR however stick with the passive voice: "ci ca lumea *să fie mântuită* prin El" (but in order that the world might be saved through him"). Moreover, the verb in a passive voice fits better in the verse exegetically speaking. The subject of the verse is God; he does the action of sending. The verse is also made up of a dualism with John contrasting two things just as in the previous verse. Namely, God gave his Son that whoever believes in him might not perish (a) but have eternal life (b) and in the same way God sent his Son not to condemn the world (a'), but that the world might be saved through him (b'). Thus, if in (a') the one doing the action is God, it is better understood to take God as doing the action of salvation, which "patient" is the world. The same idea is communicated later by John in 12:47 where it says: "And if anyone hears my words and does not obey them, I do not judge [that is, 'condemn'] him for I have come not to judge the world but to save the world."[28] Here, it is explicitly stated that he saves the world; it is not the world which does the action.

l. John 5:34—ἐγὼ δὲ οὐ παρὰ ἀνθρώπου τὴν μαρτυρίαν λαμβάνω, ἀλλὰ ταῦτα λέγω ἵνα ὑμεῖς σωθῆτε.
In this verse, σῴζω is used again in the aorist passive subjunctive, but the Orthodox translations render it as reflexive: "Iară Eu nu de la om mărturia iau, ce aceastea zic ca voi să vă mîntuiți" ("Not that the testimony I receive is from man, but I say these things so that you may save yourselves"). However, the Cornilescu reading of the verse is more appropriate: "dar spun lucrurile acestea pentru ca să fiți mântuiți" ("but I'm saying these things so that you may be saved"). In this passage, Jesus tells the Jews, the ones who earlier accused him of making himself equal with God, that John bore witness to him, and that he says these things for them so that they may "be saved."

m. John 10:9—ἐγώ εἰμι ἡ θύρα· δι' ἐμοῦ ἐάν τις εἰσέλθῃ σωθήσεται καὶ εἰσελεύσεται καὶ ἐξελεύσεται καὶ νομὴν εὑρήσει.
The future passive of "to save" in 10:9 is another case of "to save" interpreted as reflexive by Orthodox versions of the Bible. Biblia de la 1688 and other editions such as Ediția Sinodală 1914, Gala Galaction, or Anania translates the verse as following: "Eu sunt ușa: de va intra cineva prin Mine, se va mântui; și va intra și va ieși și pășune va afla" ("I am the door: if anyone enters through me he will save himself; and he will go in and he will go out and he will find pasture"). However, the context of the verse prefers the passive reading: "if anyone enters through me he will be saved." In a passage where Jesus' imagery of the good shepherd and his sheep points to dependency and talks about him as being the only way (contrasting the thieves and robbers), a translation

---

28 J. Ramsey Michaels, *The Gospel of John*, The New International Commentary on the New Testament (Grand Rapids, MI: Eerdmans, 2010), 204.

where "the sheep" would be able "to save themselves" is not the preferred reading. In a culture where you "thought of entering heaven by a gate," "the doors of heaven are the means by which knowledge and salvation are made known."[29]

n. John 11:12—εἶπαν οὖν οἱ μαθηταὶ αὐτῷ· κύριε, εἰ κεκοίμηται σωθήσεται.
This verse in the first complete translation of the Bible translates the passive σῴζω as reflexive: "Deci ziseră ucenicii Lui: Doamne, de au adormit, mîntui-se-va" ("Therefore, the disciples said to him: Lord, if he has fallen asleep, he will save himself"). Another traditional translation, Ediția Sinodală 1914, agrees with Biblia de la 1688 in translating reflexively: "se va mântui." Yet, the Bible translation in the edition of Anania, as well as other more modern translations, interprets the verb and translates it actively: "Doamne, dacă a adormit, va scăpa" ("Lord, if he has fallen asleep he will escape"). The same interpretation is given by Cornilescu in his translation of the Bible and the NTR: "he will be well."

Conclusion

When it comes to the Canonical Gospels, and especially the Synoptic Gospels, σῴζω appears sixteen times in stories where Jesus heals people. Additionally, a large number of the passages contain the verb in the passive form, with the meaning "to be saved."[30] Both the grammar and the context of these passages suggest a passive understanding. Half of the healing passages have the phrase ἡ πίστις σου σέσωκέν σε (your faith has saved you). According to Gerhard Friedrich, "σῴζω never refers to a single member of the body but always to the whole man, and it is especially significant in view of the important phrase 'your faith has saved you.' The choice of the word σῴζω thus leaves room for the view that the healing power of Jesus and the saving power of faith go beyond physical life."[31]

---

29 Andreas J. Köstenberger, *John*, Baker Exegetical Commentary on the New Testament (Grand Rapids, MI: Baker Books, 2004), 305.

30 Ten passages talk about salvation from eternal death and contain the passive: Mt 10:22, 19:25, 24:13; Mk 10:26, 13:13, 16:16; Lk 8:12, 18:26, John 5:34, 10:9.

31 *Theological Dictionary of the New Testament*, s.v. "σῴζω," § D.II.1.

Chapter 4

Soteriology in the Eastern Church Fathers

In biblical translation, the Church Fathers play an important role for the Orthodox Church. They are the first who interpreted the Bible, and the Church gave special consideration to their understanding of the Scriptures. Saint Augustine pointed to the significance of the Church Fathers, particularly for the ambiguous passages in the Bible. Augustine referred to those collections of writings of the earlier Church Fathers, as well as Church councils and doctrinal creeds for the interpretation of the Bible. He states: "the interpreter is to be firmly rooted in the church and its teaching as a safeguard against aberrant interpretations of the Bible. . . . Let the reader consult the rule of faith which he has gathered from the plainer passages of Scripture, and from the authority of the Church."[1] Even though one can argue that Augustine was not necessarily holding to such a view, the Orthodox Christians believe that a Christian should be guided by both the Bible and the sacred tradition. Having in mind the importance of the Church Fathers in dealing with biblical passages and especially their understanding of soteriology, the basic understanding of salvation in the Early Church Fathers who are revered in Romania will be presented and how the Fathers understanding can be useful in interpreting the salvation passages in the Bible

When one talks about soteriology in the patristic period, there are two main streams for understanding salvation. One is the Western church's understanding where God is righteous and just, but also loving by sending His Son to die on the cross. As a result, forgiveness of sin is emphasized. The other is the Eastern understanding of salvation where the notion of participation in God or deification is present.[2] The result of this discussion on the Eastern Church Fathers is that the Orthodox Church fails to talk about justification by faith, while the process through which Christians become united with Christ is more emphasized. The Reformed understanding of salvation would consider the Eastern view of deification to fit within the understanding of sanctification. Sanctification, however, is a result of salvation and not a way of saving oneself. In the following pages, the Early Church Fathers will be considered with their understanding of salvation, particularly as it relates to *theosis*. While the Eastern Church Fathers were teaching the doctrine of deification, their teaching is not fully in accordance with the modern Orthodox theology.

---

1 Stephanie L. Black, "Augustine's Hermeneutics: Back to the Future for 'Spiritual' Bible Interpretation?" *Africa Journal of Evangelical Theology* (January 2008): 10, accessed January 23, 2017, https://biblicalstudies.org.uk/pdf/ajet/27-1_003.pdf.

2 Donald Fairbairn, "Patristic Soteriology: Three Trajectories," *Journal of the Evangelical Theological Society* 50, no. 2 (June 2007): 289–93, accessed January 21, 2020, https://www.etsjets.org/files/JETS-PDFs/50/50-2/JETS_50-2_289-310_Fairbairn.pdf.

The concept of deification is based on Genesis 1:26 where it is said that man and woman were created in the image of God. But according to the Greek Fathers "at the fall humanity lost the likeness but retained the image, so that the Christian life is best conceived as the restoration of the lost likeness to those who have been redeemed in Christ."[3] Thus, deification is a transformative process which has the purpose of union with God. This is a union that happens not through God's essence, who is "incomprehensible in His essence," but through His divine energies:

> God, who is love, allows us to know Him through His divine energies, those actions whereby He reveals Himself to us in creation, providence, and redemption. It is through the divine energies, therefore, that we achieve union with God. We become united with God by grace in the Person of Christ, who is God come in the flesh. The means of becoming 'like God' is through perfection in holiness.[4]

For Fairbairn, deification has two patterns, one understood to be dangerous since when pushed to the extreme it has a "tendency toward impersonality," and it may argue that "believers are absorbed into the being of God."[5] Another pattern in deification, however, is more in personal terms, where the believer partakes "in the personal communion between the Persons of the Trinity. To be deified, in this view, is not to be absorbed into God in any sense whatsoever. Rather, it is to be adopted as God's child, and therefore to share in the warm communion that the natural Son of God has with his Father."[6]

One of the first Church Fathers to talk about sharing in one of God's characters is Irenaeus of Lyons, a second century Easter Church Father recognized for combating Gnosticism. For Irenaeus, the result of salvation is seen "as freedom from this sinful corruption so that humanity (body and soul) may enjoy God's incorruption," but he does not separate "one's *being* from one's *relationships*."[7] On the other side, the more mystical understanding emerges through Origen and Gregory of Nyssa. For Gregory of Nyssa salvation is seen "largely as the ascent of the human soul to God, in focusing on the soul rather than the whole person, in minimizing the personal aspects of salvation, and in viewing salvation primarily in terms of mystical participation in the qualities or characteristics of God."[8]

One of the Ancient Fathers, Athanasius, known for his explanation of the doctrine of the deity of Christ, is also well-known for his response to a heresy that eventually was condemned at the Council of Nicaea. The heresy came from Arius, a young presbyter in Alexandria who claimed that the Son of God was created; this was his understanding

---

3 Gerald Bray, "Deification," in *New Dictionary of Theology*, ed. Sinclair B. Ferguson, David F. Wright, and J.I. Packer (Downers Grove, IL: InterVarsity Press, 1988), 189.

4 Mark Shuttleworth, "Theosis: Partaking of the Divine Nature," Antiochian Orthodox Christian Archdiocese of North America, accessed January 25, 2017, http://www.antiochian.org/content/theosis-partaking-divine-nature.

5 Fairbairn, "Patristic Soteriology," 293.

6 Fairbairn, "Patristic Soteriology," 293.

7 Fairbairn, "Patristic Soteriology," 295.

8 Fairbairn, "Patristic Soteriology," 301.

on "begotten." In his book, *On the Incarnation of the Word*, Athanasius responded to Arius by giving his understanding of the deity of Jesus Christ. According to him, Christ was not a creature, "begotten, not made" and "of the same substance" as the Father with respect to his essence."[9] Moreover, "Athanasius realized that the question 'Who is Jesus?' is intimately related to the question 'How shall we be saved?' If the Son of God is a creature (as Arius maintained), salvation would be impossible."[10] This brings in discussion the question of how Jesus, a creature as understood by Arius, would save the sinners. His answer was that "by imitation," but Athanasius's understanding of soteriology was that Jesus on the cross, even though not sinning, became sin for us, a curse.[11] Only God who does this for humanity can save us, while a created being is incapable of achieving this.

In relation to the doctrine of deification, Athanasius discusses it in relation to the incarnation and atonement. For him,

> Christ's taking of a "body" refers not simply to his human conception in time, but to his suffering the cross and death. Christ's body shared the same nature with all of fallen humanity (8.2; 20.2) and was thus mortal: it "could not but die, inasmuch as it was mortal, and to be offered unto death on behalf of all: for which purpose the Savior fashioned it for Himself" (31.4). Yet "by virtue of the union of the Word with it," this body was also raised from the dead, "placed out of the reach of corruption," and rendered immortal (20.1–5).[12]

Athanasius holds to the view that deification is the fruit of Christ's atoning work, yet he also talks about deification in terms of sonship, a more personal type of deification present in Irenaeus or Cyril of Alexandria. According to the Eastern Church Father, Christians are sons of the Father through adoption through Jesus, who is the Son of God and dwells in us.

John Chrysostom

The Romanian Orthodox Church holds John Chrysostom in high esteem as one of the saints and pillars of the Orthodox Church. He was born in Antioch, learning under Libanius, a famous pagan rhetorician of that time. Soon after his education, he was baptized, and then lived as a hermit for a period.[13] After returning to Antioch, he first became an ordained priest, and then soon afterwards became the new bishop

---

9 James T. Dennison, Jr., "Athanasius, the Son of God, and Salvation," *New Horizons* (December 2002), accessed January 16, 2017, http://www.opc.org/nh.html?article_id=177.

10 Dennison, "Athanasius, the Son of God, and Salvation."

11 Dennison, "Athanasius, the Son of God, and Salvation."

12 Matthew Baker, "Deification and Sonship according to St Athanasius of AlexandriaPart 1," *Orthodox Christian Network* (December 2014), accessed January 24, 2017, http://myocn.net/deification-sonship-according-st-athanasius-alexandria-part/.

13 George H. Wright, *The Death and Resurrection of Christ in the Soteriology of St. John Chrysostom* master's thesis, Marquette University, 1966, 1, accessed January 24, http://www.marquette.edu/library/theses/already_uploaded_to_IR/wrigh_g_1966.pdf.

of Constantinople. He was named Chrysostom ("golden mouth") for his persuasive preaching, mostly against the great public sins, and is still considered one of the greatest preachers in the Christian world.

His Commentaries on the Gospel Passages

John Chrysostom is known for his homilies that speak to people even today. His homilies extend to almost all the New Testament and naturally include the canonical Gospels. Since the Orthodox Church values the Church Fathers' interpretations of the Bible, his interpretation of the passages already discussed in chapter three will now be considered.

One of the areas in which Chrysostom preached intensively was his understanding of salvation, and especially the new life of Christians in Jesus Christ as opposed to the public sins of the society. One aspect of salvation which he discusses is justification, which Chrysostom defines in relation to grace: "What is the 'law of faith?' It is, being saved by grace. Here he shows God's power, in that He has not only saved, but has even justified, and led them to boasting, and this too without needing works, but looking for faith only."[14] Even though arguably this quotation can be understood as teaching justification by faith alone, in Orthodox theology justification is just a part of a bigger doctrine—union with Christ. Thus, an important aspect in Chrysostom's soteriology is his understanding of deification. While he also talks about deification in terms of "divine likeness," "restoration of the image of God," union with Christ, imitating Christ, or adoption, John Chrysostom explains it through friendship imagery.[15]

For Chrysostom, friendship with God "is a gift immediately bestowed at baptism, indicating not just a future eschatological condition but an existential transformation," friendship as Christian life that he explains using imagery related to the angels.[16] Moreover, the friendship discourse in his writings is used to explain the union with Christ, and this is done to such an extent that "the friends are no longer two distinguishable persons but one single person," imagery that he explains by the use of the Pauline expression "to put on Christ."[17] Similar to other Church Fathers, but talking about it in terms of friendship with God, John Chrysostom also understands deification as sharing in God's characteristics. This could be understood as the believer focusing on reaching virtue, but for Chrysostom it is something personal, and God through the relationship with the believer is the one who acts, who brings "humanity back to intimacy with the divine:": ". . . . God has restored his own to himself."[18] Summarizing John Chrysostom's friendship discourse, Maria Verhoeff stresses that

---

14 John Chrysostom, *Homilies on the Epistle to the Romans* 7.27, accessed January 25, 2017, http://www.documentacatholicaomnia.eu/03d/0345-0407,_Iohannes_Chrysostomus,_Homilies_on_The_Epistle_To_The_Romans,_EN.pdf.

15 Maria Verhoeff, *More Desirable than Light Itself: Friendship Discourse in John Chrysostom's Soteriology* (PhD diss., Evangelische Theologische Faculteit, 2016), 167.

16 Verhoeff, *Friendship Discourse in John Chrysostom's Soteriology*, 171–73.

17 Verhoeff, *Friendship Discourse in John Chrysostom's Soteriology*, 174–75.

18 Verhoeff, *Friendship Discourse in John Chrysostom's Soteriology*, 185.

Chrysostom's portrayal of the union of the believer(s) with Christ in terms of friendship clearly demonstrates that his focus is not merely on the moral progress of the individual in imitation of Christ. Instead, his imagery of friendship denotes the believers' share in the divine life. Chrysostom portrays the *telos* of the Christian life in terms very similar to that of the divine life by being focused on the common good, the salvation of all, which is expressed as making all friends of God. This reflects a soteriology which envisions an appropriation of the divine life by the believer(s), not merely as an eschatological privilege but in the current age as well.[19]

a. Matthew 9:21—In the story of the healing of the woman, John Chrysostom understands σώζω to mean to heal in this context: "For she said within herself, if I may but touch His garment, I shall be whole."[20] Even though the verb is in the passive voice and Chrysostom understands it as active, nonetheless the reflexive idea is not carried by him in this commentary on the healing. For Chrysostom, the woman expects to be delivered from her disease by Jesus.[21]

b. Matthew 10:22—On this verse John Chrysostom makes the following remarks:

> "For the brother shall deliver up the brother," says He, "to death, and the father the child, and the children shall rise up against their parents, and cause them to be put to death." And not even at this did He stop, but added also what was greatly more fearful, and enough to shiver a rock to pieces: "And you shall be hated of all men." And here again the consolation is at the doors for, "For my name's sake," says He, "you shall suffer these things." And with this again another, "But he that endures to the end, the same shall be saved."[22]

As one can see, in commenting on the verse from the Gospel of Matthew, John Chrysostom understands σώζω in a passive way. Those who endure until the end will be saved, and their lives will be secure, not meaning that they will save themselves.[23]

c. John 3:17—While dealing with this verse, Chrysostom gives the following translation of it: "For God sent not His Son to condemn the world, but to save the world."[24] The verb "to save" here is in the passive voice, but Chrysostom translates it as active. However, what is worth mentioning is that he places the action of salvation into "the hands" of the Son. A reading that favors the reflexive understanding and "the world" being involved

---

19 Verhoeff, *Friendship Discourse in John Chrysostom's Soteriology*, 193.
20 John Chrysostom, *Homilies on Matthew* 31.2, accessed February 17, 2017, http://www.newadvent.org/fathers/200131.htm.
21 Chrysostom, *Homilies on Matthew* 31.2.
22 Chrysostom, *Homilies on Matthew* 33.4.
23 The same construction and interpretation are similar to Matthew 24:13.
24 John Chrysostom, *Homilies on the Gospel of John* 28, accessed February 17, 2017, https://www.newadvent.org/fathers/240128.htm.

in the action is not found in Chrysostom. Moreover, in explaining this verse, he says the following: "One says, 'You shall render to every man according to his work'; the other, 'Who will render to every man according to his work.' And yet we may see that even so the lovingkindness of God is great."[25]

d. John 5:34—In a homily on verses 31–39 from chapter five of John's Gospel, Chrysostom renders the verse as follows: "But these things I say, that ye may be saved."[26] For him, one responds to the testimony of John the Baptist, as explained by Jesus, by believing what John the Baptist witnessed about Christ. In his reading, once again a reflexive understanding of σῴζω is not found, but it is explained in a passive way.

e. John 11:12—In the story of the death of Lazarus, BDAG understands the use of σῴζω is "to preserve or rescue from natural dangers and afflictions, to save from death."[27] As seen in chapter three above, the later Orthodox translations and the Protestant translations understand the verb in this way, where an active translation of the verb as "to escape" is carried by these. Moreover, John Chrysostom uses the verb in the same way, an active understanding that does not show Lazarus as saving himself but as to escape, to do well: "His disciples said, Lord, if he sleeps he shall do well."[28]

Cyril of Alexandria

Another Eastern Church Father that talks about deification is Cyril of Alexandria. Writing in a context of Christological and Trinitarian debates, Cyril of Alexandria forms his theology on the man sharing in God's characteristics. In Cyril's understanding of salvation, one talks about salvation "with the curse of incorruption from the Spirit's departure as the central problem. Cyril portrays Christ as restoring incorruption through the Spirit. This curse is reversed through the union of believers with Christ and the restoration of the Spirit, who is the breath of life."[29] Cyril of Alexandria, like Irenaeus, talks about deification at a more personal level, the emphasis being on relationship with God. Using passages like Psalm 82:6 and 1 Corinthians 15:49, Cyril talks about "the importance of Christ as the second Adam in redemption and links adoption through the Spirit with bearing the likeness of Christ."[30] He also uses terminology as imitating Christ, while this imitation is explained as men reproducing God's characteristics.[31] According to Fairbairn, Cyril explains deification through personal communion with the Trinity:

---

25 Chrysostom, *Homilies on the Gospel of John* 28.1.
26 Chrysostom, *Homilies on the Gospel of John* 40.2.
27 BDAG, 3rd ed. s.v. "σῴζω."
28 Chrysostom, *Homilies on the Gospel of John* 62.1.
29 Benjamin Carey Blackwell, "Christosis: Pauline Soteriology in Light of Deification in Irenaeus and Cyril of Alexandria" (PhD diss., Durham University, 2010), 67, accessed January 9, 2020, http://etheses.dur.ac.uk/219/1/BCB_Christosis_Thesis_-_Final.pdf?DDD32+.
30 Blackwell, *Christosis*, 74.
31 Blackwell, *Christosis*, 74.

Although we were foreign to God, his warm love for us has led him to raise us up to the intimacy of communion which characterizes his own inter-trinitarian relationships, and the only difference is that we possess that fellowship by grace, whereas the Son has it naturally. . . . He guards sedulously against any idea of mystical absorption into God, and he tirelessly promotes a personal concept of participation in which we share in the very love between the Father and the Son. Cyril also places a great deal of emphasis on our human inability to rise up to God, and thus on God's downward action through the incarnation and crucifixion in order to make us his adopted sons and daughters.[32]

In relation to the passages analyzed in chapter three above, Cyril of Alexandria is known for his commentary on the Gospels, especially the Gospels of Luke and John. A close look at how the Patriarch of Alexandria interacted with the Greek text of the Gospels and how he interpreted the specific verses that have been examined above shows that Cyril also did not think about salvation as something in which the believer has a share; the believer's share is in his personal communion with God the Father, God the Son, and God the Holy Spirit.

Luke 8:36—In his Sermon 44 on the Gospel of Luke, Cyril of Alexandria talks about the story in which Jesus heals the demon-possessed from the country of Gerasenes. By pointing all throughout the sermon to Christ's authority over the demons, it is understandable that Cyril explains the verse as the man "had been saved" (passive voice) by Christ.[33] Thus, it is Christ who is to be praised for the miracle, and he is the one who saved (healed) the man. Such an understanding of the verse is different than a reading that aims for the reflexive voice.

Luke 8:50—The verb "to save" in this verse is understood by Cyril of Alexandria in his commentary to mean "she shall live," with the emphasis in the sermon on praising Christ, for He is "the resurrection and the life."[34] Thus, a different meaning which would not explicitly show Christ as "the Lord of life and death," and the healer is not what Cyril is communicating.

Luke 13:23—In this verse Jesus is asked by a certain man if they are few those who will be saved or not. As noted previously in the Orthodox translation, the verb is rendered "those who save themselves." It is worth looking at how Cyril interprets the passage. The Patriarch of Alexandria says the following:

> For the man wanted to learn, whether they be few who are saved: but He described unto him the way whereby he might be saved himself, saying, "Strive to enter in by the strait door." What reply then do we make to this objection? We answer as follows;

---

32 Fairbairn, "Patristic Soteriology," 306–307.

33 Cyril of Alexandria, *A Commentary upon the Gospel according to S. Luke*, trans. R. Payne Smith (Oxford: Oxford University Press, 1859), 179.

34 Cyril of Alexandria, *Commentary upon the Gospel of S. Luke*, 194.

that it was the custom of our common Saviour Christ to meet His questioners, not of course according to what might seem good to them, but as having regard to what was useful and necessary for His hearers. And this He especially did when any one wanted to learn what was superfluous and un-edifying. For what good was there in wishing to learn, whether there be many or few that be saved? What benefit resulted from it to the hearers? On the contrary it was a necessary and valuable thing to know in what way a man may attain to salvation. He is purposely silent therefore with respect to the useless question which had been asked Him, but proceeds to speak of what was essential, namely, of the knowledge necessary for the performance of those duties by which men can enter in at the straight and narrow door.[35]

It may seem that Cyril teaches a salvation that can be attained by men through the performance of some duties. By reading further, however, one understands that what he is saying is not that a man saves himself by doing these things, but the emphasis is on the path to the virtue that "is rugged and steep," and therefore every believer should strive to enter the narrow gate.[36]

The Translation of σῴζω in Regard to Soteriology

The Romanian Orthodox Church, as it has already been shown, translated the middle and passive voice of Koine Greek as primarily reflexive. A short word study on the verb "to save," used in the middle/passive voice, revealed that the Orthodox translation regularly uses the reflexive voice. For instance, in Luke 13:23–24, the translation provided is: Și I-a zis cineva: Doamne, puțini sunt, oare, cei ce se mântuiesc? Iar El le-a zis: Siliți-vă să intrați prin poarta cea strâmtă (And someone said to him: "Lord, are they few those who save themselves?") In this verse, the present participle is understood to have a reflexive aspect (the ones who save themselves). The problem with this translation of the voice is that, voluntarily or not, it promotes an understanding of salvation which is argued below as incorrect.

First, salvation is considered to be encapsulated in a main theological thought which is "God became man so that man might become a god" in Orthodox theology. This is what is called the doctrine of deification or *theosis*, which the Orthodox Church sees as a process of healing, of transformation, through which the Christian gains salvation. While the Orthodox priest Cristian Stavriu affirms that for the Romanian Orthodox Church "the state of salvation is obtained only by grace,"[37] evangelicals disagree particularly with the understanding of gaining salvation as a process. While God works salvation in a man, there is a time in the life of the Christian when he responds to "God's gracious

---

35 Cyril of Alexandria, *Commentary upon the Gospel of S. Luke*, 461.
36 Cyril of Alexandria, *Commentary upon the Gospel of S. Luke*, 461–62.
37 Cristian Stavriu, "Concepția de Mântuire Ortodoxă versus Protestantă," Catehetica: Portal Crestin Ortodox, November 18, 2011, accessed January 26, 2017, http://www.catehetica.ro/conceptia-de-mantuire-ortodoxa-versus-protestanta.

working," through faith and repentance.[38] Moreover, the conversion appears in the same time with the new birth; the believer is declared righteous, and this is a one-time event in the Christian life.

What can be agreed is that "union with Christ is a generally inclusive term for all of salvation," but the difference is on how one explains this union.[39] The Romanian Orthodox Church explains union with Christ in terms of this being mystical, such that the relationship between Jesus and the believer is "so deep and absorbing that the believer virtually loses his or her own individuality."[40] The danger with this view is that one may mistakenly believe that the Christian can become holy in this life if one strives enough for virtue. However, in what sense Christ is in a Christian or a Christian in Christ is hard to explain, but as John Chrysostom and other Eastern Church Fathers have shown, it is the personal aspect, that intimate relationship with Christ that is important. What can be said about union with Christ is to point to some of its characteristics.

Union with Christ is judicial in nature, "God always sees the believer in union with Christ," and because of Christ, the Christian is seen as righteous by the Father.[41] Union with Christ is also spiritual, meaning that it is "effected by the Holy Spirit" and is a union of spirits, and is also vital; Christ's life "actually flows into ours renewing our inner nature."[42]

Justification is another aspect of soteriology worth being discussed. According to an article in "The Orthodox Study Bible," justification is understood in three aspects:

> Justification by faith in God is part of being brought into a covenant relationship with Him, but it is first God's mercy and not our faith which saves us. Justification by faith is also dynamic, not static. For Orthodox Christians, faith is living, dynamic, continuous—never static or merely point-in-time. . . . This is why the modern evangelical Protestant question, "Are you saved?" gives pause to an Orthodox believer. As the subject of salvation is addressed in Scripture, the Orthodox Christian would see it in at least three aspects: (a) I have been saved, being joined to Christ in baptism; (b) I am being saved, growing in Christ through the sacramental life of the Church; and (c) I will be saved, by the mercy of God at the Last Judgment.[43]

The difference is not as much in theology as it is in defining it with the right terms. While in the above article salvation is addressed in three aspects, evangelical theology describes the second and third aspects in terms of sanctification and glorification. First,

---

[38] Greg Herrick, "An Introduction to Christian Belief: A Layman's Guide," ch. 7, "Soteriology: Salvation," *Bible.org*, accessed January 27, 2017, https://bible.org/seriespage/7-soteriology-salvation.

[39] Millard J. Erickson, *Christian Theology*, 2nd ed. (Grand Rapids, MI: Baker Academic, 1998), 960.

[40] Erickson, *Christian Theology*, 963.

[41] Lewis B. Smedes, *Union with Christ: A Biblical View of the New Life in Jesus Christ* (Grand Rapids, MI: Eerdmans, 1983), 112–13.

[42] Erickson, *Christian Theology*, 965–66.

[43] Evan, "Justification by Faith."

sanctification is what is addressed in the Orthodox theology as salvation in progress, but the evangelical speaks about the doctrine of sanctification in three tenses:

> With respect to the past, we have been set apart, both to belong to God, positionally speaking, and to serve him, practically speaking. We were sanctified at the moment of conversion and were declared legally holy and belonging to the Lord (1 Cor. 6:11). With respect to the future, we will be totally sanctified someday in our glorified bodies. At that time our practice will completely match our position or standing before God. At the present time we are being sanctified, that is, increasingly being transformed into the image of the Lord (2 Cor. 3:18). Thus the nature of sanctification is transformation; we are being progressively conformed into the image of the Son who died for us.[44]

Lastly, glorification as understood by the evangelicals is the final stage in the Christian's life that "involves the perfecting of the spiritual nature of the individual believer, which takes place at death, when the Christian passes into the presence of the Lord."[45] However, as one can see, there is not much disagreement on the stages that occur in the Christian's life between the Orthodox viewpoint and the evangelical one. While the Orthodox call it the process of salvation, the evangelicals call it stages in the Christian's life. The term "stages" may be more preferred in order to preserve the salvation that occurs in the Christian's life and is a one-time event. Yet, evangelicals have more to learn from the Orthodox Church in the doctrine of salvation in terms of the personal emphasis, and that once one have been saved, he is not done. In every Christian's life, sanctification and glorification must take place. Perhaps evangelicals emphasize too much the juridical aspect of salvation and justification by faith, yet evangelicals also affirm sections in James which clearly teach the role of works in the Christian's life (James 2:14–26).

Conclusion

In the above survey through some of the early Eastern Church Fathers, their understanding of salvation has been considered, focusing on the doctrine of deification. This doctrine is how the Romanian Orthodox Church explains salvation, a mystical union with God in which the Christian strives to reach virtue, in order that the image of God might be restored in him. As has been seen, however, this is not on solid ground, since deification was not that well defined in the Church Fathers. As Fairbairn notes, there are two trajectories in the Eastern Church, the mystical and the personal pattern. While the evangelical understanding of salvation is a more juridical one, the personal explanation viewpoint such as expressed in Irenaeus, John Chrysostom, or Cyril of Alexandria is something evangelicals would agree upon even if it is not that well developed. Evangelicals would agree that Christians are "partakers of the divine nature" (2 Peter 1:4), and that Christians are transformed as God dwells in them (Rom. 12:2); it is the understanding of reaching virtue and mystical absorption in God that is rejected. But as John Chrysostom explained, deification for him is about the fellowship with the Trinity

---

44 Herrick, *Soteriology*.
45 Erickson, *Christian Theology*, 924.

by grace, sharing in God's love. It is not through human effort one reaches deification, since Chrysostom clearly emphasizes human inability in this matter, but it is God's effort in the incarnation and crucifixion through which he brought one into adoption.

Conclusion and Recommendations

This work has argued through that the Romanian Orthodox translation of the Greek voice does not take into consideration some important grammatical developments, as well as the literary and theological context. While the word σῴζω with a middle/passive parsing can be mistranslated as "to save oneself," more frequently it should be translated as "to be saved." This translation finds its basis in the Greek grammar, the context of the verb in the canonical gospels, and uses in the Church Fathers, especially John Chrysostom and Cyril of Alexandria. While not explored within this study, such an understanding would fit well in line with passages in the Pauline Epistles.[1] This would be anticipated from a coherent New Testament that presents main ideas in unity with each other rather than divergent viewpoints.[2]

This study has examined passages that are representative for the understanding of σῴζω in the canonical gospels. These are representative for most of the appearances discussed in chapter three, and found to be important in terms of the context of the verse. Thus, based on the arguments already brought in discussion, the following appearances are to be subjected to revision, while the proposed translations are also given below.

Matthew 9:21—the translation of σῴζω is "*mă voi mîntui*" (I will save myself) but this translation communicates the reflexive understanding of the verb. First, the verb is in the passive voice according to the grammar of the Greek language. Second, the passive understanding of this verb will make it ambiguous to be communicated through the reflexive passive construction. As has been seen earlier, most of the reflexive passive constructions are in the third person, while in this verb is a first person singular. Last, in this passage the person who performs the miracle is Jesus, thus a passive understanding better fits the context. Thus, the translation proposed is the meaning suggested by the latter Romanian Orthodox translations, "to heal," with the NTR construction for the passive voice: "voi fi vindecată" (I will be healed).

Matthew 10:22—Most Romanian Orthodox translations of this verse provide the translation "se va mântui" (he will save himself). However, a better proposed translation because the verb is in the future passive, and BDAG also categorizes this usage in Matthew 10:22 under the passive should be "be saved, or attain salvation."[3] Moreover, while this verse can be understood to be a reflexive passive due to the use of the reflexive pronoun "se," such translation will be more ambiguous for the understanding of the

---

[1] Particularly Paul's letters to the Romans and Galatians.

[2] The unity and coherence of the New Testament is assumed throughout. For further on the unity of the New Testament, see I. Howard Marshall, *New Testament Theology: Many Witnesses, One Gospel* (Downers Grove, IL: InterVarsity Press, 2004), 29–47.

[3] BDAG, 3rd ed. s.v. "σῴζω."

verse. In the same verse, the Romanian Orthodox Bible translates the middle/passive of the verb "to hate" by using the more common construction for the passive, with the auxiliary verb: "veți fi urîți" (you will be healed). Thus, it is recommended to opt for the same construction in the case of σῴζω. Similar constructions are found in the Olivet Discourse, in Matthew 24:13, 22, and Mark 13:13, thus it is better to align Matthew 10:22 with these others.

Matthew 19:25—In this verse, the context of the passage plays an important role. As has already been seen in chapter three, the verse is found within a context where Jesus is telling the disciples that human worthiness will not allow entering the kingdom of God. Thus, the passive "să fie mântuit" (to be saved) is the better translation.

Mark 5:23—In this verse, "to save" is used once again with the meaning "to heal." The Bartolomeu edition, as well as *Gala Galaction* interpret the passage and translate it as: "ca să scape și să trăiască" (that she might escape and live). This translation is fine as it stands, having in mind the context of the passage, as in Mark 3:4 and 15:30, 31, where "saving life is synonymous with healing or making well."[4] However, the voice of the verb is passive. Thus the recommended translation would be NTR: "ca să fie vindecată" (that she might be healed). While the verb here may be seen as a reflexive passive, where a more impersonal nuance is emphasized by the translator, such a rendition of the verse will be more ambiguous than the NTR translation. However, the force of the passive construction is stronger than in other verses where the translation had a reflexive flavor. The same case is for Mark 6:56, where the verb—even though it has a reflexive construction—is communicating an impersonal type of passive, where an individual is not in mind. The reflexive pronoun *se* is found in all the Orthodox translation, but the force is not as noticeable as in the case of other examples. However, probably the best translation is to take the verb in the passive voice, just as the Cornilescu translation and NTLR renders the verse: "Și toți câți se atingeau de El erau tămăduiți" (And all as many as were touching Him were healed).

Luke 8:12—Ediția Sinodală 1914, as well as the Bartolomeu Anania translation, follows the reflexive understanding: "să se mântuiască" (to save himself). As seen previously, the context of the verse as described by Bock suggests that the responses require reflection from the side of the person, thinking about "What single type of response to the word have I given?"[5] Such a response would encourage a reading of a person who is also active in σωθῶσιν; however, one cannot ignore that the verb is in the passive voice. A reflexive passive reading of the verse, though, suggests the Anania reading, but this will leave it more ambiguous.

---

4 Robert A. Guelich, *Word Biblical Commentary*, vol. 34A, *Mark 1–8:26* (Dallas, TX: Word Books, 1989), 296.

5 Bock, *Luke. 1:1–9:50*, 734.

Luke 8:36—This verse is one of the verses that has been revised in the later Romanian Orthodox translations. Thus, in the Anania translation the verse reads as following: "Și cei care văzuseră le-au spus cum a fost izbăvit demonizatul" (And those who have seen it, told them how the demon-possessed man had been healed). This correction is not only in accordance with the grammar where the verb is in the passive voice, but also translates it in the context of healing.

Luke 13:23—In this verse, οἱ σῳζόμενοι is a participle that can be taken morphologically either in the middle or passive. The Orthodox translations take it as middle, with a reflexive understanding: "Și i-a zis cineva: Doamne, puțini sunt oare cei care se mântuiesc?" (And someone said to him: Lord, are they few the ones who save themselves?") The Synodal translations render this verse with a reflexive understanding, among them *Biblia de la 1688*, *Ediția Sinodală 1914*, *Gala Galaction*, or *Anania*.

If σῳζόμενοι is to be understood as middle voice, the Orthodox Church may have the right translation. However, the reflexive middle is just one category of the Greek middle voice to be taken in consideration with many other categories. Defining the term further, Allan understands the middle voice as

> "a marker of subject-affectedness, taken in the broad sense. This comprises, on the one hand, affectedness in which the subject is very much like a patient (as in the passive, reflexive and reciprocal middle), and, on the other hand, affectedness in which the subject is similar to an indirect object (as in the indirect middle)."[6]

The classical grammarian Moule also states that the reflexive understanding is not the norm for the middle voice and "whether or not this is true for certain periods, it is manifestly not true of N.T. usage."[7] Thus, a passive reading, "the ones who are saved," is to be preferred since both the grammar but, more importantly, the context suggests this.

John 10:9—The Romanian Orthodox Bible renders this verse as follows: "Eu sunt ușa: de va intra cineva prin Mine, se va mântui; și va intra și va ieși și pășune va afla" ("I am the door: if anyone enters through me he will save himself; and he will go in and he will go out and he will find pasture"). Yet, the verb in this verse is in the passive voice, with the subject receiving the action, while the suggested translation is "Eu sunt ușa: dacă intră cineva prin Mine, va fi mântuit." ("I am the door: if anyone enters through he will be saved").

The second argument that does not recommend the readings of the previous verses as reflexive is the context in which both of them are found. In Luke 13:23, Jesus talks about the narrow door in the light of the question of the number of the saved ones. Jesus' answer to this question is indeed a middle imperative, where the subject is directly involved by having to strive in order to enter through the narrow door. Thus,

---

6 Allan, "The Middle Voice in Ancient Greek," 12.

7 C. F. D. Moule, *An Idiom Book of New Testament Greek* (Cambridge: Cambridge University Press, 1986), 24.

a subject involved in the previous verse is made possible through the understanding of the participle as middle. Moreover, Jesus' words that follow the verse support a passive reading, that many will not be able, mainly because "the master of the house" does not know them. T. W. Manson explains the best these last verses:

> The reply of Jesus begins by asserting that the way of salvation is a door which God opens and man enters. The entry cannot be made without God. The gate of heaven opens only from the inside. But also man has to make his own way in, once the door is opened. And this is not easy. The entrance is narrow, and it is a case of struggling through rather than strolling in. If men fail to enter, it is not that God is unwilling to admit them, but that they will not enter on the only terms on which entrance is possible.[8]

Thus, as has already been seen, the participle should not be understood as reflexive, where a person works his way of righteousness to God. It is rather that one has "to labor hard at listening and responding to his message."[9]

In John 10:9, the context of the verse prefers the passive reading since this is a passage where Jesus' imagery of the good shepherd and his sheep points to dependency and talks about him as being the only way (contrasting the thieves and robbers), a translation where "the sheep" would be able "to save themselves" is not the preferred reading.

Lastly, a reflexive reading of the middle/passive rendering of the verb σῴζω is not in accordance with the most up to date understanding of the Koine Greek language and how specific Church Fathers such as Irenaeus, John Chrysostom, or Cyril of Alexandria viewed it. As has been seen in John Chrysostom's soteriology, deification is fellowship with the Trinity by grace, sharing in God's love. He makes sure to stress that as human beings, none are capable of reaching God. Rather, it is God's effort in the incarnation and crucifixion through which he makes this possible.

John 11:12—The revised translation of the Orthodox Bible and the Protestant rendition are the better readings for σωθήσεται (literally "he will be saved"). This is the recommended reading in BDAG, where σῴζω has more the meaning of "saving a life," or "to save from death."[10] This reading has been the preferred one from an early period, as another reading of σωθήσεται is ἐγερθήσεται ("he will be raised").[11] Moreover, this reading is also preferred by John Chrysostom in homilies on the Gospel of John.

In conclusion, it has been the aim of this study to analyze the translation of the verb σῴζω in the Romanian Orthodox Bible and its implication for theology. It has been seen that both the grammar and the context of the passages do not support a reflexive understanding of the verb. Moreover, John Chrysostom and Cyril of Alexandria do not communicate a reflexive understanding either. The suggested revisions of the translation of σῴζω should be considered in the context of the Romanian Orthodox Bible since it is

---

8 Manson, *The Sayings of Jesus as Recorded in the Gospels*, 125.
9 Bock, *9:51–24:53*, 1234.
10 BDAG, 3rd ed. s.v. "σῴζω."
11 BDAG, 3rd ed. s.v. "σῴζω."

the most read Bible by the people. Thus, σῴζω in the middle/passive voice understood as primarily reflexive carries theological implications for the reader. The danger in translating it reflexively is that it communicates a type of salvation outside "by grace, through faith," which is outside the meaning of other texts in the Gospels where σῴζω occurs and outside the understanding of significant church fathers. Thus, a more nuanced understanding of the Greek middle voice in relation to σῴζω in the Gospels should be considered.

Bibliography of Works Cited

Alexiadou, Artemis and Edit Doron. "The Syntactic Construction of Two Non-Active Voices: Passive and Middle." *Journal of Linguistics* 48 (2012):1–34. Accessed January 9, 2020. http://pluto.huji.ac.il/~edit/papers/Alexiadou-Doron-JL.pdf

Allan, Rutger J. "The Middle Voice in Ancient Greek: A study in Polysemy." PhD diss. University of Amsterdam, 2002. Accessed January 9, 2020. https://pure.uva.nl/ws/files/3546000/23754_Thesis.pdf.

Baker, Matthew. "Deification and Sonship according to St Athanasius of Alexandria: Part 1." *Orthodox Christian Network.* December 2014. Accessed January 24, 2017, http://myocn.net/deification-sonship-according-st-athanasius-alexandria-part/.

Barnwell, Katharine. *Bible Translation: An Introductory Course in Translation Principles*. 3rd ed. Dallas, TX: Summer Institute of Linguistics, 1986.

Bible.com. "Romanian Interconfessional New Testament Translation." Accessed April 21, 2017. https://www.bible.com/versions/1506-bint09-romana-noul-testament-interconfesional-2009.

Black, Stephanie L. "Augustine's Hermeneutics: Back to the Future for 'Spiritual' Bible Interpretation?" *Africa Journal of Evangelical Theology* 27, no. 1 (January 2008). Accessed January 23, 2017, https://biblicalstudies.org.uk/pdf/ajet/27-1_003.pdf.

Blackwell, Benjamin Carey. "Christosis: Pauline Soteriology in Light of Deification in Irenaeus and Cyril of Alexandria." PhD diss. Durham University, 2010. Accessed January 9, 2020. http://etheses.dur.ac.uk/219/1/BCB_Christosis_Thesis_-_Final.pdf?DDD32+.

Blass, F. and A. Debrunner. *A Greek Grammar of the New Testament and Other Early Christian Literature*. Rev. ed. Translated and edited by Robert W. Funk. Chicago: University of Chicago Press, 1961.

Bock, Darrell L. *Luke*. Vol. 1. *1:1– 9:50*. Baker Exegetical Commentary on the New Testament. Grand Rapids, MI: Baker Books, 1994.

———. *Luke*. Vol. 2. *9:51–24:53*. Baker Exegetical Commentary on the New Testament. Grand Rapids, MI: Baker Books, 1996.

Bray, Gerald. "Deification." In *New Dictionary of Theology*. Edited by Sinclair B. Ferguson, David F. Wright, and J.I. Packer. Downers Grove, IL: InterVarsity Press, 1988.

Chrysostom, John. *Homilies on Matthew*. February 17, 2017. http://www.newadvent.org/fathers/200131.htm.

———. *Homilies on the Gospel of John*. Accessed February 17, 2017. http://www.newadvent.org/fathers/240127.htm.

———. *Homilies on the Epistle to the Romans*. Accessed January 25, 2017. http://www.documentacatholicaomnia.eu/03d/0345-0407,_Iohannes_Chrysostomus,_Homilies_on_The_Epistle_To_The_Romans,_EN.pdf.

Cline, George J. "The Significance of the Middle Voice in the New Testament." Master's Thesis. Grace Theological Seminary, 1983. Accessed January 9, 2020. https://faculty.

gordon.edu/hu/bi/ted_hildebrandt/new_testament_greek/text/cline-middlevoice/cline-middlevoice.pdf.

Conrad, Carl W. "Active, Middle and Passive: Understanding Ancient Greek Voice." Accessed August 18, 2016. http://www.cultus.hk/latin_lessons/deponens/GreekDeponens.pdf.

———. "New Observations on Voice in the Ancient Greek Verb." Unpublished paper, 2002. Accessed January 9, 2020. https://pages.wustl.edu/files/pages/imce/cwconrad/newobsancgrkvc.pdf.

Conțac, Emanuel. *Cornilescu: Din Culisele Publicării celei mai Citite Traduceri a Sfintei Scripturi*. Cluj-Napoca: Logos, 2014.

———. *Dilemele Fidelității: Condiționări Culturale și Teologice în Traducerea Bibliei*. Cluj-Napoca: Logos, 2011.

Cornilescu, Dumitru. *Cum m-am întors la Dumnezeu*. Accessed January 10, 2017. http://www.resursecrestine.ro/eseuri/10402/cum-m-am-intors-la-dumnezeu.

Cyril of Alexandria. *A Commentary upon the Gospel according to S. Luke*. Translated by R. Payne Smith. Oxford: Oxford University Press, 1859.

Dana H. E. and Julius R. Mantey. *A Manual Grammar of the Greek New Testament*. New York: The Macmillan Company, 1957.

Danker, Frederick W., Walter Bauer, William F. Arndt, and F. Wilbur Gingrich. *A Greek-English Lexicon of the New Testament and Other Early Christian Literature*. 3rd ed. Chicago: University of Chicago Press, 2000.

Dexonline. "A spăși." Accessed April 21, 2017. https://dexonline.ro/definitie/spasi.

Erickson, Millard J. *Christian Theology*. 2nd ed. Grand Rapids, MI: BakerAcademic, 1998.

Fairbairn, Donald. "Patristic Soteriology: Three Trajectories." *Journal of the Evangelical Theological Society* 50, no. 2 (June 2007): 289–310. Accessed January 21, 2020. https://www.etsjets.org/files/JETS-PDFs/50/50-2/JETS_50-2_289-310_Fairbairn.pdf.

France, R. T. *The Gospel of Matthew*. The New International Commentary on the New Testament. Grand Rapids, MI: Eerdmans, 2007.

Friedrich, Gerhard, ed. *Theological Dictionary of the New Testament*. Vol. 7. Σ. Translated and edited by Geoffrey W. Bromiley. Grand Rapids, MI: Eerdmans, 1971.

Galaction, Gala. *Piatra din Capul Unghiului. Scrisori Teologice*. București: Tipografiile Române Unite, 1926. As cited in Emanuel Conțac, *Dilemele Fidelității: Condiționări Culturale și Teologice în Traducerea Bibliei*.

Garland, David E. *Mark*. The NIV Application Commentary. Grand Rapids, MI: Zondervan,1996.

Georgescu, Constantin. *Manual de Greaca Biblică*. București: Nemira, 2011.

Gildersleeve, Basil L. *Syntax of Classical Greek from Homer to Demosthenes*. New York: American Book Company, 1900.

Gramatica limbii române. "Gramatica limbii române pe înțelesul tuturor." Accessed August 10, 2016. https://gramaticalimbiiromane.ro/morfologia/parti-vorbire-flexibile/verbul/diatezele-verbelor/.

Guelich, Robert A. *Word Biblical Commentary*. Vol. 34A. *Mark 1–8:26*. Dallas, TX: Word Books, 1989.

Gundry, Robert H. *Mark: A Commentary on His Apology for the Cross*. Vol. 2 (9–16). Grand Rapids, MI: Eerdmans, 1993.

Hagner, Donald A. *Word Biblical Commentary*. Vol. 33B. *Matthew 14–28*. Dallas, TX: Word Books, 1995.

Hamerton-Kelly, Robert G. *The Gospel and the Sacred Poetics of Violence in Mark*. Minneapolis: Fortress, 1994.

Herrick, Greg. "An Introduction to Christian Belief: A Layman's Guide." Chapter 7. "Soteriology: Salvation." *Bible.org*. Accessed January 27, 2017, https://bible.org/seriespage/7-soteriology-salvation.

Hoarță Cărăușu, Luminița. "Un Aspect al Morfosintaxei Textelor Religioase din secolul al XVI-lea: Construcția Pasivă." In *Text și Discurs Religios.* 2nd ed., 269–78. Iași, RO: Editura Universității „Alexandru Ioan Cuza," 2010. Accessed February 7, 2017. http://www.cntdr.ro/sites/default/files/c2009/c2009a27.pdf.

IBSR. "About us." Accessed January 27, 2020. http://web.archive.org/web/20170512054431/http://societateabiblica.org/about-us/.

Jay, Eric G. *New Testament Greek: An Introductory Grammar*. London: SPCK, 1958.

Jelf, William E. *A Grammar of the Greek Language*. 2nd ed. 2 vols. Oxford: James Wright, 1851.

Jinga, Constantin. "Biblia cea mai tradusă carte: O Retrospectivă Istorică a Traducerilor Sfintei Scripturii. *Ortho-logia.*2000. Accessed November 21, 2016, http://ortho-logia.com/Romanian/Articole/Trad_Istorica.htm.

Keener, Craig S. *A Commentary on the Gospel of Matthew*. Grand Rapids, MI: Eerdmans, 1999.

Kemmer, Suzanne. *Typological Studies in Language*. Vol. 23. *The Middle Voice*. Amsterdam: John Benjamins Pub. Co., 1993.

Klimenko, Victor E. "The Orthodox Teaching on Personal Salvation." Orthodox Christianity. Accessed July 29, 2020, http://orthochristian.com/46463.html.

Köstenberger, Andreas J., Benjamin L. Merkle, and Robert L. Plummer. *Going Deeper With New Testament Greek: An Intermediate Study of the Grammar and Syntax of the New Testament*. Nashville, TN: B&H Academic.

———. *John*. Baker Exegetical Commentary on the New Testament. Grand Rapids, MI: Baker Books, 2004.

Manea, Dragoș-Ștefăniță. "A Short Exploration on the Importance of Greek Language Study for the Romanian Evangelical Church." MET thesis. Tyndale Theological Seminary, 2010.

Manson, T. W. *The Sayings of Jesus as Recorded in the Gospels According to St. Matthew and St. Luke*. London: SCM Press LTD, 1949.

Marshall, I. Howard. *New Testament Theology: Many Witnesses, One Gospel*. Downers Grove, IL: InterVarsity Press, 2004.

Miller, Neva F. Appendix 2. "A Theory of Deponent Verbs." In *Analytical Lexicon of the Greek New Testament*, Barbara Friberg, Timothy Friberd, and Neva F. Miller. Grand Rapids, MI: Baker, 2000.

Moule, C. F. D. *An Idiom Book of New Testament Greek*. Cambridge: Cambridge University Press, 1986.

Moulton, James Hope. *A Grammar of New Testament Greek*. Edinburgh: T&T Clark, 1908.

Moulton, W. F., and A. S. Geden. *A Concordance to the Greek Testament* (Edinburgh, T&T Clark, 1978.

Munteanu, Eugen. *Lexicologie Biblică Românească*. București: Humanitas, 2008.

Nicolaescu, N. I. "Scurt Istoric al Traducerii Sfintei Scripturi. Principalele Ediții ale Bibliei în Biserica Ortodoxă Română." *Studii și Articole* 26, no. 7–8 (September-October 1974): 489–521. Accessed January 5, 2017, http://forum.teologie.net/download/file.php?id=419.

Nida, Eugene A. *Toward a Science of Translating with Special Reference to Principles and Procedures involved in Bible Translating*. Leiden: Brill, 1964. As cited by Y. C. Whang, "To Whom is a Translator Responsible."

Nida, Eugene A., and Charles R. Taber. *The Theory and Practice of Translation*. Leiden: Brill, 1982.

Porter, Stanley E. *Idioms of the Greek New Testament*. 2nd ed. Sheffield: Sheffield Academic Press, 1999.

Ramsey, Michaels J. *The Gospel of John*. The New International Commentary on the New Testament. Grand Rapids, MI: Eerdmans, 2010.

Robertson, A. T. *A Grammar of the Greek New Testament in the Light of Historical Research*. Nashville, TN: Broadman Press, 1934.

Shuttleworth, Mark. "Theosis: Partaking of the Divine Nature." Antiochian Orthodox Christian Archdiocese of North America. Accessed January 25, 2017. http://www.antiochian.org/content/theosis-partaking-divine-nature.

Smedes, Lewis B. *Union with Christ: A Biblical View of the New Life in Jesus Christ*. Grand Rapids, MI: Eerdmans, 1983.

Smyth, Herbert W. *A Greek Grammar for Colleges*. Boston: Harvard University Press, 1956.

Sparks, Fr. Jack Norman, ed., "Justification by Faith." In *The Orthodox Study Bible*. Nashville, TN: 2008.

Stavriu, Cristian. "Biblia Cornilescu: Un Fals, o Înșelare, o Modalitate de Îndreptățire a Ereziilor." Accessed January 19, 2017. http://www.catehetica.ro/biblia-cornilescu-un-fals-o-inselare-o-modalitate-de-indreptatire-a-ereziilor.

———. "Concepția de Mântuire Ortodoxă versus Protestantă." Catehetica: Portal Crestin Ortodox. November 18, 2011. Accessed January 26, 2017. http://www.catehetica.ro/conceptia-de-mantuire-ortodoxa-versus-protestanta.

Stăniloae, D. *Sinteză Eclesiologică: Biserica, Organ al Mîntuirii și Sfințirii*. Accessed January 9, 2020. http://faculty.go.ro/text/text-pdf/Dumitru%20Staniloae%20-%20Sinteza%20eclesiologica.%20Biserica,%20sfintire%20si%20mantuire.pdf.

Verhoeff, Maria. *More Desirable than Light Itself: Friendship Discourse in John Chrysostom's Soteriology*. PhD diss. Evangelische Theologische Faculteit, 2016.

Wallace, Daniel B. *Greek Grammar Beyond the Basics: An Exegetical Syntax of the New Testament*. Grand Rapids, MI: Zondervan, 1996.

Whang, Y. C. "To Whom is a Translator Responsible—Reader or Author?" In *Translating the Bible: Problems and Prospects*. Edited by Stanley E. Porter and Richard S. Hess. London: T&T Clark International, 2004.

Wright, George H. *The Death and Resurrection of Christ in the Soteriology of St. John Chrysostom*. Master's thesis. Marquette University, 1966. Accessed January 24. http://www.marquette.edu/library/theses/already_uploaded_to_IR/wrigh_g_1966.pdf.

Yue L. Ng, Esther. "ἦσαν τεταγμένοι in Acts 13:48: Middle Voice or Passive Voice? Implications for the Doctrine of Divine Election." *CGST Journal* 50 (January 2011): 185–99. Accessed January 9, 2020. http://tci.ncl.edu.tw/cgi- https://drive.google.com/file/d/0B58X1TJ3bk7FZ3UwQ1kxa3hpdlk/view.

Zerwick, Maximilian. *Scripta Pontificii Instituti Biblici*. English ed. Vol. 114. *Biblical Greek*. Rome: Iura Editionis et Versionis Reservantur, 1963.